D0904110

Sectionalism in American Politics, 1774-1787

Sectionalism in American Politics 1774-1787

Joseph L. Davis

The University of Wisconsin Press

Published 1977
The University of Wisconsin Press
Box 1379, Madison, Wisconsin 53701

The University of Wisconsin Press, Ltd.
70 Great Russell Street, London

First printing

Printed in the United States of America

For LC CIP information see the colophon

ISBN 0-299-07020-4

Publication of this book was made
possible in part by a grant
from the Andrew W. Mellon Foundation

"I . . . wish the distinctions Southern and Northern were lost in the glorious name of American."

Joseph Ward to John Adams,
3 December 1775, in
Adams Mss. Trust, MHS

"we presume it to be a fact capable of demonstration, that for about twenty years past . . . the creation of new states in the south, and out of the original limits of the United States, has increased the southern interest, which has appeared so hostile to the peace and commercial prosperity of the northern states."

Meeting at Northampton,
19 January 1814, in Noah Webster,
"Origin of the Hartford Convention"

Contents

Acknowledgments

AT VARIOUS times while writing a book the historian is very much alone. Searching for clues in the past, studying the sources, trying to get as close as possible to some elusive truth, the historian struggles with frustration, doubt, and fatigue. The exhilaration and the feeling of accomplishment when the job is done could not be achieved, however, without the help of many people. I would like to thank the staffs of the Library of Congress, the Historical Society of Pennsylvania, the New-York Historical Society, the New York Public Library, the Massachusetts Historical Society, the Houghton Library, the American Antiquarian Society, the Yale University Library, the Rutgers University Library, and the Maryland Historical Society. I have been especially lucky to have had daily access to the excellent facilities of the Wisconsin State Historical Society, whose staff was extremely helpful and made long hours of research much easier to tolerate.

I consider myself very fortunate to have received my training from Merrill Jensen. His teaching, direction, support, and inspiring example made it possible for me to take the long journey from a seminar paper to a book. Jensen's seminar at the University of Wisconsin does not dissolve when the Ph.D. is received. I am proud to be part of a tight-knit group of scholars whose scholarship, friendship, assistance, and encouragement helped me in preparing this book. I especially benefited from Kenneth R. Bowling's competence as a historian, critic, and editor. His untiring support of me and interest in my work far exceeded what would normally be expected of just a colleague.

The comments and suggestions of William W. Abbott and H. James Henderson, who read the manuscript for the Press, were most helpful. This study could not have been written without the support of the National Endowment for the Humanities and the Mellon Foundation. I would also like to thank my research assistants Dale Hillerman, Joan Hammer, and Mark Weiss and the many friends and colleagues who

ix

helped me and encouraged me over the years and who listened, very patiently, to my ponderings about the eighteenth century.

Quotations from the Adams Papers are from the microfilm edition, by permission of the Massachusetts Historical Society. Quotations from the Sparks Collection and the Arthur Lee Papers are by permission of the Houghton Library.

This book could not have been written without my parents' gift of their love and respect for learning, my brother's encouragement and help when my graduate years began, and the City of New York's sixteen years of free education. My greatest debt and thanks are to Connie, who put up with the many demands made upon her while the book was being written, and whose constant support, faith, and love were and always will be invaluable.

J.L.D.

Madison, Wisconsin
May 1976

Sectionalism in American Politics, 1774-1787

Introduction

IN 1776 thirteen of Great Britain's American colonies declared their independence and became sovereign states. In 1781 they ratified a constitution which created a confederation, and in 1788 they adopted a constitution which erected a national government. This political change, which brought the United States full circle to the type of centralized authority which Great Britain had in theory exerted prior to 1776, is crucial to an understanding of the American Revolution. One of the fundamental issues during the revolutionary era was the controversy about the relationship between central and local political authority. The clash between two antithetical ideological forces, between nationalists, who looked to greater centralization of political authority to achieve their political goals, and federalists, who looked to continued decentralization of authority, precipitated a series of confrontations for control of the young nation. It is this conflict, beginning as early as 1774, which holds the key to a deeper comprehension of the developments which led to the formulation of the Constitution of 1787.*

While the ideological conflict concerning whether to have a strong or a weak central government was continual, its parameters were not fixed. Political behavior resulting from the major ideological division did not produce two clearly demarcated and structured factions. A description of revolutionary politics, especially the attempt to delineate the outlines of political behavior, needs to be balanced and qualified by the understanding that many factors (including both ideology and interest) affected the various groupings and often blurred the major divisions.

Nevertheless, for the sake of clarity, it is sometimes necessary to use

*This study is, by its very nature, limited to those men who wielded power, but their thoughts and positions did not necessarily represent all the people in their particular state or section. Moreover, we are dealing with an elite's leadership position in a changing political climate. The leaders, no matter what their political stance, were affected by pressures from below. Although this is not a primary concern of this study, it is important to remember that the elite's response to the civil disturbances in 1786 was not a new phenomenon.

3

labels to describe the political scene and identify the actors in the political arena. Although the terms *federalism* and *nationalism* and *federalist* and *nationalist* satisfactorily represent the two ideologies and their advocates, we must guard against giving them too much weight and ascribing to factions, to political alliances, a homogeneity and a consistency over time which did not exist. I have made a conscious attempt to guard against presenting a picture of stable political camps. I hope that the fluidity of factional lines and an everchanging political scene is clear in the portrayal of the conflict between the forces of federalism and nationalism during the revolutionary era.

There was, however, more to revolutionary politics than the relatively narrow limits of ideological dispute. Political differences among politicians were also affected by state and especially sectional interests which, at times, assumed a higher priority than ideological commitment or even more questionable factional solidarity. The influence of sectional politics, the conflicts between New England, the middle, and the southern states, has to be taken into account in order to give a more comprehensive picture of the reasons for the constitutional changes in America between 1774 and 1787. During those years positions were assumed, policies set in motion, and actions taken which reflected the profound influence of sectional interests. The Founding Fathers understood, accepted, and acted in accordance with the nation's sectional diversity.*

Alignments in Congress can be roughly separated into specific, though not rigid, periods. From 1774 to 1777 Congress was under a strong federalist influence primarily because of the cooperation between New Englanders and southerners in the Lee-Adams junto. From 1778 to 1782 politicians of the middle states, allied under the banner of nationalism, seized control of Congress with the support of a few New England and many southern delegates. With the coming of peace in 1783 the sectional configuration shifted, for a time, as other New Englanders and southerners turned back the nationalist thrust. Beginning in 1785 many southerners withdrew their support from New England in the face

---

*When state and/or sectional attitudes are so labeled, the intent is to simplify for the sake of description, to represent only the viewpoint of that particular segment of the elite under discussion. When a specific stance is identified as southern, northern, or New England no implication is intended that the interest of some merchants or some planters should stand for entire regions or classes. Like the terms *federalist* and *nationalist* in, for example, describing a "federalist resurgence," the use of sectional labels is not intended to create a rigid structure or to portray a level of cohesion where none existed. Indeed, a primary goal of this study is to demonstrate how the interaction between interest and ideology, sectionalism and centralism, and localism and nationalism prevents gross oversimplification and generalization.

of northern efforts to give Congress a power to regulate trade and to close the Mississippi River. By early 1787 nationalists and southerners were, as in 1781, allied against New England. This alignment and realignment of sectional blocs had a direct and powerful impact on revolutionary politics.

The American Revolution has been variously studied as an intellectual, ideological, economic, or social movement, but although the sectional nature of American politics has, in some form or other, long been acknowledged, sectionalism has been given, at best, a secondary place in most studies. Inasmuch as the theme of the Revolution, and especially the creation of a national government, is supposedly unity, little attention has been paid to the continuous impact of sectionalism on the political changes in eighteenth-century America.

Some historians have largely ignored the implications of sectional, or any other forms of internal conflict, and instead have described how a consensus and slow process of political maturation resulted in the formulation of the Constitution of 1787.[1] Others have focused primarily on the ideological struggle between federalists and nationalists to delineate the steps which led to the Philadelphia Convention. This is not to say that sectional conflicts have been totally ignored. On the contrary, the sectionally divisive problems of western lands, the navigation of the Mississippi River, and centralized commerce have been discussed. But the effect of those issues on the ideological struggle is usually overlooked in favor of citing the importance of other conflicts such as that concerning the federal debt. While sectionalism is often cited in the discussion of the formulation of the Articles of Confederation, the role of sectional interest and sectional conflict is given considerably less weight, if any weight at all, in describing the continuing story of constitutional change.[2]

A few historians have demonstrated the existence of sectional awarenesses and have analyzed sectional identities in far greater detail than any other group. Although generally in tune with the sectional forces at play in the many incidences of conflict in Congress in the 1770s and 1780s, they have failed to connect that conflict to the usually simultaneous ideological, or federalist-nationalist, confrontations.[3] Ideological and sectional conflicts did not take place in isolation from one another; they affected each other in significant ways, and this interaction is necessary in explaining the politics of revolutionary America. Although quantitative methods have recently provided us with a more rigorous description of the voting alignments in Congress, it is dangerous to rely solely on them to describe the political scene. Because the political scene was complicated by subgroups within broader ideological camps and by sectional, subsectional, and states' interests which can easily escape the static eye of the computer, analyses of congressional voting behavior can provide useful information, but not final answers to the many questions arising out of a discussion of revolutionary politics.[4]

This study is concerned with the role that sectional identity, sectional differences, and sectional interests, rivalries, and jealousies played in the political life of the new nation and the effect they had on political developments from the early days of the revolutionary movement until the meeting of the Philadelphia Convention. Rather than presenting factional behavior in sectional terms, this study is designed to show the influence of sectionalism on the forces of federalism and nationalism. Its principal goal is to show how sectionalism, in all its ramifications, complicated the struggle between the proponents and opponents of stronger central government and, in particular, how it prevented the latter from defending their ideology and the Articles of Confederation against attack.

1

The Roots of Conflict

THE IDEOLOGICAL struggle which was a constant theme in American politics during the years between the calling of the First Continental Congress in 1774 and the Philadelphia Convention in 1787 had its origins in the debates between the British and the revolutionaries. Separation from Great Britain was not supported by all Americans, and the imperial controversy concerning the authority of Parliament versus the rights of the colonial legislatures, or centralized versus local authority, was mirrored in the domestic struggle over the structure of a central government. For many revolutionaries rebellion against the British was indistinguishable from opposition to unresponsive, too-powerful central government. They wanted central government closely controlled in order to keep it a servant of rather than a dictator over the states and the people.[1] One safeguard to insure this was to prevent it from having the "power to regulate the internal Police of any Government." Although hardly democratic, the federalist perception of central government did contain the germ of a social revolution which even many of its supporters feared. Instead of looking to centralized authority, they placed their faith in "public virtue . . .[to] transcend every private consideration" and relied upon the ability of the states to maintain order. But in decentralizing political authority they ran the risk that the states might be unable to keep order and support a union.[2]

This possibility was uppermost in the minds of those politicians who worried about the effects of revolution in America. While many reluctant revolutionaries, men like John Dickinson, John Jay, James Wilson, and Robert Morris, ultimately rejected British control, they did not reject the institution of central government. A fear of social upheaval, a

7

belief that republicanism on the local level, where political change was too easy, would lead to democracy and anarchy, continually affected revolutionary politics. The rhetoric directed against Parliament and the British was easily leveled at American institutions; it precipitated a democratic response which some feared threatened to unleash "the many headed power the People." Thus, Josiah Quincy warned John Adams that his "zeal to get rid of the Reins of Government" would undeniably see "the Man of *Substance* reduced to a Level, with those who have none." After having secured "your *darling Liberty,*" he wondered, "What is to become of your Property?"[3] The desire to maintain order interested certain politicians in reconciliation with Great Britain and later moved them to advocate the creation of a central government able to exert substantial control over the states.

After Independence was declared the line of demarcation between central and local, or federal and state, sovereignty remained vague. Moreover, the revolutionary leaders faced the same complicated organizational problems which the British had been unable to resolve. They had to create some sort of political apparatus to manage interstate concerns and fill the void created by separation from Great Britain. The question of union was not, in itself, a matter of discord. Many leading federalists, though wary of central government, had long understood that cooperation was the only means effectively to combat Great Britain. At issue, however, was the amount of political power to be delegated to a central government. At stake was the freedom from central government which the Revolution at least tacitly assured.[4] The question of central government's authority, in terms of which groups would control it, was also related to the nation's sectional diversity.

Throughout the revolutionary era the sections vied for power with each other, and because the stakes were so very high sectional competition engendered jealousy and mistrust, affecting issues which, on the surface, had little to do with sectional interests. While the clash of interests between New England, the middle states, and the South became more intense later on, the impact of sectional conflict was no less significant in 1775 and 1776 than it was ten years later. Sectional interests were so strongly defended that only at those infrequent times when extraordinary pressures forced the elite, or a part of it, to stand together against a common enemy or threat to its interests, namely position and power, did cooperation replace conflict. Nevertheless, whether defending their interests against Great Britain in 1777 or against the people in 1787, the political leaders were still motivated by interests which threatened to engulf them all in a sectional conflagration.

The ideological, or factional, blocs in Congress reflected the influence of sectionalism, with federalists concentrated in New England, nationalists in the middle states, and the South split between the two. Federalists included such men as Elbridge Gerry, Samuel Adams, John Adams, James Warren, and Samuel Osgood of Massachusetts; William Whipple and Josiah Bartlett of New Hampshire; David Howell and William Ellery of Rhode Island; and Eliphalet Dyer and Roger Sherman of Connecticut. Federalist strength, in addition, owed much to the support of southerners such as Henry Laurens and Ralph Izard of South Carolina; Thomas Burke of North Carolina; and the Lees of Virginia, who, with the Adamses, formed the core of the Lee-Adams junto. Nationalists included men like Alexander Hamilton, Philip Schuyler, James Duane, Gouverneur Morris, John Jay, and Robert R. Livingston of New York; Robert Morris, James Wilson, and Thomas FitzSimons of Pennsylvania; and John Dickinson of Delaware. They too had a southern wing, which included James Madison, Joseph Jones, and Edmund Randolph of Virginia; John and Edward Rutledge of South Carolina; and Daniel St. Thomas Jenifer of Maryland. There were, moreover, such sectional crossovers as the nationalists Nathaniel Gorham of Massachusetts, Jesse Root of Connecticut, John Langdon and John Sullivan of New Hampshire, and James Varnum of Rhode Island, and the federalists Joseph Reed and the Bryans and Shippens of Pennsylvania. Despite ideological ties and the slight bridging of sectional boundaries, shifting sectional allegiances, the alignment and realignment of sectional blocs, had a direct impact on factional superiority in Congress.[5]

The disabling effects of sectional conflict were especially damaging to federalism because its influence depended upon intersectional cooperation among its supporters. Although in the early years of the Revolution the Lee-Adams junto cemented New England and the South, the differences between those sections, which demanded "the utmost caution on both sides and the most considerate forebearance with one another," were not easily resolved. Southerners, Samuel Adams noted, seemed to fear that New England aimed not only at independence from Great Britain "but of the other colonies too." They think, wrote Joseph Hawley, that Massachusetts men "affect to dictate and take the lead in Continental Measures; that we are apt from an inward vanity and self-conceit to assume big and haughty airs." Hawley thus advised his friend John Adams to avoid any conduct which might upset the southerners and hence jeopardize their support for New England's acts of resistance.[6] Adams did not face an easy task. Soon after arriving in Congress in 1774 he nervously reported an alarming "diversity of religions, educations, manners, interests, such as it would seem almost impossible to unite on one plan of conduct." This diversity led some loyalists to

venture the logical prediction that once political separation from Great
Britain occurred "commercial interests will interfere; there will be no
supreme power to interpose, and discord and animosity must ensue."[7]

Even in the face of British invasion and British attempts to split the
colonies between North and South, sectional fears abounded and
threatened to destroy the modicum of intercolonial cooperation spurred
by British transgressions and to undo the beneficial realization, which
bolstered federalism, that cooperation was vital to the Revolution, that
the lines of communication "between the northern and southern colonies" had to be maintained to prevent that disunion which could "only
give success to our Enemies."[8] The Second Continental Congress was
unhappily found to be very much "like the first," with sectional
prejudice running from North to South as well as from South to North.
While John Adams castigated southerners for their alleged fear of New
England's "Designs of Independency—An American Republic—Pres-
byterian Principles—and twenty other things," he nevertheless admitted his own "local Attachment . . . hardness . . . Prejudice in
favour of New England . . . [where] the People are purer English Blood
less mixed with Scotch, Irish, Dutch, French, Swedish than any
other."[9] Southern fears of a northern domination were strengthened by
suggestions that Congress move northward from Philadelphia. The distrust ran so deep in 1775 that some at least considered the creation of
"two grand Republics" by Congress—one southern and one northern
—as a real possibility.[10]

Some of the most serious sectional conflicts occurred in the Continental army. In order to mollify southern fears that they might eventually use their "Veteran Soldiers" to the other colonies' disadvantage, in
June 1775 the New Englanders agreed to appoint George Washington as
commander-in-chief. Washington's appointment did not, however,
allay sectionally inspired fears and jealousies to the extent which has
often been assumed. The United States might have faced a common
enemy, but only three of the fourteen senior officers in the Continental
army were southerners. Even Nathanael Greene thought that some
New England officers would have to be recalled in order "to remove any
unfavourable impressions that might arise in the Southern Colonies."[11]
With apparently no other recourse to balance the inequity but to ignore
the rules of seniority, to prevent, as the Virginia delegates said, having
the "whole Continent . . . supplied with general officers from the
Eastern Colonies," Congress promoted southern officers over New
Englanders. The promotions outraged many New Englanders in and out
of Congress and further strained relations in an army where the sections
had long since gotten into "the practice of reflecting on one another."[12]
While southerners sniped at New Englanders as "not like the Children

of the South" in either valor or expertise, New Englanders claimed that the promotions confirmed the observation "which some have had the impudence to make—'The Massachusetts men make good soldiers, but we must send to the Southward for our officers.' "[13]

Other signs of sectional conflict existed. There were reports of hostilities between New England and Pennsylvania troops. Alexander Hamilton for one did not want to have New England troops stationed in New York City because "antipathies and prejudices have long subsisted between this province and New England." There was some fear that southern objections to the high pay and bonuses New England soldiers received might "destroy that Union which now so happily Subsists."[14] These clashes, the removal of General David Wooster, and the conflicts between Generals Horatio Gates and Philip Schuyler and their supporters did little to foster the intercolonial cooperation necessary for a vigorous prosecution of the war or a successful revolution.[15]

The sectional differences which plagued the Continental army also retarded the movement for independence. New Englanders, who had no guarantee that the southerners would follow them to revolution, were afraid that they might "make their Terms of Peace and foresake us." Federalist plans for the Revolution did little to insure southern support. The revolutionaries wanted to establish a government to protect the fledgling union, believing, as Thomas Paine wrote, that "nothing but independence, i.e., a Continental form of government, can keep the peace of the Continent." It is not surprising, then, that Richard Henry Lee first proposed establishing a confederation on 7 June 1776, or that John Adams thought that for "internal concord" the informal authority of the Continental Congress had to be replaced with "a permanent Constitution."[16]

But federalism did not stop there. In order to prepare the colonies for independence and confederation, men like Samuel Adams first wanted to have new governments established "under the authority of the People." Yet this projected political change, although hardly alien to New England, was, John Adams said, accepted in the South only by men "of free Sprits and liberal Minds, who are very few." Others, including "the Barons of the South and the Proprietary Interests in the Middle Colonies," had what he called a "reluctance for Republican Government."[17] These cautious men's fears that republicanism might instill in the people expectations of further changes, that the establishment of new state governments would be "attended to with the greatest anarchy," were apparently borne out in Pennsylvania's constitution. One disgusted observer said that it introduced the dangerous notion that "any man, even the most illiterate, is as capable of any office as a person who has had the benefit of education."[18]

Despite Adams's southerners of liberal minds, federalism bore the stamp of an unwelcome, alien, and ominous New England radicalism. As late as May 1776 it was rumored that the tories were sure that the more conservative southern states would never agree to separation from Great Britain. Southern federalists were the exceptions and were sometimes castigated for blindly following "those wise Men of the East."[19] The Lee-Adams junto was a strained alliance between men with a common ideology but with conflicting sectional interests. Throughout the revolutionary era nationalist politicians tried to exploit these differences for their own ends. It was, for example, charged that a "Tiptoe Gentleman," possibly John Hancock (whom John Adams later said "had courted Mr. Duane, Mr. Dickinson and their party"), had in 1776 gone "tripping about Congress indefatigable in insinuating distrusts of the New England States . . . to make us [the southerners] look upon the New England States with a Kind of Horror."[20]

Because it was well understood that central government could, very easily, be used to further sectional ends, each section was reluctant to undermine its own interests for fear that the others might be unduly benefited. One of the reasons for New England's objection to Benjamin Franklin's Albany Plan in 1754 was purportedly the "great sway which the Southern Colonies . . . would have in all the determinations of the Grand Council." Similarly, Edward Rutledge opposed the first draft of the Articles of Confederation because he thought they would subject the southern states to "the Government of the Eastern Provinces." Before a plan of union was formulated it seemed possible that competing state and sectional interests would produce "intestine Wars and Convulsions" after separation, or, at the very least, prevent the establishment of a central government which would "be agreed to by all the colonies."[21]

Reflecting on the possibility that certain issues would block cooperation Patrick Henry warned John Adams and Richard Henry Lee to confine an intercolonial union "to Objects of Offensive & Defensive Nature . . . [for] If a Minute Arrangement of things is attempted . . . you may split & divide." Congress did not dissolve; it declared independence, and by late 1777 formulated a Confederation. The need to meet a common enemy somewhat balanced the countervailing forces of state and sectional interests. But completion of the Confederation in Congress did not signal the end of either ideological or sectional disputes. Held together by little more than a common fear the states and sections only reluctantly sacrificed their own interests. That they established a binding union was not so much a testament to their willing accord and self-sacrifice as it was a reflection of the realization that in the face of war even "an imperfect & somewhat unequal Confederacy . . . [was] better than none."[22]

The sectionally divisive problems of revenue, commerce, and western lands, which confronted Congress before October 1777, were side-stepped by a compromise borne of necessity: they were not solved. They remained troublesome throughout the revolutionary era, slowing the progress of the Articles of Confederation in Congress, stalling their ratification by the states, and causing major clashes in Congress in the 1780s and in the Philadelphia Convention in 1787. The clash between northern commercial and southern staple interests was the basic precipitant of sectional conflict. The North, with its ships and seamen, poised, ready to enter the world economy, while much of the South relied upon merchants, whether American or foreign, to carry its produce to market. The end of British rule gave northern merchants and southern land barons the promise of future wealth and power. At issue, from a sectional standpoint, were the kinds of policies to pursue and the direction to be taken by the United States. The New England merchants, who admittedly hoped to control the nation's carrying trade, wanted Congress to have a regulatory power over commerce.[23] Yet the southern delegates were so worried about northern commerical superiority that they even objected to the creation of an American navy in 1775. They were afraid that the New England merchants could too easily monopolize southern trade and charged, for example, that if New England privateering continued they would "become a devoted prey to their more formidable Eastern neighbours." Southerners, especially those who depended on competition among merchants to insure the best price for their exports and the lowest price for imports, were worried that if Congress were given a commerce power a monopoly "might be given away by those, which have no staple, as the price of commercial privelage to them."[24]

Even after major concessions mollified some of these sorts of fears, southerners remained concerned with the sectional balance in a Congress where policy could be made "contrary to the united opposition of Virginia, the two Carolinas, and Georgia; States possessing more than one half of the whole territory of the confederacy." Because of this unfavorable sectional balance, and because the direction the United States took in commercial matters was so closely related to the balance of sectional power, southerners, throughout the period, looked to the western lands to insure a degree of sectional independence. They believed that the new states which would arise in the West could more than balance northern commercial superiority by shifting the sectional balance to the southward. They therefore defended the right of individual states to determine the question of claims in the western lands, supported America's right to the free navigation of the Mississippi River, pushed for the early and easy admittance of new states into the Union, and tried to prevent their vast unimproved holdings from being included in national revenue schemes.[25]

The South's western strategy came under fire from two different groups. Middle state land speculators, who had claims to tracts in the western lands, wanted them put under congressional control to insure a return on their investments. New Englanders wanted the western lands given to Congress in order that the money realized from the sale of these lands could be used as a federal fund and thereby alleviate the need for commercial taxes. Although their own commercial interests dictated otherwise, most New Englanders in Congress acceded to southern demands: Congress, for example, was not given jurisdiction over the western lands, and state quotas for federal requisitions were to be decided by the value of only improved lands. While the New Englanders might have had little choice in 1776 and 1777, being so dependent upon southern support in Congress, some still feared that the South might eventually become "too great and powerful So as to become dangerous to the rest."[26]

These fundamental sectional differences continued to generate hostility which set the sections at odds. Southerners still railed at New England's large salaries and bounties for its soldiers. They feared that the war was enriching the northern states, which would when "possessed of the greatest part of the Money . . . lay the other States under a heavy tax." New Englanders, on the other hand, complained of inadequate assistance from the South, whose own "army seems to swallow up all the Clothing."[27] The tension between Gates and Schuyler finally erupted in 1777, with the latter, who thought his only crime was "not being a New England man in principle," dropped from command of the northern army. He was assured, though, that he had fast friends "from New York south." Not even George Washington was above the fray, and attempts to have him relieved of command were ascribed to New England resentment.[28]

The apparently uncontrollable force of sectional conflict continued to strain the intersectional accord upon which federalist strength so precariously rested. William Duer, a nationalist from New York, asserted that the one way to defeat the federalists was "in cultivating the friendship of the members [of Congress] from the Southern States." Richard Henry Lee, whose allegiances were clear, was outraged that some Virginians had accused him of favoring "New England to the injury of Virginia." He still believed that Virginia's truest ally was New England

and pointed out that "our enemies & our friends, know that America can only be conquered by disunion—The former through unremitting art had endeavored to fix immoveable Discord between the South and the Eastern Colonies, and . . . had so far prevailed that it has required a constant attention and firmness not to be shaken."[29] The accord between the two sections was violently shaken and finally destroyed during Congress's discussion of foreign policy in 1778 and 1779.

DECLINE OF FEDERALISM

The continuing sectional tensions in 1777 and 1778 added to the strain caused by the slow ratification of the Articles of Confederation. In the face of widespread state objections it seemed that changes would have to be made "and Subordinate Points either relinquished or reserved for a fairer opportunity rather than obstruct so Important and indispensable a work." There was fear, however, that once "open to debate and procrastination" the Articles of Confederation "should never live to see Ratification." Congress refused to accept the many amendments proposed by the states, but the prospect of ratification grew dimmer when it became apparent the Maryland would never ratify so long as Virginia maintained control over its western lands.[30] Failure to ratify the Articles of Confederation quickly, which raised questions about the sovereign states' willingness to readily support a union, enabled nationalists, who opposed the strictures placed on Congress under the Articles, to attack the very core of federalist ideology.

The failure to ratify the Articles also weakened the position of the United States vis-à-vis foreign nations. This was especially critical in light of the integral relation of foreign assistance to the American Revolution. Indeed, one of the strongest arguments in favor of independence had been that it was "the only means by which Foreign Alliances can be obtained." But many federalists first wanted to establish new governments in the states, then to form a Confederation, "and last of all, to form treaties with foreign powers." It was felt that any departure from this scheme would render the United States "weak, and distracted and divided in our Councils."[31] Yet even federalists like Richard Henry Lee, Ralph Izard, and James Warren were forced to admit that French assistance was too vital to American interests to risk waiting until the nation could enter into a treaty of equals.[32] This tactical decision might not have been so significant had the French been governed only by altruistic motives. Such was not the case, and they quickly sought to take advantage of America's weak and distracted condition. By 1778, moreover, the armed conflict began to fall heavily on the South, making it especially vulnerable to external dictates. During the discussion and debates on foreign policy in 1778 and 1779 the Lee-Adams junto lost all but its core support and its influence on Congress diminished.

In September 1776 Congress had adopted a model treaty designed to secure French support without "any Political Connections." Arthur Lee, Silas Deane, and Benjamin Franklin were then chosen to negotiate with the French. Their early negotiations were fruitless, partly because of French reluctance to gamble on the outcome of the Revolution. The French wanted to weaken the British and feared that premature support for America would move Great Britain to reconcile.[33] They hoped to exert a permanent influence on an independent America and were as wary of British victory as they were of the United States "becoming a great and flourishing empire." In order to influence America's foreign policy decisions, the French wanted the political connection which most federalists feared. They intended to circumscribe federalist war aims, which included control over Canada, Newfoundland, and Nova Scotia, the northern fishery, the Mississippi River, and the Floridas.[34]

The New England merchants, despite their enmity to Great Britain and their active role in bringing about the Revolution, were commercially tied to the British and envisioned normalized trade with them after the conclusion of the war. This threatened the French aim to weaken British influence while increasing their own, because the New England merchants had all the necessary mercantile tools to prevent the French from reaping major commercial benefits in America.[35] In addition, most federalists, with whom the New England merchants were identified, were extremely wary of the French. Henry Laurens, for example, advised against depending "upon a Crafty designing Court, who has never done, & who never will do, any thing for our Interest but what has been or what shall be subservient to their own." This mutual resentment increased because of the questionable behavior of Silas Deane in Europe, which resulted in his recall in November 1777. Technically Congress recalled him because he had granted hundreds of unauthorized commissions to French officers.[36] Federalists in Europe, such as Arthur Lee, William Lee, and Ralph Izard, however, also accused him of being part of a commercial "cabal" which was profiting from the war by using public money for private gain.[37]

Deane's recall was thus connected to efforts, through the medium of federalist-inspired price-fixing conventions, to control commercial speculation and defend the economic sector against the encroachment of Robert Morris's middle state mercantile combine. Deane was closely connected to Morris, whose almost total control of the Secret Committee of Correspondence and the Secret Committee for Commerce extended his influence so much that his associates in Europe were accused of using his name as if he were "King of America." Not only did Morris have close connections with such important American merchants as John Alsop and Philip Livingston of New York; John Ross, Blair McClenachan, George Mead, John Nesbit, John Nixon, Samuel Meredith, George Clymer, and Thomas FitzSimons of Philadelphia; and Carter Braxton and Benjamin Harrison of Virginia; but he also had close dealings with the French in the persons of Conrad Gérard, Beaumarchais, and John Holker. This powerful mercantile combine posed a threat to federalism. Arthur Lee, in fact, wanted to take "all the private consignments from this Country [France] & from America out of Mr. Morris's channel." He, and similarly opinioned federalists, were very worried about the connection between the French and the Morris faction.[38]

Although a war-weary nation desperately hoped for what Benjamin Rush called "a French war," Henry Laurens thought the French "specious half friends . . . who played off our commissioners and ambassadors like puppets." After America's victory at Saratoga and the news that the British were preparing to send peace feelers to America, the French finally agreed to an alliance in a treaty ratified by Congress in early May 1778. The terms of the alliance were much more binding than had been the earlier model treaty. The United States was committed to a defensive alliance and to the proviso that neither party sign a separate peace without the consent of the other. Congress was forced to accept these terms because of the critical importance of French miliatry and financial aid. There was some concern, however, that America's need opened the way for "political powers or parties, Allies or not Allies, to interfere for their own purposes."[39]

The French purposes were clear. Their enmity to the New England merchants, and federalism in general, had increased when John Adams replaced Silas Deane in 1777. Not only was Adams determined to defend New England's interest in the northern fishery, but also, at the same time, the federalist-controlled Congress had appointed William Lee commissioner to the court of Vienna and Berlin, Ralph Izard commissioner to Tuscany, and Arthur Lee commissioner to Spain. In attempting to lessen federalist, and especially New England, influence in making foreign policy, the French even accused the New Englanders and their allies of supporting and, in fact, openly soliciting reconciliation with Great Britain.[40] What they really objected to was the desire to keep America at arm's length from them. When the French threw their support to Silas Deane in 1779, Henry Laurens remarked that they disliked Arthur Lee "because he checked the unfaithful acts & attempts of Mr. Deane & his partners & because he was faithful to the United States of America & insisted upon making a better Treaty with the Court of France than Mr. Deane had submitted to."[41]

When Deane finally arrived in America in July 1778 to answer the charges leveled against him, he was accompanied by France's first foreign minister to America, Conrad Gérard, whose real mission, Arthur Lee warned his federalist friends, was "to secure you to the [H]ouse of Bourbon." The French, through Gérard, did everything in their power to aid the Morris faction and to throw the Lee-Adams junto into disrepute. James Lovell later noted that the difference between the two groups resulted "from our varying Quantum of Obsequiousness to the Dictations of a Foreigner."[42]

Buoyed by willing French support, Deane's nationalist supporters, for the first time, took the initiative. Instead of defending Deane, they argued that his recall resulted from the malicious attacks of Arthur Lee and his federalist friends. They even tried to propagate the view, which the French already believed, that the Lee-Adams junto was blatantly anti-French. Upset by Deane's contention that he and he alone was responsible for the French alliance, Henry Laurens, the president of Congress, and Thomas Paine, the secretary of the Committee for Foreign Affairs, tried, in vain, to set the record straight. Both men resigned in early January—Laurens out of frustration with Congress and Paine as a result of outright attack.[43] These resignations did not bode well for federalist influence in Congress. Morris and his cadre, reportedly using "their new formed commercial Establishments . . . [to circulate] their insinuations and falsehoods thro' the Country," were attempting, it was said, to "contract the old opinion that it is impossible to wash the black mare white." The French, moreover, continued to support Deane and the Morris faction.[44]

The Deaneites, who according to James Lovell, wanted to "get hold of the Helm & the main Stays at a critical Moment," tried to secure the removal of America's foreign ministers. Richard Henry Lee believed their attempt even to recall Benjamin Franklin, minister plenipotentiary to France, was simply part of a plan to "recall them all to make room." Obviously, they hoped to make room for their own appointees. By 10 June 1779, after almost two months of wrangling, Congress revoked the commissions of Ralph Izard and William Lee, permitted Silas Deane to leave the United States (without a commission), and took no action with regard to Benjamin Franklin and Arthur Lee. The Deaneites had judiciously avoided attacking John Adams throughout the episode.[45]

The sectional overtones of the struggle had special significance for the

Lee-Adams junto. Deane was supported by his middle state allies and by many southern delegates. The shift of the war to the South in 1778 and 1779 put increased pressure on southerners insofar as they grew ever more dependent upon French assistance. Most southerners were naturally reluctant to support Arthur Lee and eastern war aims for fear of antagonizing the French and risking the loss of the support upon which their very existence seemingly depended. At the start of the Lee-Deane controversy there were reports that "the old prejudices of North against South, and South against North" were reviving. There were even complaints that "great questions are carried every day in favor of the Eastward, and to the prejudice of the Southern States."[46] Given this situation, whether real or imagined, many southerners, once confronted with a serious military situation, looked to the French instead of to New England and were unwilling to do anything which might upset them.

The French used the budding conflict between New England and the South and the growing military pressure on the South to further their own interests, namely limiting federalist influence in America's foreign affairs and, among other things, preventing the United States from gaining entry into the fishery. The French interfered directly during Congress's discussion of peace demands and even threatened the withdrawal of their assistance to pressure Congress to pare its peace demands. New Englanders, determined not to let France dictate American war aims, were worried about "the arts . . . to hurry" Congress into a "rash" decision on the peace demands. The French were naturally supported by the Morris faction, who, said James Warren, "neither like the political principles, or manner of N[ew] England . . . [and wanted] to reduce their trade, and consequently their power and influence. What could more effectually do that than by ceding all right and claim to the fishery to get a Peace rather than see us Flourish."[47]

Those New Englanders interested in commerce argued that America needed a navy and that "the Source of Seamen is the Fishery," which was "as Valueable to America and more so to Old Massachusetts than the Tobacco Fields of the middle states or the Rice Swamps of the South." An increasing number of southerners, however, had no desire to sacrifice their own interests for something which was "of no use to any but three or at most four States." Even after Congress postponed consideration of the peace ultimata in early May 1779, the French continued to demand that the fishery not be a *sine qua non* of peace. Pressure from nationalists and the French and the worsening state of the war were too much to overcome. Richard Henry Lee concluded that only a major military victory could lessen America's dependence upon France and save the fishery "from the paws which are used to pull the

Chestnuts out of the fire."[48] Because the United States could not pull their own chestnuts out of the fire, the French were in a perfect position to get their demands met.

Not content with arguing the merits of the case against extensive peace demands, the French again accused the Lee-Adams junto of favoring the British. It was even whispered in Congress that France could engineer a peace "unless G[reat] B[ritain] should be encouraged by a faction in Congress to continue the war, in hopes, that that faction may at last, on the condition of Britain's acknowledging our Independence, prevail on the States to enter into offensive & defensive treaties with her." Thus, some saw New England's obdurate stance on the peace demands as threatening the French alliance and lengthening a pattern of warfare which was growing more and more desperate in the South. The argument was clear and compelling: the war was being almost intentionally drawn out because of demands which had "arisen in the East, but have been supported by the south side of the Potowmack." Most southerners had little difficulty in making a choice between supporting New England or the French. Richard Henry Lee and Henry Laurens, federalist stalwarts, were now viewed as "two Monsters . . . who pursue points in which the southern states have no interest." The already tottering intersectional relations were hardly stabilized by charges that New England was trying to get Vermont admitted to the Union "to gain another Voice in Congress."[49]

Although federalists continually resisted their demands, the French and their American allies eventually succeeded in withdrawing the fishery as a *sine qua non* of peace.[50] On 14 August, however, instructions were formulated for the as yet unnamed peace commissioner to negotiate a commercial treaty with Great Britain in which "the common right of fishing shall in no case be given up." New England, then, could protect the claim and possibly even insure America's entry into the fishery "if a proper person [could] be agreed on to negotiate the business."[51]

Another development put the New Englanders in a quandary. On 14 September there was a motion to make treaty overtures to Spain. Eight days later John Adams, John Jay, and Henry Laurens were nominated to make a peace with Great Britain. After an inconclusive vote Meriwether Smith and William Paca, two strongly pro-French Deaneites, moved that a minister plenipotentiary also be appointed to negotiate a treaty with Spain. The motion was approved, and Adams, Jay and Arthur Lee, already commissioner to Spain, were nominated. The contest, thought James Lovell, was really only between Adams and Jay; one "to have a post of the highest honor, and the other was to take the post of a man murdered on purpose to make room." The murdered man was Arthur Lee. On 24 September it was moved that after the word *plenipotentiary* in the instructions for a minister to Spain the words "in Lieu of a commissioner" be inserted, thus eradicating Arthur Lee's commission. In order to get John Adams appointed as peace commissioner his supporters had to sacrifice Arthur Lee. They had little choice, for if Adams were not chosen they had no doubt, as Lovell expressed it, that "the Election from another Quarter may take place. & no other New England Man will be chosen, the Interest of America requires, blind as some People are to it, that a New England Man should negotiate a Peace." Adams was elected peace commissioner, Jay was sent to Spain, and in October Arthur Lee, with his commission already taken out from under him, was recalled.[52]

The French and the Morris faction did not secure all their objectives. The French were as wary of American control over the Mississippi River as they were of the fishery, but a right to navigate the river was contained in the peace demands, and John Jay was instructed to defend America's claim in his negotiations with Spain. The Spanish consistently refused to lend their assistance to the war effort, because of America's unwillingness to relinquish its claim to the Mississippi. But they had effectively taken control of the river by 1779, and the French exerted ever-increasing pressure on Congress to secure a cession of the Mississippi to Spain. Congress did not accede to French demands. The southern states refused to back down on this issue, and the situation was stalemated, but only temporarily.[53]

The defense of the Mississippi River, which resulted primarily from southern support absent on other issues, was small compensation for the mortal wounds federalism had suffered. Silas Deane gloated that the "whole of the Family [the Lees] are disposed of . . . I say almost for the Junto tho' broken is not destroyed." William Lee wondered if the only way to secure independence was to become "the Voluntary Slaves of France." He told his brother of plots against the United States from that quarter and warned that "Your Salvation in my opinion must arise from an Union more strict than ever with New England." Too many southerners were swept along by the exigencies of war to heed Lee's warning.[54]

By the end of 1779 the balance of power in Congress was changing. The middle states' nationalists had, with strong French and southern support, forced New England to compromise its war aims and seriously rent the Lee-Adams junto. They were still unable to control Congress because of federalist delegations from Pennsylvania and New Jersey, but New England had only the barest support in other states. The South was, aside from the Lees and Laurens, almost totally committed to following Morris's lead. Richard Henry Lee even expressed a desire to eventually retire to Massachusetts, because "the hasty, unperservering, aristocratic genius of the south suits not my disposition." Although John Adams went to Europe armed with instructions to negotiate a commercial treaty with the British, which he and others hoped would recognize America's right of entry into the fishery, Congress had already shifted away from federalism. Before he left America Adams bitterly remarked that Congress "resemble[d] a picture in the gallery of the C[ount] de Vergennes."[55]

The conflict over the peace terms and the Lee-Deane dispute ushered in a new era in federal politics. Federalists were dismayed at what they termed the "spirit of party," but what they really feared was that nationalists, those "Votaries of pleasure . . . [who] Worship at the shrine of plutus," would employ the same organizational techniques they themselves had so effectively used from 1774 to 1777.[56] Federalism's period of dominance was soon replaced by a period of forceful and energetic nationalist activity. Strengthened by southern support, in 1780 and 1781 the Morris faction completed what it had begun in 1779. By 1781 the drive to further isolate and weaken New England became part of a larger effort to create a stronger central government.

2

The Nationalist Ascendancy

BY 1780 the same conditions which had earlier precipitated Congress's departure from federalist foreign policies—the pressures of war, a change in southern factional loyalties, and the effects of French interference—set the stage for a nationalist ascendancy. Some new developments also spurred the shift away from federalism. The centralizing effects of a wartime economy broadened the conservative base in America and interested many merchants and the growing number of public creditors in redefining Congress's powers. Demands for commercial and especially political centralization seemed an appropriate response to rising complaints that a lack of supplies for the army and an unwillingness of the states to fulfill their congressional requisitions were retarding the war effort. Although federalists still feared the potential for tyranny in a central government, they were hard-pressed to come up with an adequate alternative in the face of the apparent failure of voluntary state cooperation to provide for the nation's needs. They faced the problem of defending a political system which, solely upon utilitarian grounds, seemingly could not be defended.[1]

The emergence of a quite vocal pronationalist bloc in New England also affected the political scene. A growing disenchantment with state sovereignty compounded by the telltale signs of democracy in the states and sectional conflicts in Congress convinced men like Thomas Cushing, Nathaniel Gorham, John Lowell, James Varnum, Ezekiel Cornell, Jesse Root, and John Langdon that the Union was defective and needed "a controulling power, over the whole being lodged in some person or persons."[2] One of the strongest inducements, from a New England perspective, in favor of congressional centralization, was the desire to get a noncommercial source of revenue by establishing federal control over the western lands. The continuing struggle over the western lands, moreover, blocked ratification of the Articles of Confederation, which weakened federalism's credibility and kept northerners and southerners at odds. Virginia's persistent refusal to acknowledge the middle state land speculators' claims precipitated Maryland's refusal to ratify the Articles of Confederation.[3]

The increasingly apparent lack of congressional authority and national coordination, which may or may not have reflected the absence of a constitution, also raised major questions about the unratified Articles, which in turn added credence to the persistent calls to strengthen Congress. The addition of pronationalist Pennsylvania and New Jersey congressional delegations in late 1780 assured a strong nationalist influence in Congress.

But while nationalism's burgeoning power had a clear sectional component, namely southern support, intersectional alliances were transitory. Federalist influence had already diminished because of sectional differences, and it was more a consequence of the war than of anything else that southerners supported Robert Morris and his followers. The latter benefited on two counts from the fact that the war still ran heavily in Great Britain's favor. Because French support remained vital to a successful Revolution, nationalist politicians were secure in the knowledge that the antifederalist French would be able to continue to exert a great deal of influence on Congress. Moreover, the continuing military pressure on the South forced many of its leaders to support nationalist programs.

This support was invaluable in the continuing drive to weaken further the New England merchant-federalists. In order to insure their own continued prominence, leading nationalists intended to limit federalist political influence and to chart a downward course for New England by preventing its interest from being secured in a peace treaty. In 1780, in the opening salvo of their movement to strengthen Congress, nationalists set out, again in league with the French, to complete what they had begun in 1779 in a second act of the Lee-Deane controversy.

THE POLITICS OF FOREIGN POLICY

Because there was no clear factional dominance in Congress in 1779, the clash over foreign policy had ended in a fragile stalemate. Although federalist, and particularly eastern, aims and goals no longer defined America's foreign policy, some important points had been defended. In late 1779 a new foreign minister, the Chevalier de la Luzerne, assumed the direction of French policy in America. The French were not content with the partial success in circumscribing America's peace demands. They realized that the fishery and the Mississippi River were two resources vital to a commercially independent United States. The French made it difficult, if not impossible, for John Adams to begin negotiations with the British, in which he undoubtedly would have mentioned the fishery. Little more than a month after arriving in France, Adams realized that the French were playing a very dangerous game at America's expense. He told Richard Henry Lee, mixing sarcasm and cynicism, that "the Fishery and the Navigation of the Misisippi are Points of such Importance that your Grand Son when he makes the Peace I hope will secure them."[4] Adams was already sure that the French were not above letting the war continue until America was too weak to resist their permanent influence.

While the French were holding Adams in check, they used the worsening state of the war to attempt to get Congress to relinquish the claim to the Mississippi River. In January 1780 Luzerne, with greater bargaining power, emphasized anew the dire American need for Spanish assistance. He even tried to incite a fear of the danger of continued western emigration in an attempt to garner New England support. Although many New Englanders were scared by the prospect of southern expansion, they were, at this time, far more afraid of foreign domination and worried that the South might retaliate against New England's commercial aims, namely the fishery, if the Mississippi were closed.[5]

Luzerne's attempt to play off the promise of Spanish assistance against the Mississippi River was soon aided by Spain's refusal to negotiate with John Jay while America claimed the Mississippi. Congress, after being apprised of the situation, overcame considerable French and nationalist pressure and resolved on 4 October that Jay "adhere to his former instructions respecting the right of the United States to the free navigation of the Mississippi."[6]

Some new developments seriously impaired the South's ability to continue to resist French demands. By early 1780 there were reports that the newly arisen league of neutral European nations would attempt to impose a peace between Great Britain and the United States and France. This possibility, often discussed in the newspapers in conjunction with pro-French and anti-British statements, was particularly threatening to the South. If the armed neutrality was able to impose a peace *uti possedetis* there was the strong likelihood that large portions of southern states, to say nothing of the western lands, would go to the British.[7] The possibility of a peace *uti possedetis* was all the more ominous because of the questionable position of New England. There were rumors, which played right into French hands, that "G[reat] Britain will offer America, the Independence of the States except No[rth] & So[uth] Carolina & Georgia . . . & that such a proposition will be accepted."[8] If the southern states could be convinced that reliance on New England was hopeless, the French stood to increase their influence further.

Even William Lee confronted John Adams with information he had received that "it was very immaterial what became of the Southern States, or whether they were annexed to G. Britain or not, as the 4 New England States are fully capable by their own efforts to maintain & support their Independency agt. all the power of G. Britain." Adams assured Lee that despite the fact that two or three confederacies could survive the New Englanders strongly supported the Union. Adams, in fact, professed less concern about British conquest or even amicable disunion than about the possibility that "the divergent divisions of the continent, would soon be at war, with each other." He had little doubt that if sectional dissimilarity precipitated armed conflict, or uncontrollable hostility, that the French would have no difficulty in taking Britain's place as, at the least, an American overseer. Lee believed Adams, but he warned that his own too easily aroused suspicion proved that "well meaning & honest men, are too often deceived by the wicked & artful into their measures." He therefore thought it unwise for New England to increase sectional distrust and conflict by pursuing aims like the conquest of Canada while portions of the South were under British control.[9] Regardless of the source or validity of Lee's charges, the fact remained that a South battered by the storms of war could easily be misled.

The southerners had good cause for concern and good reason to doubt that they could afford New England's anti-French biases. The prospect of some sort of permanent French influence was certainly less threatening than British conquest. In the face of a deteriorating military situation John Rutledge called for "the greatest Exertions of the Northern States & of Congress." But the fall of Charles Town in August 1780 confirmed the unfavorable balance of military power. By November even America's own officers predicted "the Loss of the four Southern States." These developments compounded southern fears, increased their dependence on the French, and made them more vulnerable to French dictates.[10] They also had immediate effects on national policy.

Little more than a month after Congress reaffirmed Jay's instructions Georgia and South Carolina, "apprehensive that a *uti possedetis* may be obtruded on the beligerant Powers by the armed neutrality in Europe . . . moved for a reconsideration." There was far more at stake at this critical juncture than the question of America's claim to the Mississippi River. The southern states were being forced by circumstances beyond their control to pursue a course of action which was contrary to their own interests. There was no telling how far they would go in order to satisfy the French. James Madison pointed out that "the Eastern states must, on the first suggestion, take alarm for their fisheries. If they will not support other States in their rights, they cannot expect to be supported themselves when theirs come into question." Madison's disappoint-ment with and resentment of New England is easily understood in light of the common southern belief that the South's future wealth and influence lay to the West in the new states which would eventually enter the Union.[11]

If the Mississippi were closed, or controlled by a foreign power, there was a chance that the western territories might fall under strong foreign influence, if not foreign control. Although southerners hoped that Congress would never agree to peace "whilst the Enemy hold any part of the 13 States," they had reason to doubt northern restraint. To southerners already concerned, northern interests and British policies seemed neatly to complement each other. It was hardly a secret that many northerners feared an expanding South,and there was more than idle speculation that Great Britain intended to seize as much territory as it could "in order that if a Negotiation of Peace should take place it might probably be one of the Terms that each party should keep as much as they were then in possession of." It was thus imperative to southern interests that the war not end prematurely and that the United States get as much foreign assistance as it could—no matter what the price. The worsening military situation, the reverberations of the loss of Charles Town, and the uncertainty that New England could or would do anything to aid the South sealed the Mississippi's fate.[12]

Despite Virginia's special stake in keeping the Mississippi open, Theodorick Bland had little difficulty in convincing Virginia's leaders, among them a very reluctant Madison and Jefferson, that there was no alternative but to secure Spanish assistance by relinquishing at least part of America's claim to the Mississippi River. On 18 January 1781 Con-gress instructed Jay, if necessary, to withdraw the demand for the right to navigate the Mississippi River below 31° north latitude, or what the Americans believed to be the logical southern boundary of their terri-tory.[13] Some southerners were upset by the sacrifice of so vital a resource. But, given the state of the war and the belief that the New Eng-land states "care not for the Southern" they had little choice.[14] As condi-tions deteriorated in early 1781 southerners complained that New Eng-land was not sending troops to the South "to requite the assistance

formerly lent from hence." The situation was so grave that even Richard
Henry Lee called for George Washington to come to Virginia armed
with temporary dictatorial powers.[15] Southern cooperation with the
nationalists, and through them with the French, was determined by a
necessity which also affected other areas of policy formation in
Congress.

Southern commitment to New England's war aims, already doubtful,
was very important in light of the continuing conflict between New
Englanders and the French and nationalists. John Adams's New England allies had hoped that his selection as peace commissioner would
balance the loss of the fishery as a *sine qua non* of peace. But Adams's
avowed intention to protect New England's interests—his desire to
formulate a favorable Anglo-American commercial treaty which would,
he hoped, guarantee American entry into the northern fishery and
solidify New England's postwar commerce—threatened the French aim
to "destroy England's supremacy of the Seas . . . and give France a
necessary market for its manufactures and industry [in America]."[16]

Soon after Adams arrived in France, the Count de Vergennes advised
him not to reveal either of his commissions to the British. Adams, aware
that continued conflict with Great Britain could only weaken America
and strengthen French influence, tried in vain to change Vergennes's
mind. By March he was already complaining to Congress of "the deli-
cacy of the Count de Vergennes, about communicating my powers."
While Adams continued to warn of the dangers of too close a relationship with and dependence upon France and suggested that negotiations
with the British proceed, relations between him and Vergennes
worsened. Finally in late July Vergennes, in a very strongly worded
letter, ordered Adams no longer to concern himself with the question of
commercial negotiations and to wait until the French were ready to
begin peace negotiations. Shortly thereafter Adams left for Holland to
secure a loan in an attempt to render the United States less dependent
upon France.[17]

Vergennes, determined to erect a foundation for French influence in
postwar America, set plans to motion to draw Congress into an even
more binding alliance. All that apparently stood in his way was John
Adams, and Vergennes was determined either to secure greater control
over him or have him removed. As soon as Adams left for Holland
Vergennes forwarded their correspondence to the trusted francophile
Benjamin Franklin with a request that it be sent to Congress as evidence
of Adams's stubborn and thoughtless refusal to cooperate with
America's ally and abide by the terms of the alliance. Federalists,
though, realized that Adams and his dual commission represented the

final barrier to total French domination of America's foreign affairs.[18] They were as sure as ever that the French wanted to continue "the war, in order to weaken America as well as Great Britain, and thereby leave us at the end of it, as dependent as possible upon themselves." Arthur Lee, soon to leave Europe, warned Adams to be on guard against the French, and an equally bitter Ralph Izard suggested to Richard Henry Lee that "the political salvation of America depends upon the recalling of Dr. Franklin."[19] But Lee and his shrinking number of colleagues were in no position to strike back. Their warnings, even more so than in 1778, fell on deaf ears.

The middle states' merchants, aligned with Robert Morris, did not want to see a vigorous New England-controlled Anglo-American commerce established after the war, and many southerners would not separate interest from ideology. They were still reluctant to give any mercantile group the ability to monopolize their economy. Moreover, in attacking the French, Franklin, and Morris, federalists opened themselves to renewed charges that they were enemies to the French alliance and uncommitted to any but their own special interests. Their attacks on France's nefarious plotting sharply contrasted with Benjamin Rush's proclamation that Conrad Gérard was "still dear to the faithful citizens of America. We call him the 'Republican minister.' " The growing nationalist influence in Congress enabled the French attack on John Adams to take shape.[20]

The heated correspondence between Vergennes and Adams reached Congress in early January 1781 and was referred to a committee which quickly instructed Adams to abide by Vergennes's suggestions. Vergennes, in the meantime, sent letters to Luzerne attacking Adams and requesting that he be placed under direct French control. By May he instructed Luzerne to seek a reconsideration of the peace instructions of 1779. The French wanted Congress to have to choose between John Adams and continued assistance from them. Luzerne used the same scare tactics which had worked so effectively in relation to the Mississippi to get Congress to appoint a committee to reconsider Adams's powers. In early June this committee, strongly nationalist and pro-French, reported in favor of great French control over the peace negotiations. Congress then ordered Adams to "undertake nothing in his negotiations for peace or truce, without their knowledge and concurrence."[21]

The French and their allies were still not satisfied. They increased the number of peace commissioners, adding John Jay, Benjamin Franklin, Thomas Jefferson, and Henry Laurens. But because Jefferson had to remain in America with an ill wife and Laurens was detained in the Tower of London, only the two trusted nationalists, Franklin and Jay, went to France. At least in theory American foreign affairs were turned over to the French. The revision of the peace instructions grievously wounded New England, but because Adams's commercial commission was untouched James Lovell reasoned that "we may conclude our *haddock safe.*" Lovell's relief was short-lived. The French realized that Adams and his unrestricted commercial commission still represented a real threat to their interests, and François Barbé-Marbois, Luzerne's secretary, got James Madison to introduce a motion revoking the commission. The motion passed the same day it was introduced, 12 July 1781.[22]

The revocation of Adams's commercial commission gave the French and the Morris faction almost absolute control of the nation's foreign affairs. Many federalists were naturally disheartened by the recent turn of events. They were especially outraged at the appointment of "that corrupt old Serpent" Benjamin Franklin as a peace commissioner. The New Englanders still thought the fishery "at least as important as Tobacco yards, or Rice Swamps, or the flourishing Wheat Fields of Pennsylvania." It might have been, but not to the middle and southern states. New England's fate, its commercial future, seemed to rest on the abilities of a John Adams who was hopelessly outnumbered and whose "feathers had been plucked and worn as ornaments by others." Adams wanted them to "have the plumage, it is but a geegaw," but he, and New England, had lost far more than a geegaw.[23] Without a commercial commission, let alone the possible effects of the addition of the new commissioners, there was nothing to guarantee, or even suggest, that America and New England would gain anything from a treaty other than what the French wanted them to have.

There was little Adams's federalist supporters could do. French assistance was simply too vital and New England's interests too specialized to allow for any action other than that which was taken.[24] In addition, French propaganda, threats, and gold even induced some New Englanders to switch sides and cause what Luzerne called "the rupture of the league formed by the Eastern States."[25] The dramatic shift in the nation's foreign policy was only one indication of the degree to which the war affected the political scene. While still under its grip, Congress followed a nationalist lead in many areas other than foreign policy.

THE NATIONALIST MOVEMENT TO STRENGTHEN CONGRESS

By 1780 pleas to give the central government sufficient power to control the states became more defensible in the face of the states' reluctance fully to support Congress and the war effort. The unclear status of the Articles of Confederation and conditions which bore the signs of a national crisis supported nationalist contentions that the nation's difficulties resulted from the "political views and interests of Seperate Communities, while they profess to be members of one body." Already convinced that Congress did not possess enough power, nationalists began to argue that "such [powers] as they had, have been, from embarrassment and difficulties, frittered away to the States." Their solution was to strive for "a government with more power."[26] One way to accomplish that change was in a convention of the states.

Throughout the 1780s a convention of the states was looked to at those times when Congress appeared to be unable to handle the nation's problems. Even the earliest proposals evidenced this alternative role. The difficulty in ameliorating conflicting interests and establishing a central government in 1776 drove Edward Rutledge to the conclusion that "a special Congress" must formulate a federal constitution. By 1779 the conditions which broadened nationalism's appeal even caused Henry Laurens to advocate the calling of "a Convention in aid of 'the great Council.' " In addition to using a convention to bolster somehow congressional authority and smooth efficiency, there were calls for a "continental convention" to set the nation on a fresh course, to formulate a new constitution which would give Congress "Powers of general jurisdiction and controul over individual states."[27] This dissatisfaction with the Confederation's lack of authority spurred the calling of two smaller conventions which directed energy to and stimulated reform within Congress.

At the Boston Convention, held in early August 1780, a number of delegates from the New England states demanded that the Union "be fixed in a more solid Manner" and called for "national Concerns [to] . . . be under the Superintendancy of one Supreme Head." Even after Congress received the Boston resolutions there was still support for having "a Convention of all the States" write a new constitution to give Congress the "authority to use coercive powers" against the states.[28] Equal pressure was, however, being directed to Congress. The Hartford Convention, which met in November 1780, proposed some major changes in congressional authority, among which were a funding of the federal debt, establishment of a federally controlled impost, and the implementation of a quite radical and strong power of coercion. Despite the outcry against giving Congress too much power—empowering George Washington for example, to use force to compel reluctant states to meet their congressional requisitions—when the Hartford resolves

were defended as "temporary expedients until a perpetual Confederation," they forced even a reluctant James Warren to concede that they
"will at least shew that something is necessary to be done."[29]

The increasingly grim national situation which spawned the calls for a
general convention and the meetings in Boston and Hartford was building to a point which abrogated the need for extracongressional action.
After the Articles of Confederation were ratified in 1781 the tactic of
calling conventions gave way to less drastic methods of strengthening
Congress. Because of southern support, which continued until the war
turned in America's favor in late 1781, nationalist delegates were able to
work within the existing governmental framework to extend congressional influence.

Some nationalists like George Washington believed that Congress
had implicit authority to coerce the states, which could be effected by
"shutting the ports—by marching armed force into the States." Others
were more concerned with correcting "the Defects" in the Articles of
Confederation which John Sullivan said "were not Discovered previous
to its passing."[30] They wanted to formulate "such additional articles as
will give vigor and authority to government." The attempt to extend
Congress's powers was tactically on solid ground. From 1780 to 1783
men like Robert Morris, Alexander Hamilton, James Duane, and James
Madison needed little more defense for their proposed reforms other
than to show that strong central government was necessary to meet a
crisis. Whether that crisis was the natural state of uneasiness precipitated by a war, or a manipulated crisis like that of the public creditors in
1783, nationalists operated on the assumption that ideological objections
to political centralism carried less weight in times of stress, "while
common danger presses us together."[31]

After Virginia's land cession cleared the way for Maryland's ratification of the Articles of Confederation, the nationalist delegates were
prepared to begin their movement to restructure the Confederation.
Less than a week after ratification, in the first week of March 1781, they
attempted to revise congressional voting procedure by changing the
number of states required for a majority from nine to five. This measure,
had it passed, would have enabled nationalists more easily to push
measures through Congress, would have made Congress's activities
less dependent on the individual states, and, as some said, would have
increased "the power of Congress beyond what the States Intended."
Soon after this indirect approach failed, other measures were attempted. Congress appointed James Varnum, James Duane, and James
Madison to develop means for Congress to carry "into execution in the
several States all the acts and resolutions passed agreeably to the

Articles of Confederation." The question of giving Congress coercive powers was not without its sectional overtones. Even such a committed nationalist as James Madison showed a marked sectional bias. Madison suggested that the use of a navy would be more effective in establishing some degree of control over the states than would an army—an army which, we have seen, was forever rent by sectional upheavals. Madison reasoned that, with a navy, Congress could easily restrict a recalcitrant state's trade and thereby force it to accede to congressional orders. He also thought that a navy manned by men from all the states would not only guard the nation against foreign aggressors, but would also "protect the Southern States for years to come against the insults & aggressions of their N[orthern] Brethren."[32]

Although sectional animosity, fear, and interest motivated a southern drift toward nationalist policies during the war, a sectional identification with nationalism remained as tenuous as had been its identification with federalism. Sectional interest was a primary reason for nationalist successes in 1781, but it was also a primary reason for nationalist failures in 1782 and 1783. In a larger sense, the centralizing effects of war, upon which nationalism's increased influence depended, were not enduring. Nationalism's meteoric rise to power was too dependent upon wartime exigency. Once the pressure began to ease, it lost its tactical advantage, the key to its success. The commitment to state sovereignty was grounded in more than ideology. Each state had its own interests to advance, in addition to having certain interests in common with sectional neighbors. Strong central government thus threatened as many interests as it promised to aid. Although many political leaders were willing to enable Congress to wage a respectable war, they were unwilling to make substantive changes in the Articles of Confederation.

Between May and October 1781 three attempts to amend the Articles failed. Even before this setback James Varnum, one of the members of a committee to prepare amendments, asserted that the only way to produce change was for "a Convention to revise and reframe the Articles of Confederation."[33] It is doubtful whether any tactic would have succeeded in a quickly changing political scene. America's victory at Yorktown eased the air of impending doom which had fueled the nationalist ascendancy. The abyss into which the United States had apparently fallen in 1779 seemed, by late 1781, to have a bottom.

Nevertheless, constitutional reform was not the only means to strengthen Congress. Equal attention was paid to amplifying those powers which it already possessed. In early 1781, before ratification of the Articles and while the war was still at its height, foundations were laid for a major shift of the balance of power in the nation. Nationalist reformers tapped a quite natural frustration with the deliberate steps of a large republican body in advocating the creation of executive posts to streamline congressional efficiency, but with which they hoped to centralize and extend their own and Congress's influence. As early as 1776 there had been proposals for "distinct & precise Departments" and even suggestions that congressional inertia could be overcome by giving George Washington "dictatorial powers for a few months." Continued calls for executive centralization in 1779 and 1780 and the Boston and Hartford resolutions moved Congress to action. On 9 February 1781 it established the office of the superintendent of finance. Ten days later, after having been given the range of authority he demanded, Robert Morris was elected to that very powerful office.[34]

Although most politicians realized that Congress needed more effective means to conduct a war, some feared a possible erosion of republicanism. Thomas McKean thus ridiculed those "amongst us, who are so fond of having a great and powerful Man to look up to, tho' they may not like the name King, seen anxious to confer kingly powers, under the title of Dictator, Superintendant of Finance, or some such." Arthur Lee, believing that Congress was perhaps leaning too heavily on the French and Robert Morris, hoped that they "may prove neither broken reeds, nor spears to peirce us." But federalist charges of "*Influence*" and "the cabal" in the appointments of Morris, Gouverneur Morris as his assistant, and Philip Schuyler as secretary at war carried little weight when compared with the financial and bureaucratic distresses which so neatly supported the administrative changes.[35]

Despite the inability to secure broad substantive amendments, the new executive offices and the new peace establishment gave the Morris faction a potentially overwhelming influence. Moreover, Robert Morris, looked upon by some as the messiah who would lead America out of the wilderness, had an absolute control over federal finances with which he solidified his own power base and strengthened nationalist ties to merchants and public creditors.[36] His control over finances promised to give him even greater authority, as we will soon see, because of Congress's formulation of an impost amendment. Realizing the truth of the eighteenth-century axiom that "the power which holds the purse-strings absolutely must rule," nationalists had very early set out to give Congress an independent revenue to tighten the bonds of union and solidify their own influence.[37]

The financial problems which had plagued the nation since the beginning of the war were one of the strongest arguments for reform. News of army mutinies over the lack of pay in 1780 and early 1781 underscored the need for federal funds.[38] On 31 January 1781, after reports of yet another mutiny, Congress recommended that the states "vest a power in Congress, to levy for the use of the United States, a duty of five per cent." Congress was to appoint its own officials to collect revenue to be "appropriated to the discharge of the principal and interest of the debts already contracted or which may be contracted on the faith of the United States." A federally-controlled impost in conjunction with Morris's control of federal finances promised to give Congress almost as much authority as an explicit power of coercion. Because of this, many federalists naturally feared giving Congress the power of the purse, despite the need for revenue. It was to allay this fear, James Madison wrote, that the impost's supporters limited its duration, but "in so indefinate a manner as not to defeat the object of it." The impost was to continue until such time as the federal debt were paid, while Congress, presumably, would be increasing that very debt. The nationalist victory was not complete—the states still had to ratify unanimously this, as all other, amendments. Even giving Congress temporary powers required explicit legislation in the states.[39]

DECLINE OF WARTIME NATIONALISM

Nationalist strategy seemed foolproof, and it might have paid some immediate dividends had the war continued in Britain's favor. But the same forces which ended the drive for amendments impeded the other plans to extend congressional authority. Not only was there an increasing reluctance to strengthen Congress, but a deliberate assault on nationalist influence also began. After unsuccessful attempts in late 1781 and early 1782 to revise the peace instructions, Arthur Lee took up the fight to expose what he thought to be a plot on the parts of Vergennes, Gérard, Luzerne, Morris, Franklin, and Deane to deprive the United States of the fishery and the Mississippi River. He charged Robert R. Livingston, the secretary for foreign affairs, with taking his orders from Vergennes, who had made him "what he is," and attacked Benjamin Franklin as "the Man who I am sure sold us in the negotiations with France." Lee also made an important connection between the Morris faction's foreign and domestic programs. He complained that the scarcity of money, used to support the demand for an impost, resulted only from a concentration of wealth among Morris's own commercial followers.[40]

Not enough was as yet known about the extent of nationalist-French collusion and Morris's misuse, or intended misuse, of his powers. Therefore, Lee was too easily dismissed as an unstable lone attacker trying to correct past personal insults. He unhappily reported that the appointment of James Duane to chair a committee to investigate Robert Morris's commercial dealings suggested that "Congress do not mean the inspection should be productive of public good." Lee also moved for a reconsideration of the peace instructions. After some debate, during which James Madison argued that relations between America and France might suffer if the instructions were changed, Congress adjourned without rendering a decision.[41]

Although Madison was a leading defender of the nationalist position, the southern states, no longer under the cloud of impending sectional dismemberment, had begun to look to their own interests. This was particularly true with respect to the western lands. As we shall soon see the northerners, for various reasons, still demanded final cession of the western lands which had been promised to Congress in early 1781. By August 1782 James Madison noted that the middle state speculators' desire for the cession with provision for their claims had somewhat abated because of "*their fear* of a *coalition between the eastern and southern in a change* of *instructions for peace.*" The emergence of a more independent South was very evident in a reconsideration of John Jay's commission.[42]

During his negotiations Jay, instead of adhering to his instructions and relinquishing America's claim to the Mississippi River, promised only that the United States would forbear to use the river below 31° north latitude. The Spanish refused the offer and Jay immediately withdrew it. Congress approved his action in late April 1782. After more of his correspondence was read in early August John Rutledge moved for the appointment of a committee to revise Jay's instructions. James Lovell, seeing an opportunity to defend federalist war aims and New England's interest at the same time, moved that Jay's letters and the peace instructions of 1781 "be referred to the same committee." Lovell's motion was divided: Jay's letters were referred to a committee, but "the other part of the motion was put off by adjournment." On 6 August Congress formulated new instructions upholding America's claim to the Mississippi River.[43]

Two days later Arthur Lee reminded Congress of its unfinished business, and he again moved for a reconsideration of the peace instructions. After a series of proposals and counterproposals Congress appointed a committee not to formulate new instructions, but to report on "the most advisable means of securing to the United States the objects claimed by them and not included in their ultimatum for peace." The question of the northern fishery remained in limbo. For the moment, the old Lee-Adams junto failed to reclaim the direction of American foreign policy.[44]

Morris and his friends were not nearly so successful in an even more important confrontation. The winding down of the war had retarded passage of the impost amendment by the states. Shortly after it was sent to the states, Connecticut ratified, but stipulated that its duration be limited to three years after the conclusion of the war. Within a few months it appeared that Rhode Island would not ratify at all.[45] If the impost was not passed before the end of the war, there seemed little chance that it would be passed at all. Its supporters did what they could to speed ratification, but to no avail. A letter from Robert Morris, pamphlets by Thomas Paine, and a committee of congressmen sent to the states failed to secure passage.[46]

By late October 1782 Rhode Island stood alone and resolute in its opposition. There were indignant attacks at "this perverse sister," and "the obstinancy of Rhode Island" was used as additional proof that the Confederation was inadequate to the task of controlling and directing a union of independent and sovereign states.[47] But it was the very question of whether or not Congress should be able to dictate to the states which, on one level, was at the very center of the impost controversy in Rhode Island. The Rhode Islanders believed that the impost "derogated from the Sovereignty and Independence of the State." They charged that the real purpose in establishing a fund "over which the people have no control" was "to serve the purpose of aristocracy and perpetually enslaving the common people for the aggrandizement of a number of families in each state, by population & fraud."[48] A clearer enunciation of the connection between the impost and nationalism cannot be found than the Rhode Island delegates' assertion that its passage would "empower Congress, by their own officers, to bear with their own weight directly on individuals. This would disturb the harmony, derange the elegant proportion, and endanger the welfare of the whole building."[49]

Ideology alone did not account for Rhode Island's refusal to ratify the impost. An equally important factor was the still unresolved question of the western lands, which, it was said, was "an object of so great magnitude and Expectation that . . . it influences the Politicks of almost all the States." The land-poor, revenue-hungry New Englanders wanted Virginia's cession given to Congress to be used as a source for federal revenues. Following tacit acceptance of Virginia's cession in 1781, however, the land speculators had continued to defend their claims in the western territory. Virginia refused to complete the transaction with the inclusion of those claims, thereby only changing "the name and place of Residence of our Tyrants." The result was that the New Englanders saw the southerners holding a major resource, while they were being asked to support the federal government with commercial taxes. This slight departure from the more usual conflict between New England and the middle states had serious implications for the southerners not only in 1781 and 1782, but throughout the revolutionary era.[50] The potential for cooperation among likeminded northerners was a constant fear for some southerners. Madison's assertion that "an agrarian law is as much covete[d] by the little members of the Union, as it ever was by the indigent Citizens of Rome," was realized when a congressional committee composed of New England and middle state delegates upheld the land companies' claims.[51]

By early 1782 information began to come out of Congress that "the *Northern* interest is all prevalent; their members are *firmly united,* and carry many measures disadvantageous to the Southern Interest." At least with respect to the western lands, the southerners did not differentiate between the middle states and New England. Madison accused Pennsylvania, Maryland, Delaware, and Rhode Island of being the prime movers in the attempt to seize Virginia's territory. Southern fears increased in light of New England's continuing attempt to get Vermont admitted to the Union—allegedly because of "the accession of weight they will derive from it in Congress." Naturally, the southerners were loath to admit Vermont until "they can admit one to the Southern likewise."[52]

New Englanders, and particularly the Rhode Islanders, were more upset than ever that the southern lands were immune from federal revenue schemes. Even merchants outside New England complained that they had and were suffering because of the war and angrily pointed to the wealth of the "Men of Landed Property." Moreover, the New England merchants had had their commerce seriously curtailed by a successful British blockade in 1782, and they did not want the added weight of a commerical tax pressing down upon them.[53] Thus, rather than having the impost stand apart from the rest of the federal revenue system, they wanted the revenue from an impost to "be carried to the credit of each State . . . and deducted from their annual Quota of continental requisitions." The Rhode Islanders, determined not to pay more than a fair share of congressional expenses, believed that the most direct way to spread the revenue burden among all the states was finally to get control of Virginia's cession lands. The Rhode Island delegates in Congress questioned the wisdom of passing a commercial tax "whereby these same engrossers of land will also be disproportionately benefited." The North Carolina delegates, in response, questioned the Rhode Islanders' ideological objections to an impost while "they contend for the participation of the Western Lands, which is contrary to the express terms of the Confederation."[54]

The issue of the western lands was not to be decided for more than a year, and Rhode Island rejected the impost in November 1782. The Rhode Islanders saw no need to pass an impost which would simply make it easier for land-rich southerners to continue to withhold an untapped source of massive funds "important for restoring public credit." David Howell, however, warned the delegates "not to assign the withholding the Back-Lands as a reason [for the refusal to ratify]. That reason was better calculated to influence the State than to satisfy Congress." It was simpler for Rhode Island to base its rejection on the more easily defensible ideological grounds. But five months later one writer tried to explain the rejection with an argument which demonstrated the impact of sectional interest. He maintained that Rhode Island was "possessed of few native products, [and] industrious merchants . . . sailed cheaply and . . . sought out and procured the commodities of indolent people, and reexported them in considerable quantities, to their own emolument. An impost of 5% must at once extinguish all hopes of reviving the branch of trade above stated. A *Virginian* or *Carolinian* . . . may not have averted to the sacrifice which Congress called upon Rhode Island to make."[55]

Rhode Island's rejection of the impost was not solely responsible for its ultimate defeat. Had it been the only state to reject, it might have been possible to force it in line. In fact, after the rejection Congress appointed a committee to go to Rhode Island in the hope of securing a reconsideration. Congress recalled the committee after the news that Virginia had rescinded its previous ratification. The Virginia legislature, in a resolution passed on 7 December, held that the levying of taxes by any body "other than the General Assembly of this Commonwealth . . . is injurious to its Sovereignty and may prove destructive to the rights and Liberty of the people." Although the ideology expressed was similar to Rhode Island's, and doubtless played a role in the action, sectional interest, in this case support for the western lands, was equally important in deciding the impost's fate. In the same way that some southerners attacked Rhode Island for rejecting the impost while trying to give Congress control over the western lands, some northerners attacked Virginia for rejecting the impost while continuing "the futile claim to the immense Western Region."[56]

Whereas the Rhode Islanders were afraid that passage of an impost would destroy any chance to secure the western lands, George Mason angrily warned that passage of the impost would set a precedent for congressional authority which could easily be transferred to the matter of the western lands. The only way, then, to prevent Congress from trying to "dismember Virginia" was to keep it "within the lines of the Confederation, and to resist and reprobate their first attempts to exceed them." This concern gave Richard Henry and Arthur Lee the opportunity to restrict Robert Morris's influence. They were the instigators of the revocation.[57]

Although the opposition to the impost in both Rhode Island and Virginia was partly motivated by antithetical interests, the ideological accord, the common opposition to Robert Morris and nationalism, was a foreshadowing of things to come. For a time in 1783 and 1784 northern and southern federalists regained enough strength to throw nationalists into a full retreat. Nevertheless, they faced one final test. The defeat of the impost did not end the movement to strengthen Congress. While the impost was meeting stiff opposition in the states in 1782, a few influential nationalists began to set plans in motion for the formulation of another impost and an even more comprehensive revenue system. Although sectional concerns were not forgotten, conflict between federalists and nationalists over the limits on Congress's authority took precedence in late 1782 and 1783 politics.

3

A Federalist Resurgence

WHILE RATIFICATION of the impost amendment by the states was haltingly underway in 1782, nationalists remained convinced that a funded national debt was the key to a stronger central government—that "the loan office books [were] . . . a much stronger cement to the States than the labored Articles of Confederation." A series of developments, some intentionally triggered and some not, kept the question of revenue alive and created the foundation for yet another effort to extend congressional authority through the medium of revenue reform. Shortly after a financial settlement enlarged the federal debt and broadened Congress's fiscal responsibilities in early 1782, Robert Morris created an interstate administrative system of tax receivers and called for a poll tax, a land tax, and a liquor excise to pay the now enlarged federal debt. Because of the uncertain state of the impost, however, Morris's proposal was premature, if not redundant, and in early March a committee composed of Arthur Lee, Samuel Osgood, and Abraham Clark gave it an unfavorable report.[1]

But federal finances still precariously rested on requisitions and foreign loans. While requisitions had never been a satisfactory replacement for an independent revenue, from a creditor perspective, French bills of exchange, used to pay the interest on loan office certificates, had at least stifled complaints about the domestic debt. Robert Morris, however, saw to it this French support ended. He wanted to add to Congress's already broadened financial burden to support the need for an independent revenue. In response to his request that they pay bills of exchange without deducting the amount from money previously loaned to the United States, the French decided to issue future bills of credit only out of American funds in France. This action justified Morris's

report in early June that payment of the interest on loan office certificates had to cease. This not only increased concern about the slow
ratification of the impost, but also "caused great commotion and clamor
among the class of public creditors against Congress." The obvious
remedy seemed to "be notification that all the States had granted the
impost." Morris lost little time in using the creditors' anxiety to insure
this. He discouraged the Philadelphia creditors from appealing to the
state for payment of their share of the federal debt and urged them to
direct their energies to and focus their discontent upon Congress by
making "one common cause with the whole of the public creditors of
every kind."[2]

The public creditors were not the only discontented group. In late July
Congress began discussion of a memorial from the officers of the
Connecticut Line demanding action on the unfulfilled promise of a
pension of half-pay for life. After some debate Congress, hoping to shift
the burden of responsibility to the states, told the memorialists that it
had neither the authority nor the money "to make a general arrangement
for liquidating and paying the half pay." It was problematical whether
this was a good enough answer. The day before the half-pay discussion
Morris, quickly taking advantage of the growing uneasiness, informed
Congress of the demands of the public creditors, that "numerous,
meritorious and oppressed body of men." Conditions seemed to
support reconsideration of the question of federal revenues to meet
what now appeared to be a snowballing financial crisis.[3]

On 5 August Morris sent Congress a Report on Public Credit in which
he stressed the need for funding the debt, pointed out that collection
machinery already existed (his new interstate system), and called for a
federal impost and the other forms of taxation he had earlier suggested.[4]
A few weeks after Congress referred the report to a committee, the
Philadelphia creditors sent a circular letter to creditors in the other
states asking for their support in pressuring Congress for a national
revenue system. The mobilization quickly spread. There was a meeting
in Albany on 30 September at which plans were laid to petition Congress. In October a group of creditors in Hartford petitioned their
congressional representatives to find means to pay the public debt.
There was a similar call from a creditor assembly in New Jersey. Morris
and his fellow Republicans even got the Pennsylvania Assembly to inform Congress that if a national revenue were not established, it would
assume that part of the federal debt owed to its citizens. Faced with the
dilemma of having its legitimate authority usurped by the states, Congress asked the legislature not to take any action until the fate of the
impost amendment was decided. In early September, obviously react-

ing to the seriousness of the situation, a grand committee favorably responded to Morris's report.[5]

In the meantime the army officers had begun to demand that their grievances be heard. Initially, they only wanted Congress's support in pressing their demands on the states. Benjamin Lincoln, the secretary at war, believed that the states were "jealous of Congress and they will reluctantly lodge in their hands such ample funds as shall inable them to discharge their debts to their officers." Nevertheless, the existence of financially inspired discontents in the army had serious political implications. Without federal funds and some method of payment there was a distinct possibility that the army might be as hard "to disband as it has been to raise."[6] By mid-October Morris, emphasizing the relationship between the officers' demands and a national revenue, had convinced a few officers in Philadelphia that the proper focus for their grievances was Congress and the proper goal the attainment of a national revenue system. Whether or not this information was circulated is unclear, but by the end of October there were predictions of a "dangerous eruption" unless the army were paid.[7]

Finally, in mid-November the officers stationed at Newburgh petitioned Congress. There was an implicit, and possibly even an explicit, threat that some of the officers might eventually resort to "the sword to determine who ought to be responsible to them." The officers, however, were not of a single mind. Benjamin Lincoln thus still believed that the officers' demands were really a matter for state attention.[8] Yet the potential for trouble was unmistakable. At roughly the same time that the Newburgh petition arrived in Congress, Pennsylvania agreed to postpone funding its portion of the federal debt until passage or defeat of the first impost. Congress thereupon sent its soon-to-be-recalled delegation to Rhode Island to secure ratification of the impost. Pennsylvania's postponement of its funding plan, contingent upon the establishment of a federal revenue, the Newburgh petition, and continued pressure from the public creditors unquestionably made "the great political question . . . payment of the public debt."[9]

NEWBURGH AND A SECOND IMPOST

A major problem nationalists faced in trying to increase Congress's powers was defending the right of a government of states to exert control over its own sovereign, and very jealous, constituents. In early 1780, setting the tone of wartime nationalism, Alexander Hamilton had suggested that only with the "attachment of the Army to Congress . . .

would [it] then have a solid base of authority." There was, however, a
great difference between Congress using an army to enforce its dictates
in 1780 and the federal government using an army to quell the Whiskey
Rebellion in 1794. The latter was the act of a government exercising its
supreme constitutional authority within an inferior political entity. The
former would have been the act of a government clearly abrogating its
constitutional limits as established by the states. During the war men
like Morris, Hamilton, and Madison were able to defend giving Congress additional powers and the right to implement those powers with an
effective, if not perfect, tactical argument based upon the need to protect the nation. Inasmuch, however, as the Confederation was a league
of sovereign states, it operated most effectively as a self-motivating
central government, when extraordinary circumstances forced the
states to bow willingly to congressional authority. Even in the darkest
hours of the war it was difficult to exceed the limits, grounded in revolutionary ideology, which girded the Confederation and protected the
states from the threat of tyrannical central government. In late 1781
Gouverneur Morris had even gravely predicted that the Articles of Confederation would most surely not be reformed if the war did not continue. The distrust of centralized power and the attendant support for
state sovereignty which had muted the appeal of political centralism during the war showed every sign of growing even stronger in peacetime.[10]

Nationalists were under no illusion that a people tired of war and the
sacrifices it had demanded would willingly "submit to burdens they
bore at the beginning of it." They understood the implications of the
defeat of the impost amendment and the countless other examples of the
futility of stimulating what Robert Morris called "the exertions of the
States" while the war was winding to a close. Thus, the defeat of the
impost amendment had the beneficial effect of adding to the mounting
pressures for reconsideration of revenue reform.[11] It was unimportant,
then, how that pressure, the reason for reform, was exerted. What was
important to those involved was that instead of passing laws without
teeth which merely substituted "Deception in the Place of Denial," a
federally run impost would have drawn "by degrees the bands of
authority together." It would have done so not only by establishing
machinery for Congress to exert its authority, but also, and even more
important, by creating "a numerous class of citizens . . . interested in
the preservation of the Federal Union."[12]

In the last week of December 1782 the arrival of a delegation from
Newburgh brought the matter to a head. The presence of the delegation
was not, in itself, a dire threat. Robert Morris, however, had little
difficulty in persuading Alexander McDougal and his co-petitioners to

join with the public creditors in supporting a new revenue system. Gouverneur Morris and McDougal, in turn, tried to elicit Henry Knox's invaluable support. Morris, declaring to Knox that "after you have carried the post the public creditors will garrison it for you," intended to test his earlier assurance that the army really was "a Hoop to the barrel."[13] Morris might even have had more in mind than using the army's vocal support. He confided to John Jay that "the army have swords in their hands. You know enough of the history of mankind to know much more than I have said, and possibly more than they themselves yet think of." There is no telling how far some nationalists would have gone to accomplish their immediate ends. Abner Nash spoke for many, however, when he admitted that if a vocal, dissatisfied, or even mutinying army could produce constitutional reform "we shall by and by say, as we have often had reason to say before, all is for the best."[14]

On 6 January 1783 the Newburgh delegation outlined its demands for present and past pay and for commutation of the half-pay claim to a retirement bonus of five years at full pay. The immediate referral of the petition to a grand committee was interpreted as evidencing "the important light in which the memorial was viewed." It appeared that the only way to avoid a crisis was for Congress to find the necessary funds to satisfy the army. Things took a critical and probably calculated turn the following day when Robert Morris reported that there could be no "advances of pay in the present state of finances."[15] A week later the Newburgh delegation advised the grand committee that the situation among the troops at Newburgh was serious and that "a disappointment might throw them into extremes." Alexander Hamilton, James Madison, and John Rutledge were then appointed to draft a report on the officers' claims.[16] The pressure on Congress continued to mount as first Robert Morris tendered his resignation as superintendent of finance, although he did not leave the office for quite a while, and then Nathaniel Gorham, Richard Peters (both of whom were deeply involved in the impost scheme), and Ralph Izard reported that there could be no further loans from France "until solid funds are put into the hands of Congress."[17]

A week later the committee on army claims proposed that "Congress . . . make every effort in their power to obtain from the respective States *general* and substantial funds." Theodorick Bland, unwilling to sanction extensive reform, moved the insertion after the words "in their power" of the words "consistent with the Articles of Confederation." There were also objections voiced to the idea of a pensioned military—smacking, as it did, of European armies and foreign aristocracies. On 25 January the question of commutation was referred to a committee on which sat Hamilton and Madison.[18]

Emotions ran high during the continuing revenue debates. James Wilson called again for an impost, to "be collected under the authority of Congress," as necessary to overcome what was "more of a centrifugal than a centripetal force in the States." But Hamilton's attempt to make the ultimate statement in defense of an impost did more harm than good to "the cause it was meant to serve." He indiscretely argued that a federally controlled impost was vital to the continued existence of the Union because it would "introduce the influence of officers deriving their emoluments from, and consequently interested in supporting the power of Congress." There were immediate charges that "a collection by officers appointed under Congress [was] . . . repugnant to the Articles of Confederation" and warnings of "surrendering the purse into the same hands which held the sword." Most of the impost's opponents wanted to ease the nation's financial burden and satisfy the creditors and the army, but not at the expense of the Articles of Confederation or to the benefit of Robert Morris and his associates. Despite the pressures being brought to bear in support of revenue reform, they limited the proposed second impost to a twenty-five-year duration and still refused to accept commutation. Alexander McDougal and Samuel Ogden, reacting to the apparent stalemate, informed Henry Knox that "the zeal of a great number of the members of Congress to get continental funds while a few, wish to have us referred to the States, induced us to conceal what funds we wished."[19]

The situation remained unchanged through mid-February. Federalists continued to assert that rather than acting as a "cement of union" a large debt and an independent revenue would "tend to its dissolution." They even blocked an awkward attempt to increase the pressure on Congress by admitting some public creditors to the debates.[20] But even stronger pressure, not so easily handled, was exerted by "the terror of a mutinyzing Army." Arthur Lee and Theodorick Bland tried to cripple this strategy by moving that an impost be used only to pay the army. Although the arguments of Hamilton, FitzSimons, Wilson, and Madison against dividing "the interests of the civil & military Creditors" prevailed, the proposed impost was not to be an amendment like the first. It remained limited in duration and collectible by state-appointed officers.[21]

Almost on the heels of this restated opposition to a broad revenue power, there were stirrings about the possibility of a mutiny in the army. It is inconsequential, in terms of congressional politics, whether or not a mutiny or coup d'etat was ever seriously contemplated. That Alexander Hamilton advised or warned Washington to handle carefully the army's "endeavor to procure redress" or that Colonel John Brooks might have carried instructions or information from Philadelphia to Newburgh does, however, suggest that the army was not leading but being led and that its officers were mere pawns in a very dangerous gambit. It is fairly obvious that nationalists were the source of McDougal's report that "the Sentiment is daily gaining ground, that the Army will not, nor ought to disband till Justice is done them."[22] Even before the army took a stand on the matter, there was talk of an imminent mutiny. On the evening of 20 January James Madison went to Thomas FitzSimons's lodgings to meet with Gorham, Hamilton, Peters, and Daniel Carroll. Hamilton and Peters "informed the company that it was certain that the army had secretly determined not to lay down their arms until due provision & a prospect should be afforded on the subject of their pay." Within a day the news that the army had "resolved not to lay down their arms" was provoking the reaction that the Union was "a Barrel of thirteen states without a hoop to keep it together."[23]

The tactic seemed quite effective in increasing the possibility of revenue reform. It was reported that "the fears of Congress are awake" and that the pressure to find a solution was like that "felt in any period of the Revolution."[24] This anxiety, however, was produced by a still illusory threat. Although Horatio Gates, who probably harbored visions of toppling his old enemy George Washington, joyously wrote to Richard Peters about the furiously boiling "political pot in Philadelphia," Henry Knox refused to stoke the fire. Knox, who undoubtedly had a fair share of the New England resentment of the middle states' nationalists, did not think that a combination of the army and the creditors was an effective way to stimulate reform. As we shall soon see he had a quite different idea of how to go about extending congressional authority.[25]

By early March one of Knox's temperate letters was circulating in Philadelphia, and it seemed to place "the *temper and affairs of* [the] *Army in a less alarming view* than some preceding *accounts.*" Despite all that had been done to create a mood favorable to revenue reform, by 6 March the second impost was still in a federalist format. The optimism generated by Knox's letters was, moreover, soon bolstered by a tactical reversal in Newburgh. After John Armstrong, Jr., the anonymous pamphleteer, called a public meeting of the Newburgh officers to make a firm statement about the army's resolve to support the nationalist position, George Washington called his own meeting on 15 March at which he succeeded in regaining control over his men.[26]

The effect of Washington's success was immediately apparent in Congress as it dissipated "the cloud which seemed to have been gathering." The pressure for revenue reform dissipated with that cloud. Congress passed an impost, but one far more restricted than nationalists had wanted. On 18 March debate on the impost, one part of a larger revenue package, ended. It was recommended that the states give Congress the power, for a term of twenty-five years, to levy a duty of 5 percent "provided that none of the said duties shall be applied to any other purpose than the discharge of the interest and the principal of the debts which shall have been contracted on the faith of the United States, for supporting the present war." Unlike the unratified impost amendment of 1781, the states would not have been under the constant pressure of an increasing federal debt. Within a few days Congress also agreed to a commutation of half-pay into a grant of full pay for five years. This was a small price to pay to satisfy the army and keep it out of politics.[27]

While Congress was considering an impost, there had also been considerable discussion of more effective ways to raise additional funds. Congress had the authority, under Article 8 of the Articles of Confederation, to raise a revenue from the states in proportion to the value of their improved lands. On 11 February the committee of the whole reported on a method to secure the information necessary to put Article 8 into effect. The funds thereby produced were to be "applied only for allocating among the states the sums required for '*supporting the public credit and other* contingent expenses,' and for adjusting all accounts between the United States and each particular State." A variety of problems prevented speedy action. Jonathan Arnold charged that the "mode for obtaining a general estimate . . . meets with Violent & stubborn opposition from those who wish to engross more power to Congress and —change the present Constitution."[28]

There were, however, other interests at play which were even more troublesome than the ideological. Article 8 had been a hotly contested issue in 1776, and the question of land valuation was no less volatile in 1783. In order to balance the sectional inequity of Article 8, namely the immunity of unimproved lands, some New Englanders tried to substitute population for land as a determinant of state quotas. There was insufficient support for amendment, however, and Congress tentatively agreed to the original report. Within a week, after more nonproductive debate, the report on supplementary funds was adopted, but, as Madison noted, "with great reluctance by almost all."[29]

The report, "which the Southern States have carried with great difficulty," was a stopgap measure at best. Northerners were still upset because the valuation scheme would "not Opporate Justly," excluding, as it did, the vast southern holdings. But James Wilson's motion to levy a one-quarter-dollar tax on every acre of land in the nation was defeated, with every state south of Delaware voting against it. In late March an amendment to have the states raise, for a period of twenty-five years, two million dollars annually reopened debate on Article 8.[30] Another amendment to substitute population for land in determining state quotas forced consideration of an old problem: what proportion was to be accounted for by slaves? After a great deal of debate, during which sectional interests were balanced by the need to provide funds which would not overwhelmingly strengthen Congress, the proposed amendment, which counted slaves as three-fifths of freemen, was easily passed.[31]

Finally, on 18 April Congress passed the entire Report on Public Credit. Robert Morris and his supporters, however, had been forced to accept a much less powerful impost than they had wanted. They had, said Joseph Jones, ''to take a middle course with respect to its duration, and the appointment of collectors, or hazard ultimately the loss of the measure.'' This forced concession had far greater import than simply reflecting a slight tactical setback.It signaled the beginning of a powerful antinationalist movement in and out of Congress.[32]

WARTIME NATIONALISM IN RETREAT

The gamble to force congressional reform before peace undermined the need for reform not only failed, but also provoked a storm of antinationalist sentiment. Although there was no hard evidence to single out the perpetrators there was ''good ground for suspecting that the civil creditors were intriguing in order to inflame the army into such desperation as would produce a general provision for the public debts.''[33] After Alexander Hamilton admitted that it was ''partly true'' that the late agitation in the army had been begun in Philadelphia, Washington berated him for his part in the affair and attacked ''Mr. Morris, to whom or rather to Mr. G[ouverneur] M[orris] is ascribed, in a great degree, the ground work of the superstructure which was intended to be raised in the Army by the Annonymous Addresser.'' Arthur Lee charged that Robert Morris and ''his friends have been the prime movers of all the disturbances in the Army.''[34]

The allegations about the origins of the Newburgh conspiracy merely added to a growing case against wartime nationalism and especially Robert Morris, who had ''been entrusted by Congress with greater powers than Ld. North possessed.'' Arthur Lee, who still had an old score to settle, had a good deal more credibility than he had had in 1782 in attacking him. Lee even charged that Morris's earlier attempt to make his resignation public was simply a ''manouvre to force the system of funding upon the States'' to secure payment of the federal debt, ''in which Mr. Morris & his friends are so deeply interested as to hazard the destruction of this Country rather than not realize the immense wealth, which large purchases of Loan Office Certificates at an infinitely low depreciation, has offerd to their hopes." In an attempt to diminish Morris's influence Lee and Theodorick Bland, "disparaging the administration of Mr. Morris, and throwing oblique censure on his character," moved in early March to rearrange the Department of Finance. The defeat of the motion did not end the effort "to re-establish a *board* in place of a single minister."[35] As late as August 1784 Arthur Lee was still arguing that America's financial problems resulted only from "placing two men [Robert and Gouverneur Morris] in the first Offices of trust & power, who have constantly aimed at exalting themselves by depreciating the public."[35]

Even without a formal declaration of the fact, Morris's influence was already seriously impaired. He was no longer vital to a war effort, and he was no longer immune from attack. His prestige suffered for his having failed to deliver on the promises he had made to the officers and creditors. In Pennsylvania his power base dissolved as the Constitutionalists began to reassert themselves.[36]

Although on the verge of defeat, nationalism still had committed and active supporters. After formulation of an impost, which still required state legislation, some nationalists made a final effort to strengthen Congress. This time there was no doubt; they intended to use a convention of the states. New York had given them a model for action in mid-1782 when Hamilton, Schuyler, Duane, and Jay secured passage of a resolution calling for the "assembling of a general Convention of the States" to formulate amendments to the Articles of Confederation. Most delegates were cool to the idea, and nothing came of the proposal.[37]

By early 1783, however, the revenue crisis began directing some attention to a convention. Too often historians have failed to describe adequately the reasons for this and especially the motivation which drove some federalists to advocate calling a convention. The increased interest in constitutional reform and especially in a convention did not really reflect increased support for nationalism. Henry Knox, instead of supporting the drive for an impost, advocated "a convention of the states to form a better constitution." John Francis Mercer, who opposed passage of an impost and feared the creation of "a monied interest in the U.S.," still felt that it might be necessary "to new-model the Constitution." Knox distrusted men like Morris, and, according to Madison, Mercer apparently believed that as the impost's supporters, while "right in principle . . . had no plan, and it was essential something should be done . . . [it was necessary to] strike in with the other side." But Mercer's decision to revise the constitution rather than establish an impost did not necessarily imply total acceptance of nationalist theories. On the contrary, support for a convention in the critical days before the danger of mutiny passed might have been a way to sidestep the uncertain effects of extensive revenue reform.[38]

It is likely that those men who were following the two Morrises believed that constitutional reform in a convention would be unnecessary if Congress were given an independent revenue. This was evident when Nathaniel Gorham revealed Massachusetts's invitation to the New England states to meet in a revenue convention. While most of the delegates attacked the notion of resolving federal problems outside of Congress, Alexander Hamilton and Stephen Higginson called instead for a general convention of the states. Hamilton, with scant encouragement, had been talking about such a convention as a means to further nationalism since 1780. But Higginson was a bitter antinationalist. Many years after the fact he pointed out that when he supported the call for a convention "Madison and others . . . were as much opposed to this idea, as I was to the measures they were then pursuing, to effect, as they said, the same thing." Higginson, like his close friend Henry Knox, did not think that those measures, namely passing an impost and establishing a federal revenue system, were intended to repair the Confederation. He, and other federalists, differentiated between strengthening Congress and the Union and the "attempt to strengthen the federal government by influence . . . [to] greatly increase an influence which is by far too great & enable a few individuals to give law to Congress."[39]

After passage of the impost Morris's enemies no longer had to accept the lesser of two evils. But the very reasons which turned them away from constitutional reform spurred others to action. Before the Newburgh affair peaked the Marquis de Lafayette had alerted Washington to his duty to support the movement to strengthen Congress, while elsewhere confessing his desire to see a convention of the states reform the Articles of Confederation. Washington probably needed little persuading. He might have opposed armed action, but he was most definitely in favor of strengthening Congress. Possibly driven by a sense of obligation to his men or heeding the whispers of Hamilton and Lafayette, or afraid of the prospect of an impotent peacetime Congress, Washington soon admitted his intention to try to avert the evil of conflicting state interests by writing "a new Constitution." He called upon the states to transform the Confederation into "an Indissoluble Union of the States under one Federal Head" and privately wished to see this change accomplished "by a Convention of the People."[40]

Washington's great prestige, which it was assumed was "the first Attribute necessary" for constitutional reform, was not enough to overcome a snowballing federalist resurgence. The circular letter's effect in Virginia was judged to be "momentary" and prone to future "disgust." David Howell attacked it as "the sheet ancor of the cause."[41] Even more damaging to the prospect of calling a convention than these re-actions was Congress's hasty retreat from Philadelphia in June 1783 (see Chapter 4). Soon after Congress reconvened in Princeton Hamilton had to abandon a resolution for a convention "for want of support," and in early September New York's 1782 convention resolution was shelved.[42]

Once Congress was safely out of Philadelphia, the acknowledged hot-bed of nationalism, attacks on Morris, that "dominus Factotum, whose dictates none dare oppose," increased. There were open criticisms of the governmental excesses which Morris and his faction had pro-pounded. The attacks not only condemned nationalism's departure from the Articles of Confederation, but also insisted that the nation had been threatened by a despotic movement whose center was Robert Morris, who was "a King, & more than a King." By early November Stephen Higginson reported that "it is a general Opinion now, that our Affairs have been much under the direction of a venal senile Junto . . . that it is time for independent men, to look around and attend to the public safety."[43]

In attacking Morris and nationalism men like Higginson, Gerry, Os-good, and the Lees realized the scope of their adversaries' influence—and their offensive was as wide-ranging as that influence. One of their first targets was the army officers' new interstate hereditary organiza-tion, the Society of the Cincinnati, because they saw in it the same organization, tactics, and ideology which formed the structure of the nationalist movement. The publication of Aedanus Burke's inflam-matory pamphlet sparked a very vocal effort to prevent the "unsus-pecting people," who had too high a regard for the officers, from being swayed by nationalist ideas conveyed through the society. Elbridge Gerry, certain that the nationalists had "created this political Wolf and presented it in Sheeps Cloathing" to change the Constitution, was afraid that the officers might once again be led down the garden path and "by degrees be [slowly] drawn into Measures; which they would not shudder at the thot of."[44] Even after the society changed its constitution to an-swer such charges Samuel Adams thought it "the same Serpent still, but its sting is hid."[45]

Opposition to the impost reflected an identical concern with the intru-sion of influence in government. Because they believed "the treasury, the Cincinnati and other public creditors, with all their concommitants are somehow or other . . . inseperably connected," federalists worried that a federal revenue would "draw the attention of . . . all the aristocracy, of all the unprincipled and subtle intriguers of America, and their power will be an overmatch for the honest and independent."[46] One of the most significant aspects of this perceived threat was that it was equally evident in the southern states and New England. As early as June 1783 David Ramsay assured Benjamin Rush that he would do his best to build support for the second impost in South Carolina, but he warned that "M. Morris has his enemies here as well with you." Alexander Gillon, while probably overreacting, assured Arthur Lee that Morris's character was "so well known in these three southern states" that even if the first impost had passed it would not have been "remitted to Congress whilst such a Man as R[obert] M[orris] was to have the handling of it."[47]

Virginia, which, by mid-1783, was under federalist control, simply continued what it had begun in late 1782. Soon after the impost was sent to the states, charges were levied "from the Leeward" that the impost was designed for no other purpose than to give Congress "an undue Influence in the States."[48] The Lees' old colleagues in New England were just as determined to diminish nationalist influence while blocking a commercial tax. Even Silas Deane issued a warning to "let each State guard well the strings of its own purse." Rhode Island was now lauded for having singlehandedly saved the nation by rejecting the first impost in 1782. Antiimpost county conventions met in Connecticut which were reminiscent of preindependence revolutionary bodies.[49]

By early July the impost was stalled in the Massachusetts General Court owing to a refusal to raise "Monies to pay the commutation . . . The Idea of Pensioners . . . is abhorrent." After a hotly contested, but unproductive, struggle during the summer the legislature adjourned without a decision. Instead, it sent Congress a memorial attacking commutation in "as plain a language as they formerly spoke to Great Britain."[50] Emotions ran so high that in June 1783 Stephen Higginson, Samuel Holten, Nathaniel Gorham, and Samuel Osgood, the delegates who had reluctantly voted for the impost and commutation, were turned out of office. Their attempt to defend their action on the grounds that they had not been instructed to oppose commutation and that there had appeared, at the time, no other way to avert a serious crisis had little effect against the argument that "the impulse of temporary exigence" ought not to be permitted to erect "a system, which experience has found to be productive of undue influence, inordinate power, national corruption, and public ruin."[51]

Soon after the General Court reconvened in October Governor Hancock called upon it to pass the impost. Stephen Higginson, however, was confident that because of his own warnings about "the Designs of the Aristocratic Junto in Congress,'' the members would be on their guard against its ''plans and insinuations.'' Higginson did not reckon with that junto's tenacity and political expertise. On 9 October Hancock again addressed the General Court, but this time he produced some extracts of letters, forwarded by Robert Morris, in which John Adams called for stabilizing America's credit situation in order to enhance America's bargaining position and respect abroad. Adams, who was at the time concerned about relations with French financial houses and worried about anything which might hurt America's chances for commercial treaties, had used language which, by editing, enabled Morris to demonstrate his support for passage of the impost.[52]

Adams's letters had an immediate impact on a deadlocked General Court, as interested as he in commercial treaties. Higginson, noting that his own testimony had ''been much more than balanced, by the extracts of John Adams's Letter,'' was outraged at the ''scandalous practice . . . to send extracts of letters and mutilated information to the States, in order to hurry them into measures.'' Nevertheless, on 17 October the impost was adopted, with Adams's letters apparently turning ''the point by a majority of five.''[53]

The Massachusetts federalists did not intend to let the matter rest simply because of ''a few Individuals attentive to their business, & properly instructed from the great source of intelligence & power.'' Shortly after passing the impost the General Court framed a remonstrance ''complaining of the excessive Power of the Office of Finance'' and in late October instructed its delegates in Congress to ''urge for a new arrangement of that Department.''[54] Stephen Higginson, for one, had little faith that Morris would willingly ''give up the Reins and Retire.'' It was widely accepted now that there was no alternative but finally to take the nation's finances out of his hands and keep them out by putting the treasury ''in Commission by rotation.'' By June 1784 the office was dissolved, and the formal reign of Robert Morris ''& his immoral Assistant'' was over.[55]

IDEOLOGICAL CONFLICT IN POSTWAR AMERICA

The federalist resurgence had little lasting effect on many nationalist thinkers other than reinforcing their political theories. They were hardly surprised that the states were beginning to begrudge Congress the modicum of sovereignty that they had given to it—that with ''the common danger being removed we are receding instead of advancing in a disposition to amend its defects.'' They asked the obvious question that ''if an union could not be formed until we were driven to it by external oppression and tyranny, is it likely such an union will hold when that pressure is removed?'' They knew the answer: it would not, and the nation would quickly lose that ''public spirit which up to this time made good the want of energy in government.''[56]

The alleged appearance in some states of ''almost an entire independence of Congress'' and efforts ''to ruin what is called the aristocratical influence'' caused certain nationalists to ponder the likelihood of major erosions of congressional authority. They worried about rumors that Congress might be dissolved once the federal debt was paid and believed that radical segments of the population wanted to ''expunge all public debts.'' The regression from the forced centralism of the war years signified, to many nationalists, the beginning of a progressive weakening of the bonds of union leading to the ''general anarchy'' they had so long feared.[57]

Yet charges that federalists wanted an even weaker Congress and that they did not intend to honor Congress's financial obligations were groundless. Opposition to the impost and the fear of setting precedents which might be used later to abrogate the Articles of Confederation evidenced a desire to reaffirm the power of the states, to get the Confederation to where it had been in 1777. While federalist writers admitted that many of the changes wrought during the war had been necessary ''& even good Men were obliged to concur in it as a lesser Evil,'' they nevertheless pointed out that those powers which ''Princes and magistrates, eagerly seize, in time of war'' did not have to be sacrificed ''in a time of Peace.'' ''INDEPENDENS,'' for an example, was certain that if Congress supported ''the dignity of the States,'' they, in turn, would willingly support Congress. He was, however, opposed to Congress making ''ordinances carrying the force of laws'' and maintained that he was ''subject only to the code of laws of that state wherein I live . . . I revolted from the British government, because I would not be subjected to two codes of law . . . when Congress are empowered to grant pensions and salaries, and multiply their dependents, the Government of America becomes an Aristocracy, and the People lose their *majesty*.''[58]

Federalism was not antiunion, but it did balance the view that ''the Confederation must be adhered to'' and that Congress was ''the cement of the union'' with a still very healthy distrust of centralized authority. State sovereignty was thus not a defect of the Confederation, but ''our greatest *safeguard* . . . [it]is the *fence* and *check* . . . for the safety and security of the states.'' Supporting the Confederation was one thing, but Congress's ''lusting after power'' and a desire for ''arbitrary government'' were quite another.[59]

Nevertheless, the distrust of men in power, and an intention to guard against "the Infirmities of the best as well as the Wickedness of the worst of Men," did not mean that federalists blindly and dogmatically accepted the Articles of Confederation as inviolate and absolute. Tristram Dalton, who had learned the hard lesson that "the follies and carelessness of the *many* first suggest to Knaves the benefit that may accrue to themselves by the exercise of their cunning," argued that had the states acceded to Congress's demands during the war they might have "stopped the Mouths of our internal [or] . . . infernal Enemies." The danger for him remained that if the states did not, for example, supply the treasury, the resulting turmoil would aid the "party [who] seem disposed to heave all into confusion, that their deep laid plans may take place." Some federalists perceived clearly that if unresolved problems cast doubts on the Confederation's stability "power must finally be given to Congress" as a last resort which would "in the End, deface the Altar of Liberty, so happily erected in this Hemisphere."[60]

Henry Laurens seemed certain that a future choice between Scylla and Charybdis could be avoided by measured responses whereby the Articles of Confederation would "undergo revisions, amendments will be made & new laws enacted in each State as the Interests and well-being of each & of the whole shall require." Stephen Higginson was more emphatic that complacency not take hold and that "the good Sense of the States lead them to revise the Constitution before such general confusion takes place." The crucial thing was that the Confederation respond to crises and problems without changing its basic structure; that it work to insure that having "finished the game with Great Britain" the nation would not "be bilked out of the stakes by any single state whatsoever."[61]

The dilemma was that if the Articles of Confederation did not respond to changing needs nationalism could very easily reap the benefits; if the Articles of Confederation did respond there was an inherent risk of "overleap[ing] the fences established by the Confederation to secure the liberties of the respective States." The ideological question was only part of the problem. The Confederation's stability, and federalists' ability to defend it, depended upon the states supporting each other as well as Congress. It was very soon apparent that trouble lay ahead. Thus the unwillingness of the states to adopt the supplementary fund showed some "how fond men & States are of one another."[62] There were federalists who wanted nothing to do with strengthening Congress, who, instead of formulating alternatives to nationalist proposals, gave faint lip service to the hope that Congress would be "generally disposed to adopt economy and good measures." They advocated state-controlled imposts without seeming to care that "quarrels will surely arise" among the states.[63]

Although passage of the impost might have given Congress too much power to suit most federalists, nonpassage and the increasing reluctance of the states to meet their federal requisitions seemed to confirm the oft-repeated accusation that the Articles of Confederation could only operate as an effective central government when danger pressed the states together. Complaints about the need for congressional funds, demands for passage of the impost, and continued creditor activity had only a slight effect. William Grayson's complaint that the people would only "give you the skin louse" if asked contrasted sharply with continued warnings that giving Congress "both purse and sword" would "subvert the liberties of America."[64] By 1785 New York took the place Rhode Island had had in 1782 in substantiating nationalist charges that a single state could confound federal programs. New York passed the second impost in 1786, but so qualified and amended it that it was not even "considered as a compliance with the same."[65]

Although federalist-nationalist conflict shaped the immediate post-war political scene, sectionalism retained its powerful influence. To a certain extent the federalist resurgence was as dependent upon an imposed, even artificial, intersectional cooperation as had been the nationalist ascendancy. In a way Robert Morris and nationalism replaced the British in binding northern and southern federalists against a common enemy. David Howell, for example, remarked in mid-1783 that his "good friends Mr. A. Lee & Col. Bland received me with a smile [in Congress] & cooperate in every measure for maintaining the Sovereignty of the Individual States." But the Articles of Confederation had not provided solutions to the many sectionally divisive problems facing the nation. The issues of revenue, commerce, and western lands were side-stepped by a compromise born of necessity in 1776 and 1777. There still were no workable solutions to these potentially troublesome issues. Northern and southern federalists' cooperation in repelling a nationalist threat did not mean that they were less committed to, or less concerned about, their own antithetical interests. On the contrary, northern and southern federalists did not exhibit a similar sense of accord and cooperation on those issues which were related not to the question of political balance in the constitutional system, but to the question of sectional balance.[66]

Although the end of the war revitalized federalism, it also produced a climate conducive to renewed conflicts of interests. With national defense no longer pressing the states and sections together, the old conflicts began to rise slowly to the surface in an even more virulent form than in 1776 and 1777. In the end, it was this conflict which prevented solutions to the many problems facing the nation in the postwar years. At the same time that its defenders were turning back the Morris faction and all it represented, the Confederation was being battered by the almost uncontrollable forces of interstate and especially intersectional conflict. The resulting discord eventually breathed new life into nationalism. While fighting with each other northern and southern federalists let their special interests disrupt the cooperation upon which the Confederation, federalism, and their own influence depended.[67]

4

The Capital Fight

AN ISSUE which graphically demonstrated the connection between ideology and interest in revolutionary America was the more than two-year fight over the location of a federal capital. Long before the federalist resurgence was in full swing, some federalists already had an awareness of the powerful impact that Congress's residence in Philadelphia, "the bosom of Toryism," had had on national politics.[1] Shortly after the collapse of the Newburgh Conspiracy William Gordon suggested to Arthur Lee that a residence in New York City would effectively stifle further nationalist influence. He reasoned that while Virginia could "watch the motion of Pennsylvania and prevent our becoming provinces to that power," the New Yorkers, who were also "for lording it over their brothers," would be kept in check by Pennsylvania, which having lost "the seat of continental government . . . [would] become a counterpoise to the York patrones." Gordon, however, had more in mind than simply splitting the two centers of nationalism. Although he might have been sure of Arthur Lee's federalist commitment, he was very dubious about most other southerners. Gordon was not simply defending federalist ideology when he opposed George Washington's suggestion to call a convention of the states to revise the Articles of Confederation in 1783. Gordon said that he could not envision a better system "considering the opposite cases of the people in the different states," but what he really meant was that he distrusted the South. In September 1782, echoing the fears of 1775 and 1776, a cynical and paranoid Gordon warned John Adams that the United States had to "remain a collection of Republics, and not become an Empire . . . [because] if America becomes an Empire, the seat of government will be to the southward, and the Northern States will be insignificant pro-

59

vinces. Empire will suit the southern gentry; they are habituated to despotism by being the sovereigns of slaves: and it is only accident and interest that had made the body of them the temporary sons of liberty."[2] The location of a capital had far broader implications than ideological conflict. Northern nationalists were just as anxious as northern federalists to keep Congress away from the South.

Although Philadelphia had been the site used for Congress's residence during the war, provision had never been made for a permanent capital. With the war ended attention began to be directed to the question. In early April 1783 New York offered a site at Kingston on the Hudson. Within a short time the Virginia and Maryland delegates in Congress agreed to have their states offer a joint site for a federal residence. It seemed quite logical for them to offer a suitable alternative to a northern site. But Maryland, in order to further its own interests, backed out of the agreement and instead offered Annapolis as a prospective site for a capital. Not about to be outdone, the Virginians planned to enter Williamsburg into the growing contest. Because the federal residence promised to enhance greatly the commercial and political influence of the state and section in which it was located, the capital fight brought to a head and was one of the foci of the increasing interstate and intersectional conflict in the nation in the postwar years. One writer offered the common view that wherever Congress situated "it will advance the interest of the State." Another, trying to build support in Virginia to counter Maryland's offer, judged that "the advantages that will derive to any State, in which Congress shall establish the seat of their future Sessions, will, we doubt not, be totally weighed by the Legislature." The capital was a prize which many states eagerly and jealously sought.[3]

By early June it seemed that many congressmen were convinced that the selection of a permanent residence was necessary. But with offers beginning to pour into Congress, discussion on the selection of a site was postponed until October.[4] Within a short time an unexpected event dramatically catapulted the residence issue back to the fore. In early June several hundred soldiers of the Pennsylvania Line came to Philadelphia demanding a redress of grievances. On 21 June between 200 and 250 disgruntled soldiers surrounded the Pennsylvania State House, where Congress met. Congress, however, was not in session. When the delegates hastily convened, after the outbreak of the disturbance, they appealed to John Dickinson for assistance from the state government, but the request went unanswered. Congress, purportedly rankled by the direct affront to the nation's central government, quickly passed a resolution castigating the state of Pennsylvania and resolving to adjourn either to Princeton or Trenton within the week.[5]

Congress's hasty retreat from Philadelphia spurred some thoughts of conspiracy. One Philadelphian charged that the entire business had been engineered to embarrass the nationalists in Pennsylvania and get Congress to another state. There was some conjecture that if the matter were sifted to the bottom Congress would discover "some Capital movers." There were even insinuations, which Alexander Hamilton vehemently denied, that he had instigated the trouble because he "wanted to sow dissension among the delegates . . . and hoped to get Congress in New York."[6] Although there is no way to determine whether or not there were ulterior motives to or dark forces behind the removal, there seems little doubt that many influential men were hardly displeased with leaving Philadelphia. It is fairly certain that Elias Boudinot, the president of Congress, used his influence to get Congress to Princeton, because of his desire to have Congress in New Jersey. Certainly other claimants for the federal residence were more concerned with advancing their own interests than they were about Philadelphia's loss of stature. Robert R. Livingston was especially glad that Congress was no longer in Philadelphia. In late June both Virginia and New Jersey offered prospective sites for a capital.[7]

The removal from Philadelphia also had major political repercussions. The angry Philadelphians, who tended to be nationalists, cited the removal as a dramatic example of congressional impotence. It was, for example, argued that Congress could have easily avoided the present crisis had it fully accepted Robert Morris's revenue plan. Even Tristram Dalton, concerned that a lack of congressional authority would further the cause of nationalism, hoped that Congress's retreat before a few hundred soldiers would finally stimulate measures to "render the Confederacy still respected." Dalton was clearly in the minority. Most federalists were more concerned with limiting nationalist influence. One way to do that was to keep Congress out of Philadelphia, where its "wisdom has long been question'd, their virtues suspected, and their dignity a jest." One writer even accused Robert Morris and Benjamin Lincoln of having precipitated the army mutiny in order to secure a revision of the Articles of Confederation.[8]

There seemed good ground for the belief that a Philadelphia residence was dangerous to the Confederation. David Howell relayed the information that a Rhode Island delegate, who had voted for commutation, when asked why he had ignored his instructions replied that "he could, as things were circumstanced vote no otherwise." Howell hoped that "things will take a different run in Congress now it is removed from the unhealthful & dangerous atmosphere of Philadelphia." Things quickly took a different run. Stephen Higginson reported that since the removal

the "members act with much more independence" and that he had
gotten motions passed "which but one would support me when in
Philadelphia." He further noted that Congress had escaped at the precise moment when "the spider's web is so nearly finished, so many of
our members have got entangled in it, and so artful are the Manoeuvres
made use of to draw others into it, that I see no way of getting rid of the
danger . . . but that of destroying him who has the management and has
placed it at his will" This desire to destroy Robert Morris and nationalist
influence guided much federalist activity in 1783, and the capital fight
was a vital part of the struggle.[9]

A short time after Congress convened at Princeton, Hamilton and
John Francis Mercer moved for an immediate return to Philadelphia.
Congress instead passed a motion by Higginson and Ralph Izard to
remain in Princeton until Congress received an assurance of protection
from Pennsylvania. The Philadelphians believed that with such assurance Congress could be made to return, but a federalist-controlled
committee refused to respond to their petition urging a return.
Federalists had no intention of returning to a city upon which Robert
Morris's "undue and wicked influence depends so much." They were,
moreover, prepared for Morris to use "his utmost authority" to effect a
return.[10] By the end of July it seemed certain that Congress would
remain in Princeton through the summer.

Federalist opposition, and Philadelphia's negative image, were not
enough to account for Congress's willingness to delay the question of a
return to Philadelphia. The growing competition for the capital doubtless did more to keep Congress in Princeton. Because Morris and his
colleagues were so influential and because they could quite easily defend Philadelphia as the best site for the federal residence, many competitors for the capital wanted to choose a location in relative tranquil-
ity. Madison noted that they "now make a common cause agst.
Philada."[11] Although it was certain that Congress would not leave
Princeton within the near future, a few delegates wanted to make sure
that an anti-Philadelphia bias was publicly declared.

On 1 August Jacob Read of South Carolina moved that Congress
return to Philadelphia. Madison, who was in that city, doubted that
Congress would return, or that the matter would come to a vote. He
supposed "that no question will be taken when the probability of a
negative is fully discovered; though it will be pushed by those who wish
to multiply the obsticles to a removal South of the Delaware." Sure
enough the motion to return to Philadelphia was "hurried . . . with
unbecoming precipitation" by federalists.[12] On 11 August David Howell
and Theodorick Bland moved the question, and two days later it was

defeated. Madison was shocked by their vile behavior. He later reported that "the more moderate opponents concurred in the inexpediency of proclaiming unnecessarily an aversion in Congs. to Philda., But some of this class were so keen in their hostility that a motion was made by two men to return, who on the question voted solid agt. their own motion."[13]

The Philadelphians, however, continued to work for a return. An easy way was to incite sectional fears in order to crack the strained accord among the dissimilar anti-Philadelphia delegates and get Philadelphia to again be chosen as the most central and hence the most acceptable site for the federal residence. Benjamin Rush thus warned Elias Boudinot that if "you have availed yourselves of an ostensible excuse only to detach Congress from their stronghold in Philadelphia, then stay where you are till you are duped and laughed at on Hudson's River." Boudinot, however, was quite confident that "some Village in Jersey near N[ew] York would be preferred." In fact, federalists, who had no intention of returning to Philadelphia, did back a capital in New Jersey.[14] Their strategy was vulnerable on two points. The Philadelphians, and some of their nationalist supporters, equated a smoothly running Congress with a Philadelphia location; Congress, they felt, would be a mere cypher until it returned "to that Sweet Paradice from which they hastily took Flight in June." But the possibility that Congress might return to Philadelphia, that there would be a triumph of "art and cultivation over right and judgment," did not spring solely from the pro-Philadelphia forces.[15] Although the Lee-Adams junto was finally making headway in limiting nationalist influence, sectional difference, as always, threatened its ability to carry out policy. William Gordon was continuing to report that "the Southern Gentry are going back to their aristocratic or monarchical principles . . . It will require much wisdom to keep the states united. The South is foolishly jealous of the North."[16]

Southern jealousy was not without some foundation, especially in light of New England's alleged desire to build a capital in New Jersey, with a temporary residence in New York City. Madison, who was convinced that the New Englanders opposed a southern location for Congress, objected to a temporary residence in New York City not only because it was "farther from the South," but because it would make "a removal to the Southern position finally more difficult, than it would be from Philada."[17] Although there was little likelihood that the capital would "be fixed further South than Pennsylvania," some southerners were not about to give up the fight. William Grayson even charged that all "the Northern Gentry" had in mind in attacking the nationalists was "to dupe the Southern States by making Philaa. a bug-bear & so pull you further North, if in their power."[18] Not all southerners agreed with

Grayson or Madison. Joseph Jones, who was no less committed to
southern interests than any of his colleagues, was busy trying to convince Madison of the importance of Pennsylvania's apologizing for the
affront to Congress. One consideration in the New Englanders' favor
was the strong resentment some influential Virginians had for the
Philadelphia merchants.[19] Yet it was still highly doubtful whether northern and southern federalists could overcome the pull of sectional interest and continue to keep Congress out of Philadelphia. In the face of a
projected northern capital and a temporary residence in New York there
was a chance that many southerners would opt for Philadelphia as the
lesser of two evils.

The Philadelphians had, in the meantime, not been idle. It was reported that "great pains had been and are taking place to get Congress to
return." In mid-August John Dickinson had proposed that the General
Assembly offer some site in Pennsylvania for a permanent residence,
with Philadelphia the temporary residence. Although Philadelphia was
never placed in contention, Gouverneur Morris had suggested that
because of the fear the mention of Philadelphia inspired, it might be
more effective to propose a site somewhere near, but not in Philadelphia. When Congress finally began discussion in early October Morris's
suggestion had evidently been heeded, as Germantown, but "another
name for Philadelphia," was submitted for consideration. But Germantown and all the previously offered sites were rejected.[20]

Congress began voting on a permanent residence on 7 October. The
congressional delegates from Delaware supported the original motion,
which called for an undesignated site on the Delaware River. The first
vote for a specific site near Wilmington, however, was overwhelmingly
defeated. Congress then passed Elbridge Gerry's motion that it erect
buildings either on the banks of the Delaware near Trenton or on the
Potomac. Maryland, Virginia, North Carolina, and South Carolina opposed the measure. These southerners probably realized that the
Potomac site hadn't a chance of being selected, and their fears were
soon realized when it was immediately resolved that the Delaware site
be the location for a capital city. The selection of a location for the
capital on the Delaware near Trenton rankled the Delaware delegates,
who had hoped for a Wilmington site. They quickly voiced their unwillingness to have a capital anywhere on the Delaware but at Wilmington
and on 8 October supported a motion to reconsider the matter in order to
select a site "more central, more favourable to the Union, and [which]
shall approach nearer to that justice which is due to the Southern
States." Although the motion was defeated, southern displeasure had a

major impact on further discussion as Congress turned its attention to
the selection of a temporary residence.[21]

After passage of a motion for adjournment on 10 October Hugh
Williamson moved that Congress adjourn at the end of October to
reconvene in Philadelphia. New York, Pennsylvania, Delaware, Virginia, and North Carolina all voted in favor of Philadelphia; had South
Carolina's and Maryland's delegates not split, thanks to the old Lee-
Adams junto ties and James McHenry's desire to get Congress to
Annapolis, Congress would have returned to Philadelphia. The following day William Ellery moved that Congress adjourn to Annapolis until
June 1784, at which time it would return to Trenton. Gerry and Holten,
apparently seeking to alleviate southern fears, moved to insert "the
place of their temporary residence" instead of Trenton. Although it was
in their best interest to get a temporary residence in or south of Philadelphia, a major rift prevented Maryland and Virginia from agreeing on a
suitable location. Influential men in each state were beginning to set
plans in motion to navigate and improve their inland rivers, the Susquehanna and the Potomac. Each group had hopes of capturing the lucrative
backcountry trade and neither wanted to enhance its competitor's position by situating Congress in a commercial center. The Gerry-Holten
amendment carried, but the original question was defeated, with New
York, New Jersey, Pennsylvania, and Virginia in opposition. Two days
later a Mercer-Lee motion for adjournment to Williamsburg was
soundly rejected.[22]

THE DUAL RESIDENCE

The discussion of a temporary residence, especially in light of the
narrow defeat of a Philadelphia removal, affected the previous selection
of a permanent residence on the Delaware. Federalists, more specifically New Englanders, faced a dilemma: they were happy with the
choice of a northern capital city away from either Philadelphia or New
York's immediate spheres, but there was the danger that if Philadelphia
were chosen for the temporary residence "Congress will never again
make their escape from that City." A Philadelphia removal, moreover,
seemed quite likely because of the southern displeasure "that the federal Town is not more South."[23] Madison even confessed his own
surprise that New England had joined with the middle states in favor of a
Delaware site which, he thought, would stand "unless a conversion of
some of the Eastern States can be effected."[24]

It was soon evident that such a conversion had, indeed, taken place.

The probability of the selection of Philadelphia as Congress's temporary residence required some modification in the previously passed resolution for erecting a capital on the Delaware near Trenton. Elbridge Gerry's motion on 17 October that additional buildings for Congress's residence be built at Georgetown on the Potomac had grave import for the Philadelphia backers. Charles Thomson, the secretary of Congress and a staunch nationalist, reported "that in order to engage the Southern States not to vote for a temporary residence in Philadelphia the eastern Members had it in contemplation to propose two places for erecting buildings for the residence of Congress, one in the South & one in the eastern or middle states. Mr. Gerry who had taken an active lead in this business, yesterday broached the matter." George Clymer quickly relayed the news that an "arrangement had taken place out of doors to be ratified within, between the Eastern and Southern Members, to which the middle is to be sacrificed."[25] These fears were realized when instead of waiting until 22 October, the date which had been scheduled to take up the matter, Gerry's motion was considered on 20 October, with New Jersey, Pennsylvania, Delaware, and New Hampshire absent from Congress. After some minor revision of the temporary residence clause a dual residence was established. Capitals were to be erected near Trenton on the Delaware and near Georgetown on the Potomac, and until construction was completed Congress was to move from Trenton to Annapolis.[26]

In order to understand the continuing conflict on the question of a federal residence, it is necessary to examine the factors which led to the dual-residence compromise. Although the compromise was important in limiting nationalist influence in the immediate postwar years, too much cannot be made of its effect on intersectional relations. The term *compromise* may even be a misnomer, because New England and the South did not really resolve their differences. The New Englanders, by their own admission, had no other alternative but to give the South a share in the federal residence in order "to prevent the return of Congress to Philadelphia, for a temporary residence." They were convinced that if Congress returned to Philadelphia a capital would never be constructed and Congress would never again be able to leave that city.[27] Although Elbridge Gerry proposed the dual-residence resolves and was generally considered to be the father of the scheme, it was the southerners who were in the position to set terms. Their willingness to return to Philadelphia forced New England to compromise its own interests; the South gave up nothing and stood to gain a great deal. Southern reaction to the dual residence pretty much confirmed Elias Boudinot's assertion that the southerners had "maneuvered in such a manner as to take in the

Eastern Members to conform entirely to their views." The North Carolina delegates optimistically reported that having gotten "Congress to the Southward for Six months . . . some future Congress will prevent their return to this side [north] of the Waters of the Chesapeack." Joseph Jones appeared confident that "in the end George Town should be solely established as the seat of Congress."[28]

Southerners believed that the future lay with them, and their behavior during the whole of the residence issue and during the later Confederation period attests to this. Although they did not have the votes and ability to set policy, they followed a strategy of obstructionism in relation to those matters which, from their viewpoint, could be better solved when their own and not northern interests predominated. It seemed certain, and not only to southerners, that the great migration to the trans-Allegheny in the 1770s and 1780s was inexorably tilting the weight of population and influence to them. "A True American" noted that "it must be obvious to everyone, that emigration from abroad prevails much more in the Southern States than those of the eastward, especially in the back settlements; no one therefore can falsely venture to predict, which part of the Continent will be consequential [in] a century." It was, moreover, easy to foresee a powerful southern influence in Congress much sooner than that, given the effect of the admission of new western states to the Union. The interest of some southerners in improving the navigation of the inland rivers was partly motivated by a desire to speed the process of sectional integration between the West and the South. They wanted a residence chosen only when they could insure its location in the South, as Jefferson said in late 1783, to "cement us to our Western Friends when they shall be formed into separate states."[29] Although there was hardly any chance of a single southern capital in the 1780s, some southerners at least hoped to prevent the erection of a capital in the North.

The unstable foundation upon which the dual residence rested was not lost on some observers. Edward Bancroft, the sagacious British agent, predicted that not only would the residence "doubtless give occasion to much future Contestation," but that the Union would surely dissolve and it was only a "question whether [to] have thirteen *separate* States in *alliance* or whether the New England, the middle, & the Southern States will form three new Confederations." Bancroft was not alone in his pessimistic view of the probable results of sectional conflict. William Gordon, certainly not motivated by Bancroft's desire to see the Union collapse, was no less cheerless in his assertion that the Union "by not suiting the Northern climate however well adapted for the southern will after a time bring on fresh wars and fighting among ourselves, and make the whole one great [nation], or break us into smaller ones, instead of remaining separate states, united by a confederation, under a Congress freely chosen by the powers of each state." These dire predictions were balanced by a more optimistic though less realistic view. Stephen Higginson, for one, did not believe that sectional conflict was systemic. He instead argued that the Morris faction had tried to "assume the Reins and Lord it over the States . . . [by keeping up] a jealousy between the Eastern and Southern States . . . calculated to subjugate both." He had every confidence that because they "now understand the Views of the Junto . . . in future the southern & eastern States will in general be united."[30]

The capital fight was, however, only part of a larger sectional clash concerning western expansion, governmental policy, and the future of the nation. The issues of commerce and western lands, which were as closely related to sectional dominance as was the location of a capital, slowly began to revive what were aptly called the "old partialities."[31] Yet Higginson's conspiratorial view of the origins of sectional conflict continued even in the face of increasing sectional tensions. He still believed that sectional conflict, while grounded in real differences, was politically instigated. Because they could not keep "their tools properly instructed" in Trenton or Annapolis, Higginson was certain that nationalist leaders intended to get Congress back to Philadelphia by setting New England and the South at odds. He warned Theodorick Bland that they might try to persuade the southerners that they "may secure for themselves a permanent residence" by refusing to vote for an adjournment to Trenton. This action would naturally excite a jealousy in the New England delegates which might lead them to join with the nationalists "in removing congress to trenton, and fixing them there permanently." The next step, of course, would be a manipulation of angry southern delegates to effect a return to Philadelphia. Higginson wanted to "guard against their schemes for dividing us, and renewing our jealousies of each other."[32] To a certain degree Higginson's alarm was warranted. Nationalists did believe that a single congressional residence, preferably in Philadelphia, was vital to a restructuring of the Confederation.[33] Moreover, conflict between New England and the South was, once more, disarming federalist resolve. The fact remains, however, that there were major differences between New England and southern interests, and the continuing struggles on a federal residence were as much an effect as a cause of sectional conflict. Certain nationalists might have sown some seeds of distrust, but they had very fertile ground with which to work.

A CHANGING POLITICAL CLIMATE IN 1784

Even before the intensification of sectional conflict in 1784 the dual residence, admittedly an awkward, unprecedented arrangement, was criticized. The fact that congressional influence was divided led to charges that the central government was a mockery and that the dual residence was weakening the Union. In early January 1784 Charles Thomson and Robert R. Livingston reported that many congressmen were now "ashamed of their two federal towns." Thomson, who unlike Livingston wanted Congress back in Philadelphia, was especially critical of Elbridge Gerry, "the father of the project," whose pleasure, he said, "seems proportioned to the absurdity of his schemes."[34] There was even a piece in the prints "in which a *moving town* was proposed, to which the equestrian statue of General Washington was to be attached." Some New Englanders were also displeased with the dual residence. Samuel Osgood, for example, believed that the southern states would try to get Congress back to Philadelphia if they could not obtain a capital either in Maryland or Virginia. He warned about their "aristocratical principles" and doubted whether there would "be a coincidence of political views in some matters of great importance to the Eastern States." Osgood clearly and very early realized that the sections' antithetical commercial interests would spell trouble for New England. New Englanders like Osgood saw the dual residence as simply a means to an end. Even Elbridge Gerry reasoned that if the dual-residence resolves "only exist in Idea, untill We have effectually opened the despotic System so warmly pursued to destroy the Liberties of our Country, they will have answered a great, & political purpose."[35]

By early 1784 the dual residence had performed that purpose. With plans underway to create a Board of Treasury and nationalists apparently in full retreat, there was less need for New England to placate the South. New England's desire to leave Annapolis was shared by Virginia. As plans for the Potomac navigation swung into full gear, it became more important than ever for Virginia to lessen Maryland's influence. Thomas Jefferson, who was deeply involved in the Potomac navigation, advised Madison that Congress should move "to some place off the waters of the Chesapeak where we may be ensured against Congress considering themselves as fixed." He wanted Congress to adjourn, "not to meet again till November, leaving a Commee. of the States" to sit in Philadelphia until Congress reconvened. Jefferson surmised that the choice lay between Trenton and Philadelphia and would "depend on the vote of New York." Madison agreed, believing that if New York had the deciding vote "it is not difficult to foresee into which scale it will be thrown, nor the probable effect of such a decision on our Southern hopes."[36]

It appeared by mid-March that Congress would most probably select Trenton for its temporary residence.[37] It was reported, though, that the New Englanders really wanted to situate in New York City, with only a committee of the states sitting in Trenton during the recess. A temporary residence in New York City, which William Gordon had proposed in mid-1782, would have stifled Philadelphia's designs, and having a committee of the states sitting in Trenton would, the New Englanders hoped, prevent any shady dealings during the recess. Southern jealousy was still a fly in the ointment; the New Englanders were reportedly "on thin ground and very causions in speaking of " their plan.[38]

On 14 April Congress began to discuss adjournment. After Newport, Philadelphia, and Alexandria were rejected, it was resolved, on a motion by Beatty of New Jersey and Sherman of Connecticut, to adjourn on 26 May and reconvene in Trenton in late October. Jefferson made it known that the southern states would not accept adjournment unless "a committee of the States shall have been previously constituted." Less than two weeks later, both Philadelphia and Trenton were still in the running for the temporary residence. Because Georgia and Delaware were soon expected in Congress, Jefferson thought that Philadelphia would be selected. But those states never arrived, and in late April Gerry and Howell moved for adjournment in early June. Congress was to convene in Trenton on 30 October, with a committee of the states to sit in the interim. Only the five southern states supported a motion to give such a committee "all the powers exercised by seven states in Congress assembled." The sectional lines were being clearly drawn. A motion by James McHenry and John Francis Mercer to take up the question of the erection of federal buildings on the Delaware and the Potomac was defeated, as was a motion by Samuel Hardy and Jacob Read to remain in Annapolis until the two residences were completed. The southerners failed to prevent Congress from adjourning to the north. Howell and Gerry's motion to adjourn to Trenton was carried.[39]

The New Englanders had won a questionable victory. John Montgomery admitted that the Pennsylvania delegation had only supported Trenton "as we were certain we could not [obtain] a vote (having tried it) for Philadelphia." The Pennsylvanian's waiting game was bad enough, but in keeping Congress out of Philadelphia the New Englanders had antagonized the southern delegates, who had good reason to believe that Congress would never again come south of the Delaware. It was intimated that the southerners intended to remain in Annapolis throughout the summer on the committee of the states and that they might try to adjourn to Philadelphia and get Congress to convene there instead of in Trenton. This possibility was at the center of the debates on the powers of a committee of the states.[40]

Although the Articles of Confederation provided for a committee of the states, it had never before been necessary to call one together. A committee was appointed on 18 July 1783 to consider the power which a committee of the states ought to possess. Its report of 17 September was not acted on until 23 January 1784, when on Jefferson's motion the business was referred to a new committee composed of Jefferson, Osgood, and Sherman. Jefferson wanted the committee to have wide-ranging powers, but Osgood and Sherman's influence prevailed in their report on 27 May. Two days later a resolve was passed giving a committee of the states power to act only so far as seven states in Congress assembled could act, which, of course, meant that it would be unable to take any sort of policy initiative. The committee was also enjoined from doing anything, save adjourning, without nine states present. David Howell was relieved that its proscribed powers provided "ample Security against the Committee's sitting in Philadelphia, unless infatuated."[41]

Congress's decision to adjourn to Trenton further aggravated relations between the sections. Joseph Jones, who had previously opposed a return to Philadelphia, was now convinced that New England was never "serious in the proposition of two residences and that it was merely introduced to shun Philadelphia as the temporary residence—they will never come south of Delaware if by any means they can avoid it." The Virginia delegates completely supported Jones's view. They complained that the sectional balance in Congress lay with the northern states, and "untill the admission of Western States into the Union, we apprehend it will be found impracticable to retain that Body, for any length of time, Southward of the middle States." They were also worried that because Congress's alternate removal between Trenton and Annapolis depended upon New England, the residence compromise might "be productive of concessions in favor of the Northern members of this confederacy on other very important points and indeed give them an unequal weight in the Scale." Certainly uppermost in their minds was the northern merchants' growing demand for commercial reform. This issue, despite the political differences and commercial competition between New England and the middle states, was beginning to draw merchants and politicians in those two sections together.[42]

Ephraim Paine, noting the deep-seated conflicts between "the southern nabobs . . . [and] the great spirits of the Northern gentry," feared that "some matters must be left undone, or they will be ill done." Paine was correct. A commerce act was passed in Congress on 30 April 1784, but it was only a proposed embargo power to enable Congress to combat British trade restrictions. It did not meet the needs of the northern merchants. Likewise, northern plans for a national western land policy were unacceptable to the southern states.[43] In self-defense some southerners again began to look to the middle states. Hugh Williamson complained to James Duane about New England's attempt to admit Vermont into the Union. Because the like admittance of two southern states seemed remote, Williamson was loath to "see a phalanx of 5 dead Votes against us on every interesting Question till we are enabled to preserve the Balance." He hoped that "the Southern States shall support and be supported by N[ew] York on Federal Questions."[44] It turned out that New York was the wrong place to turn to try to break the very recent New England-middle state accord. But the South's interest in aligning with the middle states against New England was to have a great impact on politics in the later Confederation period.

During Congress's recess intersectional relations took a turn for the worse. The committee of the states, which some expected to adjourn to Trenton, remained in Annapolis. New England federalists had hoped that the committee would not be well attended. But, through early August it almost consistently had nine members. Although little business was undertaken, there was still talk of a removal to Philadelphia.[45] On 11 August, with the excuse of "private affairs," the New Hampshire, Massachusetts, and New Jersey deputations left the committee of the states. The real reason for their departure, said James Sullivan, was that "the locus in quo [the location] became a serious question between the Southern and Northern members." Richard Dobbs Spaight even thought that New England planned to leave the Confederation.[46]

Congress was supposed to reconvene in Trenton on 30 October, but the delegates filtered in slowly and a quorum was not achieved until late November. Even before Congress convened it appeared that it would not remain long in Trenton. The two alternative sites mentioned were New York City and Philadelphia, with the latter apparently clearly in the lead. In the meantime, two of the three commissioners appointed to the Board of Treasury had resigned. One anxious New Englander even thought that Congress might "be brought to replace Morris" if it returned to Philadelphia.[47]

On 10 December South Carolina and Pennsylvania moved for an adjournment. Although no mention was made of the place to reconvene, Rufus King and Richard Henry Lee both thought that Philadelphia was clearly intended. The following day the motion was defeated, with New England and New York aligning against Pennsylvania, Virginia, North and South Carolina, and Georgia.[48] Ten days later John Jay and David Howell proposed that Congress appropriate $100,000 for the erection of federal buildings with the proviso that "it is inexpedient for Congress at this time to erect public buildings for their accommodation at more than one place." Probably fearful that if Congress returned to Philadelphia a capital might never be constructed, Jay and Gerry tried to postpone discussion of the above resolution to take up the motion that Congress remain in Trenton until "the place near the falls of Trenton at which the federal buildings . . . shall be fixed and ascertained and Commissioners for erecting the same be appointed." On the 24th three commissioners were appointed to find a site on the Delaware. The only remaining business was to choose a temporary residence. After William Churchill Houston and David Howell failed in an attempt to keep Congress in Trenton, Samuel Hardy and Richard Dobbs Spaight moved for an adjournment to Philadelphia. Their motion was defeated with the same sectional breakdown as the 10 December vote. Finally, Howell and Spaight's motion for a temporary residence in New York City was passed with only three dissenting votes.[49]

The fact that Spaight sided with a New Englander, or that the southern states supported the new residence plan, did not mean that the South had given up its fight. Although Spaight had wanted Congress to go to Philadelphia, he believed that a New York residence would "prove advantageous by cementing all of the states to the southward of Connecticut together." A bitter Joseph Jones found little to change his view that the New Englanders had used the dual residence "as well as the removal to Annapolis, to keep clear of Philadelphia . . . until they had gained sufficient strength" to locate Congress "at Trenton or near it."[50] The southerners, as the Virginia delegates felt obliged to point out, had had no alternative but to agree to adjourn to New York. Obviously feeling that they had to justify their behavior, the delegates reported that when the residence was first discussed they had hoped "to decline a decision on it for the time." Without Maryland and Delaware in Congress they could not overcome the weight of numbers. The Virginia delegates, specifically Hardy and Monroe, did see one good result from a location in New York City. They believed that Congress's residence there would better enable the United States to secure "the furr trade." They were also sure that "before any competition can arise between the communication down the Mohawk, thro' this port [New York], and the Potowmack, we shall have removed hence to the falls of the Delaware." They reasoned, then, that New York's commercial advantage would be temporary and that Congress's eventual move to Trenton would not harm Virginia's interest in reaping as much of the backcountry trade as it could. Hardy and Monroe hardly represented the majority southern position. In fact, they did not even represent the majority position in Virginia. As we shall later see the men involved in the Potomac navigation took positions in 1784 and 1785 more in keeping with their own special commercial interests than with the dominant southern staple interest.[51]

The New Englanders had good reason to be pleased with the residence arrangement. They thought that the dissolution of the office of the superintendent of finance and Congress's locating in New York City would finally "put an end to the Influence of our political Monster." They were convinced that had Congress returned to Philadelphia, that "sink of corrupt Influence," their old enemies would "have impeded every measure for the completion of the federal buildings, and thereby kept Congress in that city."[52] They had little reason to fear New York's designs on the residence, because there was too much opposition to a capital that far north. In addition, New York was controlled by the Clintonians, decidedly anti-Philadelphian, who sided with New England on many issues in 1784 and 1785.

SECTIONALISM AND A FEDERAL CAPITAL

The 1784 residence plan lasted little longer than the dual residence, as increased sectional conflict rocked the nation. Added to the problems of commerce and western lands was a conflict over the payment of the federal debt. The impost was not yet passed and the supplementary funds, designed to make the former "palatable" to the commercial states were faring just as poorly. During and after the war the domestic debt changed hands, and by 1785 southerners held roughly one-eighth of the loan-office certificates held by speculators in Pennsylvania, Massachusetts, Connecticut, and New York. When Congress discussed the federal debt in early 1785, the southern states favored separating the foreign and domestic debts "because they have little in the foederal Funds."[53] The congressional requisition passed in March 1785 called for specific payment of money from each state to pay off the interest on the debt. William Grayson's typical reaction was that it was "formed on principles to suit only the Eastern and some of the middle States."[54]

The requisition also included the allocation for federal buildings now in the sum of $30,000. While a few New Englanders opposed construction because of a general reluctance to have Congress spend money, southerners had special concerns. They were reluctant to spend money to build a northern capital, while being called upon to pay northern speculators and while the northern states seemed intent upon setting up obstacles to settlement of the southwest. On 5 April Grayson and Abiel Foster, of New Hampshire, tried to strike the residence allocation. To some this move seemed designed to get Congress back to Philadelphia, and it was therefore assumed that the allocation would stand.[55] Despite Grayson's vow to do everything in his power "to frustrate the measure," the allocation was included in reports on 24 April and 18 July.[56] By August, however, Grayson was sure that a few penny-wise New Englanders would support striking the capital allocation. This suited his design to prevent the northern states from dominating the nation. He would, he said, even have moved for an adjournment to Philadelphia as "the properest place at least until we can see our way clearer to the Westward" were it not for "fear of the imputation of instability."[57]

Grayson's analysis proved correct. The New Hampshire delegates did not want to waste federal money on the construction of a capital. They were confident that no matter how long construction was delayed the capital would never be located in the South. Other New Englanders disagreed, and on 22 September Elbridge Gerry and David Howell unsuccessfully moved to reinsert the $100,000 allocation. The same day New Hampshire sided with Delaware, Maryland, Virginia and South Carolina to block rentention of the allocation in the congressional requisition.[58]

Grayson's statement about his unwillingness to impute instability reflected a fairly common feeling that the nation needed one congressional residence to regain "that influence at home and respectability abroad" which it had purportedly lost during its recent trouble finding a home. The notion was especially evident among nationalists that "a foederal Town will be a Kind of Center of the Union." The centralizing tendencies of one capital were certainly lost on no one in the 1780s. Southerners, however, were not about to accept a northern capital. George Washington, for instance, thought it inadvisable and foolish to construct "what may be call'd the permanent *seat* of Congress at this time . . . for without the gift of prophecy I will venture to predict that under any circumstances of Confederation, it will not remain so far to the Eastward long."[59] The southerners were playing a by now familiar game, waiting until the seeds of western expansion began to bear fruit. By the fall of 1785 strained intersectional relations made southerners exceedingly uncomfortable in New York, and they were again considering a return to Philadelphia.[60] In the end the question of a permanent residence was not settled until 1790 after the creation of a national government. Thus, southern obstruction was successful in the long run —and it was to be equally successful in blocking commercial reform of the Articles of Confederation.

5

Commercial Reform

AMERICA'S WELL-DESERVED exuberance at the close of the war in 1783 was quickly shaken by the realization that it was an upstart, a huge but weak second-rate power in a world of empires. America might have won recognition of its political independence, but it had no assurance that it would be treated as an equal in the commercial world. Particularly damaging was Great Britain's refusal to enter into a commercial treaty with the United States and its erection of a navigation system which discriminated against American shipping. By late 1784 New England merchants, who had the most at stake, concluded that the European states, and most important Great Britain, would not enter into commercial treaties unless Congress was given a power to regulate foreign and interstate trade. The refusal of the southern planter interest to accede to commercial reform had a tremendous impact on the political scene. It irreparably split federalist ranks and helped demonstrate the inability of the Confederation to respond to specific needs. Although by 1785 conflict between northern merchants and southern planters prevented commercial reform and exacerbated relations with the British, the seeds of Anglo-American contention had been planted much earlier. Ideological conflict and the antagonistic interests of New England and middle state merchants in the earlier 1780s had as great an effect in blocking commercial accord with Great Britain as southern intransigence did later.

Before New England's mercantile plans began to threaten the southern economy, northern and southern federalists cooperated in trying to establish a commercial treaty with Great Britain in order to break the nationalist and French grip on the nation. Their efforts in 1781 and 1782 to lay the necessary foundation for commercial negotiations failed to

76

weaken France's secure position. In early 1782 François Barbé-Marbois assured the Count de Vergennes that no matter how much what he called the party of Samuel Adams stormed, America would never gain entry into the fishery.[1] There was little this group could do besides thunder at "being in leading strings or pinning our faith upon others' sleaves." In October 1782 Congress reassured the French that its commissioners would not negotiate a treaty or sue for peace without their prior approval. If change were to come it would not come from America. Even Richard Henry Lee was reluctant to put his political ideas on paper for fear "that-Some penetrating eye may see it, or curious ear may hear of what I have written; and with lengthened face, shrug'd shoulders, and important air, whisper 'an enemy to the French Alliance.' "[2] Lee, whose own brother had been a sacrificial lamb before the altar of Bourbon, did not have to wait long for his revenge.

The flaw in French/nationalist strategy was the peace commissioners themselves. Adams, who had fought with the French since his arrival in Europe, was not about to see America become a semidependent French satellite. Realizing this, the French and nationalists had added Jay and Franklin to the peace commission in 1781. But by September 1782 Jay was also convinced that the French wanted "to postpone an acknowledgment of our independence by Britain to the conclusion of a general peace in order to keep us under their direction, until not only their and our objects are attained, but also until Spain shall be gratified in her demands to exclude everybody from the gulf." In late December 1782 one of Jay's letters, containing some very damning anti-American comments from an intercepted letter from Marbois to Vergennes, "awakened strong jealousies" in Congress. It was therefore postulated that if Great Britain yielded the "fisheries and the back territory, America will feel the obligation to her, not to France."[3]

The commissioners did negotiate a peace treaty with England which secured those rights and the acknowledgment of America's claim to the Mississippi River. Jay and Adams felt themselves relieved of the obligation to abide either by the peace instructions or the terms of the French alliance because, as Jay said, "our allies don't play fair." He was shocked that the French did not want America to secure either the fishery, the western lands, or the navigation of the Mississippi and were not above bargaining "with the English to deprive us of them." Adams, of course, was not shocked by anything the French did. He charged that their assistance was geared "to keep us from succumbing and nothing more; to prevent us from ridding ourselves wholly of our enemies; to prevent us from growing rich or powerful . . . to prevent us from obtaining consideration in Europe." Adams hoped that the favorable treaty would be sufficient excuse for the commissioners having ignored their instructions.[4]

The French did not intend to give up without a struggle. Soon after the American and British commissioners completed the preliminary treaty in late 1782 Vergennes ordered Luzerne to inform "the most influential members of Congress . . . of the very irregular conduct of their commissioners." About a month before the preliminary treaty arrived in America Robert R. Livingston read some dispatches to Congress from John Adams. Livingston might very well have asked Adams to write freely about the French alliance in order to give him enough rope to hang himself. In a quite candid dispatch written before the peace negotiations were concluded Adams warned Congress not to follow blindly the French, who, he argued, wanted America "to accept such terms of peace as they should think would do for us." In order to free America from French control, he suggested that Congress appoint ministers to reside in foreign capitals and charged it either to support its commissioners, and not France, or to recall them. Adams's comments, much more so than Jay's, were easily written off by some as nothing more than "a display of vanity, his prejudice against the French and his venom against Doctr. Franklin."[5]

Nevertheless, buoyed by a favorable treaty, insinuations of French anti-American policies, and the end of the war, Adams's colleagues now held the tactical advantage. After the preliminary treaty arrived in America in early March 1783 Robert R. Livingston tried his best to support the inviolability of the French alliance. He denounced the commissioners' abrogation of authority and requested permission to censure them and inform them that the preliminary treaty would not be ratified until peace was concluded between Great Britain and France. He even tried to incite anti-British feeling in a letter to the governors by warning that "Britain still seeks rather to divide her enemies than to be reconciled with them." Livingston was stretching America's responsibility to France to the breaking point. It was true that a separate peace conflicted with the express terms of the French alliance. America, however, stood to gain little and lose a great deal in placing its allegiance to France before its own interests. There was also the matter of past conflicts. During the debates on the preliminary treaty John Francis Mercer, for example, defended the commissioners by pointing to the peace instructions of 1781 as "the greatest opprobrium and stain to this Country which it had ever exposed itself to." The problem, as even Madison saw it, was that if Congress "abet the proceedings of their ministers, all confidence with France is at end . . . if they disavow the conduct of their ministers . . . the most serious inconveniences also present themselves." The choice between a favorable treaty and a self-interested unscrupulous ally was not hard to make. On 22 March Congress decided only to censure the commissioners mildly.[6]

Much more than duty caused men like Livingston to disparage the preliminary treaty and defend the French alliance. In early April Stephen Higginson noted that those delegates who were responsible for the "memorable instructions to our ministers which threw them entirely into the hands of Mons. Vergennes . . . [and for] the Revocation of the Commission for a Treaty of Commerce" could not conceal their "surprise and chagrin" when the preliminary treaty was first read. He said that they realized that the commissioners no longer felt obliged to honor their instructions "and that if they remained in Europe commercial negotiations would next engage their attention, though not sufficiently commissioned to complete them. They have endeavored to remove such *dangerous persons,* by passing an unjust censure on their conduct . . . in this also they have failed." Higginson was certain that the signing of the definitive treaty, the tacit sanction of the commissioners' actions, would lay "open the way for a commission to negotiate a commercial treaty with Britain." France, he warned, "had been, and still is, exceedingly afraid of such a connection. She wishes if possible to prevent it."[7] So did middle state nationalists. They had just as much reason as the French to deplore a vigorous and equitable trade between Great Britain and New England.

That the United States was no longer bound by "the officious advice of distant Friends" did not insure clear sailing for federalist policies. Higginson, attacking Morrisonian foreign policies with as much fervor as he did its domestic plans, reported that there were some men in Congress who were sorry "that peace has taken place, or rather perhaps, that the terms are so good & we thereby rendered so independent of all foreign power—these persons seem very anxious to find fault with it . . . & retard the complying with the Articles of the Treaty." This was especially true, he thought, with respect to the articles concerning loyalists. The British were adamant about protecting loyalists from American recriminations and persecution. They had even managed to insert two articles in the peace treaty prescribing congressional attention to the matter of the treatment of loyalists and their property. Although many Americans harbored antiloyalist feelings, in addition to desiring confiscated loyalist property, Higginson accused the French of taking "great pains . . . to prevent their [loyalists] return," because they wanted America "saddled with the Refugee Article—Their object is to divide & perplex us by it, having done this, They use the same principles in an endeavor to encourage our opposition to it, & if they can by this means prevent or delay a friendly, commercial intercourse between us and Great Britain, They gain a great point . . . They expect in this way to retain their influence over us, & prevent any connexion with others." Higginson, attempting to set some priorities among the forces and issues at play, warned that entering into irresoluble disputes with the British would only delay and possibly end any hope for a commercial treaty. He was sure that even without the formulation of a commercial treaty, "individuals here will eagerly desire a Trade with them, & they will see that important concessions on their part will not be necessary—Our policy should be to perfect the Treaty of peace & comply with the several articles on Our part, at least in appearance, that no objections may arise to their engaging with us readily in the treaty of Commerce."[8]

ANTINATIONALISM AND FOREIGN AFFAIRS

A commercial treaty with Great Britain was important not only because of the danger of continued French influence, but also because of the possibility of a commercial dependence and impotence as stultifying as colonial status. Because there were no commercial clauses in the peace treaty, relations between Great Britain and America depended upon future negotiations. At first it appeared that the establishment of an equitable trade would quickly follow completion of a definitive treaty. William Lee was confident that America had only to await favorable offers from the British "for they will certainly receive more benefit with a Commerce from us, than we shall." Lee was right about Britain's interest in America, but he misjudged America's response to the cessation of hostilities. The British were very interested in trading with the United States, but upon their own terms and, if possible, without granting commercial concessions. The British, with London reportedly "in a hurry and bustle, unknown at any former time," wasted no time literally in flooding America with large amounts of goods sweetened by major extensions of credit.[9]

Some merchants were very reluctant to begin trading with Britain in the face of an expected "revolution in Commerce." They planned to suspend their commercial activities until the "prodigious Shock" had passed. Others were not as circumspect. America was hungry for British goods—so hungry, in fact, that there had been complaints about trading with the British well before the coming of peace.[10] It was difficult to stifle an Anglo-American trade which one Frenchman bitterly reported was "protected by habit, custom, mercantile avarice, and Toryism." The last charge probably reflected more the influence of dashed French hopes than fact; however, the analysis was, on the whole, quite valid. At the same time that Henry Laurens was advising his European correspondents that trade between the United States and Great Britain would not begin until the former could decide upon a precise course of action, many merchants were throwing caution and good sense to the wind. It seemed as if peace unleashed a pent-up force in the mercantile community. There were reports that Baltimore was "crowded with Vessells from all ports" and that others were "open to British ships."[11]

The merchants' too willing receptiveness to renewed trade had just the effect on the probability of an Anglo-American commercial treaty that Stephen Higginson had predicted. With American trade "returning rapidly to their arms" and their "ships . . . admitted to an entry to the ports of America, particularly Philadelphia," the British quickly withdrew from their alleged "eagerness and desire" for a commercial treaty.[12] A new ministry, less amenable to making concessions, came to power in early 1783 and formulated a series of navigation acts culminating in the Orders in Council, passed on 2 July, which closed the lucrative West Indies trade to American shipping. Henry Laurens bitterly complained that although "America's Ministers had in April the vantage Ground, America by her folly has given them the uphill task."[13]

There is little doubt that America's willingness to trade without the benefit of a treaty undercut the chances for fruitful negotiations. Yet America's "hunger and thirst after cheese and porter" did not completely account for the failure to reach a commercial accord. America's foreign ministers, at least those in the Lee-Adams junto, were in complete agreement that "if there had been a Commission in being We should have had a provisional Treaty of Commerce with Great Britain, Signed at the Same time with the provisional Articles of Peace."[14] In December 1782 Thomas Jefferson had finally been free to go to Europe. His earlier appointment as peace commissioner was renewed, and he was also given a new commercial commission. After news of the preliminary treaty was received, however, both commissions were revoked.[15]

Although America's foreign ministers were still formally constrained by French and nationalist policies, Francis Dana's initiative promised to upset a well-structured plan to restrict America's commercial freedom. By early 1783 Dana, who had earlier been appointed to secure military and financial assistance from Russia, was attempting to negotiate a commercial treaty with that country which would have opened the door to American commercial responsibility. After Dana complained to Adams that Congress refused to send him money to support his venture, Adams advised him to give up the attempt. He thought that Dana had no

chance of reaching a commercial understanding with the Russians because the French had formed "a Congress here, in order to have all your
Business done by the 'Pacificateur de L'Europe' [Vergennes]." Dana,
in the meantime, had continued to plead his case before Congress. On 1
April a committee weighted in favor of federalists advised him to continue his negotiations if they were still in progress. Less than two weeks
later, after Congress determined that the foreign ministers were not
empowered to negotiate commercial treaties, John Rutledge "thought it
wd. by well for the U.S. to enter into commercial Treaties with all
nations and particularly with G.B." Madison, Gorham, and FitzSimons
were then appointed to prepare a report on commerce.[16]

By the end of the month Congress received another of Adams's
dispatches. In this letter, which Madison categorized as "a long and
curious epistle," Adams accused the French of revoking his commercial
commission; charged that they were still determined to prevent the
United States from gaining any commercial consideration in Europe;
and suggested that Congress, in order to disarm French policy, should
lose no time in formulating a commercial commission in order to begin
negotiations with the British. Congress acted very quickly. On 1 May
Robert R. Livingston was ordered to prepare commissions for Adams,
Jay, and Franklin, "authorizing them . . . to enter into a Treaty of
Commerce, between the United States of America, and Great Britain."
Although Livingston presented Congress with a plan for treaties and
commissions on 6 May, his report was referred to a committee and
eventually tabled. Further action was not taken for more than four
months.[17] With the question of commercial commissions still unclear, it
was relatively easy for a few nationalists to stop Francis Dana before he
did any damage.

By late May Dana's authority to obtain commercial consideration
from Russia was still in doubt. Within a few weeks it was even learned
that Adams had probably never informed his colleagues about the revocation of his commercial commission in 1781. In early July Congress
ordered that because there was no longer a need to secure assistance for
the war and because the United States "should be as little as possible
entangled in the politicks and controversies of European nations, it is
inexpedient to renew the said powers to either Mr. Dana, or the other
ministers."[18] Livingston then wrote to Dana "telling him that Congress
did not wish to form a treaty" and that he was not empowered to conduct
commercial negotiations. Dana had no choice but to return to America.
Stephen Higginson, however, accused Livingston of writing "that which
was false . . . [because the] Junto had determined that Mr. Dana should
come home, and that no treaty should be made with Russia, perhaps by
the order of the Count de Vergennes."[19]

In the meantime, Adams, still frustrated over the lack of a commercial commission, tried to reduce French influence by divulging fully his version of America's recent foreign policy. While Adams's charges were not materially different from his earlier ones, except in detail, they were important in directing attention toward another area of nationalist influence. He villified the French for placing America in a "shackling and clipping system" and accused Vergennes of wanting to deprive the United States of the fishery, the western lands, and the Mississippi River so that "he might have Us in his Power, that he might have the miserable Gloriole of being the Pacificateur of Europe, of having America, Holland, Spain and France in his Pocket." He further maintained that the attack upon his character, behavior, and commissions in 1780 and 1781 was really "an Attack upon the Fishery and Western Country." Vergennes's charges that Adams had overstepped his authority and offended the French was, as far as Adams was concerned, "a mere Fiction" to give Francophiles in Congress the opportunity to "carry their Point." Vergennes was aware that Adams was "too much attached to the Western Countries and the Fisheries, and to be a Man, who would neither be decieved, wheedled, flattered, or intimidated into a Surrender of them. Franklin he knew would let him do as he pleased."[20]

Adams was especially worried about Franklin, because even though the French might not hold a great sway in a peacetime America Franklin, whose prestige bordered on adoration, could easily continue to look out for French interests. Although Franklin was naturally enraged by Adams's "ravings," the latter had a singular purpose in exposing French duplicity to his own countrymen and to the British. While clearly venting frustrations built up over long years of abuse, Adams, above all, wanted to destroy America's unwarranted affection for the French—an affection which Adams thought all the more dangerous when he and Jay met with "a Fearful looking Judgment and a fiery indignation from Philadelphia" for having signed the preliminary treaty.[21]

Adams believed that the United States would never be able to secure their own interests in a world of empires "until they consider their interests as distinct and keep them separate, from those of all other nations." He was ablaze with the desire to convince Great Britain and, more important, the United States that the French were intent upon promoting disharmony between the two nations in order to protect their own interests. Adams accused the French of communicating their own jealousy of "American Ships, Seamen, Carrying Trade, Naval Power" to the British and of using their still considerable influence to dissuade the British from giving "up the cause of the refugees [loyalists]" in order to prevent amicable relations between Great Britain and America.[22] He thought that having a British minister at Versailles, a Frenchman in London, but no American minister at the Court of St. James was "admired at Versailles . . . but not because they think it for our Interests." He warned that the Confederation was "a brittle Vessell . . . [and] an object of Jealousy to France. Severe strokes will be aimed at it; if we are not upon our Guard to ward them off, it will be broken."[23]

Adams advised Congress quickly to send a minister to London while permitting the two nations to trade. After the Orders in Council he modified his position. Certain that Britain would never have acted this way "but from an opinion, that We have no Common Legislature for the Government of Commerce," he suggested that the United States levy a duty of 5 percent on the West Indies trade; cultivate West Indian produce; manufacture iron and wool; "Lay Duties on Exports & Imports by British Ships"; and enable Congress, "by a grant of necessary power, to regulate the commerce and general concerns of the Confederacy." Speed was and continued to be uppermost in Adams's mind. Every day lost was another in which the distance between the United States and Great Britain increased. By September he even accused the French of having told the courts of Denmark, Sweden, and Portugal that only Benjamin Franklin had "the power to treat with them and he alone" and of then informing Congress that those nations would only "treat with the great Philospher."[24]

Adams's attack on the French neatly complemented the growing antinationalist movement, for any information that damned the French also cast aspersions on those "who have made large fortunes during this war" and without whose help the French would never have been able to play such a dominant role in American affairs. One writer, alluding to Robert Morris and his Philadelphia base, hoped that no "one mart" would ever again be able to "rule other place's trade, through the medium of commercial intercourse, so as to dictate to the rest of the union, in important matters of government." By October many New Englanders were convinced that the revocation of Adams's commercial commission, "the plan of a Monopoly now subsisting in Favor of France," and the absence of an American minister at London resulted from "Foreign Influence (or the French and Frankleian Politicks)."[25] Because so much of the Morris faction's influence rested on its ability to "engross all the foreign business to themselves & their Connections in the different States," some federalists believed that if in addition to keeping Congress out of Philadelphia, establishing a Board of Treasury, and destroying the Society of the Cincinnati "a System of Commerce" was established the nationalists would "very Soon [be] without a Pilot &

fast aground." Without such a system they would, it was felt, be free to "promote the Individual at the expense of that of the public."[26]

The New Englanders faced a difficult task in trying to limit nationalist influence by organizing an American economy which was, as Robert Morris described it, split into "three different heads, as carried on from the eastern middle and southern states . . . to these may be added the circuitous trade, which last but never the less must be confined to the eastern states." There was as little likelihood in 1783 as there had been in 1776 and 1777 that a system of commerce could be established for "13 States each sovereign and whose exports & imports will be of nearly 13 complexions." In order, however, to stabilize their own commerce, and especially to protect the carrying trade, the New Englanders had to make the attempt.[27]

At first it appeared that Congress's "Removal from Philadelphia and the Prohibitory Restrictions passed in Great Britain" might produce an atmosphere favorable to commercial reform. It is true that the differences between New England and the South had been used for political ends, but the causes of sectional conflict existed apart from such tactics. Moreover, Great Britain did not threaten the United States in the same way it had during the war. The nation was not faced with conquest—New England stood to suffer the most from British trade restrictions. James Warren, for instance, was worried that "the other states will be indifferent" about "the Transport Trade." He pointed out that the southerners would probably not support New England's effort to reopen the West Indies trade, "because they may get their goods to Market cheaper if our Ships have nothing else to do."[28]

To be sure, there were southern merchants who were as interested as their northern fellows in "repairing their losses." The southern states were no less affected by the burst of commercial activity in early 1783; however, more southerners, and more influential southerners, were planters who were dependent upon all merchants, whether foreign or American, to carry their goods to market.[29] Many southerners thus believed that formulating a commercial treaty with Great Britain, or restricting the nation's trade, or opening the West Indies commerce, would benefit the "*powerful* and rapacious" New England merchants "*whilst* the privelage to be ceded *will chiefly* if not alone affect the southern states." They had no desire to destroy the policy of free trade and open competition which assured them of being able "to buy cheap & sell at profitable rates." Added to the old jealousies and mistrusts was a new fear that the northern states, which held most of the "paper money, and other continental securities . . . might be tempted by their naval superiority to pay themselves out of the rich commerce of the Southern States."[30]

Even Richard Henry Lee began to draw away from his New England friends. While sympathetic to New England's situation, he believed that "to embarrass Trade with heavy imposts or other clogs is effectually to demolish it." He and other southerners were willing to protect the nation against foreign intrusion, even to the extent of meeting foreign trade restrictions with unified responses. But rather than supporting measures which would only benefit northern merchants, Lee suggested that the establishment of a merchant marine manned by men from all the states could effectively repel foreign aggressions without forcing southern staples to be carried in northern ships. His proposal might have been a way out of what soon became a stalemated situation. By early 1784 it was becoming increasingly clear that interest was splintering ideological bonds, that "Southern and Eastern Republicans" were drawing in opposite directions on the question of commercial reform.[31]

The "Confidence between the extremeties of the Union," supposedly solidified by the dual residence and which a few New England federalists had hoped would unify the Confederation, could not endure the clash of basic sectional interests. It was certainly not in the southern interest to have Massachusetts, for example, disrupt Robert Morris's commercial network by forming "an opposing [system] in the mercantile line" and extending "their System thro' the Continent." While many New Englanders agreed with Stephen Higginson that "a liberal conexion with Britain" would increase their "weight in the Union," there was a growing realization that only if southern interests were as intimately connected to Great Britain as were New England's would there be "less difficulty in settling commercial treaties & very much less ground to apprehend a disunion of the States."[32]

THE DRIVE FOR COMMERCIAL RESPECTABILITY

Congress began to respond to Great Britain's navigation system in September 1783. Late in the month a committee, composed of James Duane, John Rutledge, Thomas FitzSimons, Elbridge Gerry, and Stephen Higginson, called for establishing "such general systems and arrangements, commercial and political, as our own particular circumstances, may from time to time require." After they suggested that the only way to counteract Great Britain's navigation system was to give Congress "a general power for regulating their commercial interests," FitzSimons, Duane, and Arthur Lee were instructed to prepare a report on extending Congress's commercial powers. The same day Lee, Duane, and Samuel Huntington were appointed to formulate instructions relative to commercial commissions. In late October they reported a set of instructions designed "to meet the advances and encourage the disposition of the other commercial powers in Europe for entering into treaties of amity and commerce." The proposed commercial commission did not fulfill federalist expectations. Commercial treaties were to be limited to a fifteen-year term, and the commissioners were enjoined from entering into any agreements without prior congressional approval.[33] On 15 December Thomas Jefferson, who was very sympathetic to commercial reform, Elbridge Gerry, and Hugh Williamson were appointed to report on letters received from the foreign ministers. Five days later, noting that the commissioners were still complaining of the lack of commercial commissions, they moved for immediate action. This report superseded the October report, which a few New Englanders thought "calculated to defeat every treaty . . . [and] intended purposely to delay." They believed that "the Anti-American System was to have no more commercial treaties" and wanted "to amuse the commercial Interest by issuing Commissions & giving Instructions . . . to form projects of such Treaties, to be viewed & altered by Congress—& then to make such alterations as the other contracting Parties never would agree to."[34]

Although Adams kept writing letter after letter in 1783 and 1784 calling for the immediate formulation of commercial commissions, there was a serious barrier to Anglo-American commercial relations that had very little to do with foreign intrigues or domestic politics. According to Article 9 of the Articles of Confederation Congress was not permitted to enter into commercial treaties in which the states would be prevented "from imposing such imposts and duties on foreigners as their own people are subject to." It was obvious that foreign nations would be reluctant to enter into commercial agreements with a government which was not able to compel obedience to the stipulations in a treaty.[35] In order, said Jefferson, "to prevent Great Br. from applying her navigation act against us separately," the 20 December report declared that "these United States be considered in all such treaties and in every case arising under them as one nation." When the report was again considered in late March 1784 the clause "upon the principles of the federal constitution" was added to the above article in order, said Jefferson, "to satisfy the jealous members." Doubtless there were New Englanders who were still afraid of a too powerful central government. But the qualifying clause was proposed by Hugh Williamson, whose "attachment to the interest of the Southern States . . . where they clash with the middle and Eastern ones" was, according to the Virginian Samuel Hardy, beyond doubt.[36]

When debate resumed John Francis Mercer and Richard Dobbs Spaight, who supported the removal of Congress from Philadelphia in 1784, proposed that commercial treaties be approved by the individual states, in addition to Congress, and that negotiations be carried on only in America. Although their proposals were not accepted they and Ephraim Paine of New York prevented passage of the report on 12 April. Jefferson later accused Mercer of getting "a young fool from North Carolina [Spaight] and an old one from New York [Paine]" to oppose the report and divide the states so that Mercer might become secretary for foreign affairs. Although Mercer's motives may have been self-seeking, they also bespoke the determination of some southerners to play an active role in the formulation of America's foreign policy. Even James Monroe, who soon became one of the leaders of the commercial reform movement, wondered whether it was advisable to "join three men all of whom are northern" to negotiate commercial treaties. There was, in addition, a special distrust of John Adams because of his reputed aversion "to the Slave Trade."[37]

On 5 May Hardy and Spaight moved for the appointment of two additional "ministers from the Southern States." After a great deal of debate and conflicting motions between a New England wing and a Pennsylvania-southern wing nothing was resolved.[38] But two days later commercial instructions were finally passed. The same day John Jay was relieved of his commission and appointed secretary for foreign affairs. After this action, which presaged final passage of the commerce report on 11 May, Thomas Jefferson was chosen to replace Jay, to the great relief of many southerners. As it turned out, though, Jefferson remained a resolute supporter of commercial reform long after most other southerners turned into strong opponents.[39]

The formulation of commercial commissions had little effect on America's relations with Great Britain. In the first place Great Britain was not one of the nations to which America's ministers were to make overtures. In addition, Britain's navigation system and America's overimportation in 1783 still placed major barriers in the way of commercial accord. The overimportation produced a situation which was, in the long run, far more costly than merely dissuading the British from dealing with America. Britain regained its dominant position in America without the benefit of a commercial treaty; goods flowed into America and specie flowed out at unprecedented rates; and by 1784, despite earlier warnings, the United States, and particularly the northern mercantile community, was in the grip of a severe commercial depression.[40] Although America was largely responsible for the depression, it was far easier to vent frustrations by attacking the British. Thus, Congress first responded to the British in mid-1783, not in an attempt to foster accord and cooperation, but to defend against Britain's commercial assault.

Within a short time the defensiveness about the apparent challenge to "the wisdom firmness and union of the States" inflamed anti-British feelings.[41] There were accusations in Virginia that Britain's plan to "monopolize the trade of these states" was being aided "by plans formed by the refugees." Henry Remsen also complained that returning loyalists had "engrossed the Commerce" of New York. The easily rekindled enmity to Great Britain was attested to by anti-British riots in South Carolina, an embargo on British goods in New Haven, and anti-British duties passed in Maryland and New Jersey.[42]

This normal reaction to British policy did, however, decrease the likelihood of commercial negotiations. The widening gulf between the two nations also seemed to substantiate earlier, almost paranoid, federalist warnings that the French and their American friends had carefully sown the seeds of Anglo-American conflict. Very few politicians were willing to follow the advice that "it is more easy to make sores than to heal them" and that "to adopt restrictions with marks of resentment" could only aggravate an already tense situation.[43]

There was too much reason to support the establishment of a system "to counteract the Commercial System of G[reat] Britain." The newspapers were filled with reports of discrimination against American merchants in the West Indies.[44] The British, whose dealings with America had by their own admission risen "to a much greater value" than they had anticipated, had no need to do anything to satisfy American merchants.[45] The news from the West Indies was not totally gloomy. Commerce, albeit illegal, was carried on, and there is every reason to believe that many merchants were benefiting from a very lucrative trade. The lack of a commercial treaty, however, still bothered most New England merchants. But at the same time that they were hoping to get legislation enacted, on the state and federal levels, to crack Britain's resolve, anti-British resentment continued to mount and demands for action were increasingly voiced, especially by southerners and allies of Robert Morris.[46]

A COMMERCE AMENDMENT

In an effort to combat British trade restrictions Congress requested the states on 30 April 1784 to vest in it "for the term of 15 years the power to prohibit any foreign goods from being imported into any of the United States, except in vessels belonging to or navigated by citizens of the United States or subjects of foreign powers with whom the United States may have treaties of commerce." It was expected that this commerce act would dispel "the idea in Europe of impotency in the federal Government in matters of Commerce."[47] It did not have this effect partly because the states were slow in passing it and partly because the British were still opposed to a commercial treaty.[48] Although it is doubtful whether any American action would have had an effect on the British, the merchants began to demand more extensive commercial reform. They believed that the major barrier to a commercial treaty was Congress's inability to compel the states to adhere to the stipulations in any commercial treaty. While they supported the commerce act of 1784 as a partial solution, they questioned the "propriety of individual states interposing" in what was essentially a national concern.[49]

The movement in Congress for a comprehensive commerce power got off the ground in early December 1784. On a motion by James Monroe Congress appointed a committee to prepare an amendment to Article 9 of the Articles of Confederation to give Congress "the power to regulate the commercial intercourse of the States with other powers." Monroe reasoned that Congress could exercise such a power by erecting "duties upon exports and imports," with the revenue from the duties going into state coffers. This attempt to avoid the problem of permitting Congress to collect and use an independent revenue met only one of the lesser objections to commercial centralization. Far more important was the intention to give Congress the power to regulate interstate as well as foreign commerce.[50]

Merchants throughout the nation quickly supported commercial reform. In January 1785 a meeting of Philadelphia merchants appointed "a standing Commercial Committee." By April, responding to the merchants' petition, the Pennsylvania Assembly supported giving Congress a "full and entire power" over commerce.[51] In March there were reports that merchants in New York City were clamoring for action. By June, at a public meeting called by the New York City Chamber of Commerce, a corresponding committee was appointed and a desire was expressed to "vest in Congress full and ample power to regulate the commerce of the said United States."[52] There were similar calls for commercial reform from merchants in New Hampshire, Connecticut, and New Jersey. Rhode Island even passed the commerce act of 1784 with the proviso that it not go into effect "untill Congress was given a power over inter-state trade."[53] The most vociferous demand for com-

mercial reform came from Boston. The Boston merchant committee
sent a circular letter in early 1785 which was responsible for a great deal
of the merchant organizing in other states, and in April it petitioned
Congress. Boston's petition reached Congress after the Monroe committee had already made its initial report. It was read in early May, but
by that time serious problems had arisen; the petition's effect was
minimal, as it was tabled pending consideration of the Monroe
committee's proposals.[54]

The Monroe committee had been renewed on 25 January 1785. It
reported in February, and a month later was instructed to prepare a
circular letter to accompany the proposed commerce amendment.
There was the hint, though, that passage of an amendment was not going
to be easy—that "Jealousy or perhaps a worse passion . . . will still
[prevail]." Richard Henry Lee, for instance, didn't think that the
nation's commercial problems could be solved by courting still greater
importations, "which impoverish by increasing the balance of trade
against us." Lee worried that the cure might be worse than the disease
and argued that as "contrary indications threaten danger to human
life . . . contrary indications threaten danger to the Political Body."[55]
Lee was not opposed to commercial reform because of the adverse
effect it might have on foreign relations, he was simply scared of the
merchants.

Some of his fellow Virginians were not. Monroe, leading the reform
movement in Congress, Jefferson, Washington, and Madison consistently supported the need for commercial reform. Unlike those southerners opposing reformation, their involvement in plans to navigate the
Potomac River stimulated interests which paralleled those of northern
merchants. In addition, they tended to support Congress on ideological
grounds. Their belief that western expansion was inevitable, and that
the South would be strengthened because of it, made them much less
fearful that an increased congressional influence would be an increased
northern influence. They were to remain unquestioning supporters of
commercial reform until the northern attempt to close the Mississippi
River in 1786 forced them to reevaluate their position.[56]

On 28 March the Monroe committee proposed an amendment to the
Articles of Confederation to give Congress

> the whole and exclusive power of . . . regulating the trade of the States, as
> well with foreign Nations, as with each other, and of laying such imposts and
> duties upon imports and exports, as may be necessary for the purpose;
> provided that the Citizens of the States shall in no instance be subjected to
> pay higher imposts and duties, than those imposed on the subjects of foreign
> powers; provided also that the Legislative power of the several States shall

not be restrained from prohibiting the importation or exportation of any
species of goods or commodities whatsoever; provided also that all such
duties as may be imposed, shall be collected, under the authority and accrue
to the use of the State in which the same shall be payable.

They warned the states, in a circular letter, not to "become victims of
their indiscretion." The proposed amendment was carefully worded so
as not to depart too radically from the Articles of Confederation. The
states were still to possess quite a substantial degree of independence.
Nevertheless, within three weeks Monroe advised postponement of
further discussion on the amendment for fear that "if carried further
here prejudices will take place."[57] These prejudices were strictly sectional. The proreform northerners in Congress tended to agree that
Congress ought to be given extensive commercial powers before any
commercial treaties were formulated.[58] Richard Henry Lee, the president of Congress and the South's primary spokesman, doubted whether
giving Congress such a power would aid the economy or result in
commercial accord with Great Britain. He regretted that "the avari-
cious, monopolizing Spirit of Commerce and Commercial Men" could
interrupt free trade and accused the merchants of "poisoning the minds
of men with plausibilities and theoretic reasonings, that are opposed to
the true state of things."[59]

By early June it appeared that commercial reform was impossible. A
writer from Boston pointed out that "each province is jealous of that
adjoining to it, they draw in discord, the Southern are in interest diametrically opposite to the Northern States; hence perpetually bickerings are
continually happening." The southern delegates refused to consider
passing the amendment unless it was modified to "make it Palatable."
But if it was changed to suit the South, it would then be unacceptable to
the North. Monroe noted that the amendment's fate hung upon the
question of whether or not the southern states thought "the obtainmt. of
the carrying trade and the extension of our National resources is an
object." It was clear they did not. By mid-July the commerce amendment was, for all intents and purposes, a dead issue.[60] The New Englanders were especially dismayed and frustrated. They complained that
they had come out of the war with little trade advantage, that commercial treaties were necessary to revive their economy, and that without
commercial reform European nations, and especially Great Britain,
would "esteem our Confederacy a rope of Sand.'[61]

The southerners were not as concerned with this eventuality as they
were with the danger that giving Congress a power to regulate trade
would create "a monopoly of the carrying business . . . in favor of the

northern states." Rufus King chided his constituents, who attacked him
for Congress's inaction and who clamored for reform without realizing
that the southern states had to keep their ports open to all merchants to
produce "competition among purchasers." Many southerners were
certain that the eight northern states would "combine and shackle and
fetter others."[62] In order to prevent this from happening some southerners were willing to accede to commercial reform if eleven and not the
usual nine states were required to set policy in Congress. A few Virginians hoped that this would enable them to prevent the eight northern
states from securing the support of either Baltimore or Charleston
merchants to complete their domination. Other southerners refused to
modify their position at all.[63] Yet there was a third position which
evidenced the desire of some southerners to stabilize the economy,
without running the risk of a northern monopoly, by giving Congress a
limited power to counteract foreign navigation systems. James
McHenry admitted that "the Southern States should give up something," but he also thought that "the other States should not ask everything." In early August he talked with some delegates about a navigation
act to combat foreign aggressions "which would gradually and slowly
tend to augment the seamen and shipping of the States without sensibly
wounding in its progress the interest of any State." McHenry did not
make a formal proposal, Monroe noted, as it was readily apparent that
the New Englanders "wish something more lasting, and will, of course,
in the first instance not agree to it."[64]

McHenry was not at all surprised by the northern states' "anxiety to
obtain a monopoly of the carrying trade of the Union," but he did not
intend to let them have their way. Richard Henry Lee was also unmoved
by the merchants' reasoning, or by James Madison's argument that
there was little Great Britain could get "by concession which she is
unwilling to make, which she does not enjoy." For Lee, and many other
southerners, the problem was still British recalcitrance and not a defect
in the Articles of Confederation. He was willing to have a "considerate
restraining of their Trade," but he was unwilling to expose southern
"freightage and shipping to a most pernicious and destructive
Monopoly." Lee was certain that commercial centralization would
"shut close the door of Monopoly" and place the southern states "at the
Mercy of our East and North."[65] By late summer he had won the first
round in what proved to be an increasingly volatile conflict between the
sections. Too much was at stake for either side to give in. With neither
willing to compromise, the situation intensified, and even more serious
conflict, with implications which touched the very foundation of the
Confederation, was in the wind.[66]

6

Commerce and Sectionalism

ONE OF the foundations of the commercial reform movement was the merchants' unswerving belief, even in the face of Britain's intransigence, that the nation's "wretched condition" could only be improved by securing an Anglo-American commercial treaty. The attempt to give Congress the power to regulate trade was itself stimulated by the conviction that Britain would revise its policy and negotiate a commercial treaty if finally faced by a unified America.[1] Although giving Congress the power to regulate trade was a primary goal, it was only one alternative to which merchants and their supporters looked to revive the nation's ailing economy. That Congress was so slow in acting increased the importance of and necessity for state action. It was, in fact, suggested that "the supineness of Congress" motivated organization not only to press for federal legislation, but also to "forbid the entering and unloading of any British vessels whatever." It was widely believed that if the states could pass "uniform laws" Great Britain might be prodded, even in the absence of congressional action, to see and, more important, to feel the necessity of relaxing its trade restrictions and formulating a commercial treaty.[2]

Both sides of the commercial reform movement affected each other. Congress's inability to respond to the commercial depression spurred the demand for reform on the state level, and the states' inability, in turn, redirected attention to Congress. Although this further worsened intersectional relations, the conflict between the North and the South was only one result of the various attempts to remedy the nation's commercial ills. Merchants were not the only northern commercial group affected by the depression, and the formulation of commercial treaties was not the only solution offered to correct the commercial distresses. The merchants' support for anti-British legislation evidenced a dis-

94

pleasure with the pervasive and strangling influence of Britich merchants, but in no way did it reflect an opposition to the continued importation of foreign goods. On the contrary, they looked to a more structured and formalized foreign trade to revitalize the nation's sagging economy. They were, however, opposed by the burgeoning manufacturing class, the artisans, tradesmen, and mechanics, who decried the nation's dependence upon foreign trade and blamed the merchants for the commercial depression. Because the tradesmen believed that the depression was caused by "money daily exported, goods imported, both of which tend to impoverish the United States," they asserted that the only way to "make us prosperous at home, or respectable abroad" was to stop buying large quantities of imported goods on credit, even to the extent of a self-imposed deprivation. They saw trade restrictions not as a means to insure a healthy foreign commerce, but as a way to cut the nation loose from a dependence on foreign wares and further their own interests.[3]

The demand for protective tariffs, as opposed to restrictive duties, was as much a reaction to the merchants' political influence as it was a response to the commercial depression. It is not surprising that tradesmen and merchants battled for control of some state legislatures. Whether on the federal or the state level control of government insured, at the least, the ability to set policy. Two states which had some of the strongest mercantile activity, Pennsylvania and Massachusetts, also had some of the most violent intergroup conflict. The experiences in these two states demonstrate the complexity of the issue of commercial reform and the degree to which merchants' demands were stifled within their own states.

The conflict in Pennsylvania was essentially a variation on the theme of struggle between the Constitutionalists and the Republicans. Many of the Republican leaders were on the Philadelphia Merchant Committee, in addition to being directors of the Bank of North America, and by early 1785 the Constitutionalists, with the support of artisans, mechanics, and manufacturers, began to oppose their economic policies. The Constitutionalists, unlike those "yellow whigs" in the Assembly who were allegedly blocking action, quickly and wisely seconded the call for protective tariffs. They also got behind the growing paper money movement and attacked the merchants' hard money policy and the Bank of North America with the "ostensible Reason [being] . . . that it is incompatible with a free government, but the real Reason is that Mr. Morris and the Directors of the Bank are not of the present ruling party."[4]

As the state's commercial distresses continued to generate factional conflict and as the demand for tariffs from special interest groups increased, the Republican position deteriorated. The Philadelphia Merchant Committee had already been meeting for some months when in early June a meeting of the citizens of Philadelphia empowered a committee of thirteen to coordinate state action and to call a town meeting which seconded the merchants' demand for a congressional power over commerce. It also supported, however, the need for protective tariffs and added seven mechanics to the committee of thirteen. George Bryan, a Constitutionalist leader, was very pleased with the results. He believed that "Mr. Morris's friends, fearing some thing they might not like would ensue, opposed it [the meeting], and have rather suffered with the people. They would have gotten credit and advantage by promoting it."[5]

Bryan was probably correct, but the merchants could hardly have been expected either to heed the mechanics' advice or to support protective tariffs. In September, but a short time before the state election, the Constitutionalist Assembly finally passed an act "to encourage the manufacture of this State, by laying additional duties on the importation of certain manufactures which interfere with them." The Republicans' political stock was falling lower and lower. Only the election of Thomas FitzSimons, William Irvine, and Robert Morris, in Philadelphia, blocked a Constitutionalist sweep.[6] While the roots of the Republican-Constitutionalist conflict existed apart from the differing attitudes toward commerce, the effect on the merchants and their ability to match southern obstinance with northern solidarity was costly.

The picture of a disharmonious North was just as clear in New England. Very early in 1785 the Boston merchants, confronted by a hostile and unmoving Europe on one side and by a recalcitrant South on the other, began to act "with their wonted Spirit" to demand that Congress "counter act the anticommercial plans of the British." There were proposals that Congress be empowered to regulate trade, that the importation of British goods which could be manufactured in Massachusetts be prohibited, and that duties be laid "on all importations in British bottoms." It was even suggested that Massachusetts set an example for the other states and unilaterally boycott British merchants and factors.[7] At a public meeting at Faneuil Hall in April 1785 the merchants decided to petition Congress, to convince merchants in other states of the necessity of "uniting in one request to Congress," and to boycott "such British merchants factors, or agents, who may hereafter arrive either from England, or any part of the British dominions." They even appointed a committee of seven to see to it that no merchant would "let or sell an warehouse [to British merchants] . . . *as we conceive that all such British importations are calculated to drain us of our currency, and have a direct tendency to impoverish this country.*"[8]

The British factors apparently got the message. It was soon reported that "the poor D[evi]ls are packing up." They became the physical embodiment in America of the British navigation system and the target for the populace's frustration and anger. The continual arrival of full-freighted British ships and only half-freighted American ships "roused the Spirit of 1775." There was a major riot on the docks on 19 April during which the British factors came dangerously close to being tarred and feathered and run out of town. At a critical juncture cooler heads prevailed and the public outcry was directed to a meeting, with Governor Hancock in the chair.[9] At first there was some feeling that this violence was just what the mercantile reform movement needed—that "the flame will communicate from State to State." But by mid-May only eight states had passed the commerce act of 1784, which, being only a power "to *prohibit,* and not to regulate," did not satisfy the merchants anyway.[10]

The merchants, moreover, soon realized that there were groups which believed that the economy was suffering only because commerce had "extended itself beyond its natural supports . . . its Extravagant Imports greatly Exceeding Exports . . . while Luxury keeps pace with the manner of older more affluent countries." The problem from this anti-merchant perspective was not that trade restrictions stifled the economy, but rather that "an avidity for Pleasure . . . and a thirst for acquisitions . . . pushes to the most dangerous Experiments."[11] The conflict between these two groups, with their diametrically opposed positions, was soon involved in a hotly contested struggle for the governorship.

Governor Hancock, probably angling for a vote of confidence from the General Court, tendered his resignation at almost the same time that the commercial depression was beginning to affect state politics. His enemies refused to let an unexpected opportunity to topple him pass. The General Court accepted his resignation at face value.[12] The ensuing race, which pitted Hancock, his hand-picked candidate Lieutenant Governor Thomas Cushing, and their supporters against the merchants and their choice James Bowdoin, produced a marked increase in anti-British propaganda. The people were enjoined to "refuse to purchase of those hirelings, or barter the blood, the treasures of a dignified Republic, for gewgaws of luxury, or even the necessities of life," while the tradesmen were called on to "extirpate the viper that is gnawing at our vitals."[13]

Of course, the British would have been unable to gnaw at Massachusetts's vitals had it not been for the state's own merchants. The connection between British imports, the depression, and the merchants was implicitly made, and the "jarr between the Mercantile Interest &

others'' became increasingly more pronounced. Less than two weeks after the merchants' public meeting, the tradesmen appointed their own standing committee, which prepared an address complaining of the large importation of foreign goods, calling for a protective tariff, and pledging their support for the election of men who best represented their views. They also sent a letter to the merchants requesting their assistance in repelling the British menace, in the form of goods, while declaring that they were "in duty bound to prevent, if possible [importation of] those supplies either by foreigners or our own merchants." Although the merchants were unwilling to restrict their enterprises, Hancock, their chairman, pledged his support to the tradesmen. The lines were drawn, but neither leading candidate captured a majority in the election.[14]

The jockeying for position started again as soon as the inconclusive election was held. The press was filled with attacks upon the British and the allegedly anglophile Bowdoinites. Finally, the General Court took up the matter. The House supported Cushing 134-89, but the Senate supported Bowdoin 18-10. The House caved in, Bowdoin became the new governor, and the merchants set out to right the tottering economy.[15]

THE POLITICS OF COMMERCE IN NEW ENGLAND

The situation in Europe continued to influence the mercantile reform movement both on the national and state levels. The mood of foreign nations, especially Great Britain, was critically important to the merchants' attempts to strengthen the nation's economy. In early 1785 John Adams finally secured his long-awaited appointment to the Court of St. James, and Thomas Jefferson replaced the duplicitous Benjamin Franklin as minister plenipotentiary to France. Both Adams and Jefferson were very active in trying to correct America's commerical problems. Adams believed that Britain's policy was determined by a more serious concern than a desire to monopolize American commerce. He likened Great Britain to "a Dancer on a slackrope [who] shudders at the opening of a Door against him lest a Blast of air should rush in and Blow him over. Ireland India are already blowing a storm." If America was an example for the empire, even more resolute responses seemed justified and necessary than simply commercial competition. Although Adams offered the alternative of discriminating against British shipping and goods, he demanded more from America than only discriminatory legislation. He argued that the nation had to take "an higher Ground, a Vantage Ground. We must do more than lay on Alien Duties." Adams did not want any state to "stop at a Navigation Act" instead of empowering Congress to regulate foreign and interstate commerce and even "the internal commerce of the States."[16]

Jefferson, who was just as anxious to "take the commerce of the states out of the hands of the states," proposed another way to give Congress a power over commerce. Rather than waiting for a grant of power which might never come, Jefferson wanted to manipulate Congress's restricted, though workable, treaty power. He reasoned that "the moment these treaties are concluded the jurisdiction of Congress over the commerce of the States springs into existence." By the end of July Jefferson sent Adams the draft of a model commercial treaty which, by his own admission, went "beyond our powers; and beyond the powers of Congress too," because in it he ignored the specific limits on Congress's treaty-making power, namely that Congress could not formulate such treaties which exempted foreigners from duties Americans had to pay and which prevented the states from blocking the importation of certain goods.[17] Adams did not agree with Jefferson. He continued to call for "Prohibitions, Exclusions, Monopolies, and Imposts" as the only means to provide the United States with economic leverage by giving "a clear advantage to their own" and the manufactures of other nations. Jefferson reluctantly concurred, but he would rather have seen Congress given a power to regulate trade by whatever means necessary. Jefferson's reticence was warranted.[18]

Despite the pressure brought to bear by the British navigation system, the individual states were unable to succeed where Congress was failing. It was impossible for the states or Congress to develop coordinated programs while "Each State acts an independent for all its needs and interests." It appeared that the British were correct in assuming that their policy was secure because of the "Interference of Commercial Interests among the States, and mutual jealousy arising therefrom." State navigation acts, without strong interstate accord, let alone congressional guidance and sanction, proved more trouble than they were worth. They seemed to be "always contracting each other" and merely "kindle[d] heartburnings on all sides."[19] This was especially so in New England.

Even before James Bowdoin was officially chosen governor, Massachusetts merchants and tradesmen had attempted to interest him in supporting their economic programs—a navigation act to restrict British shipping and tariffs to reduce the quantities of goods imported into the state. Although Bowdoin actually wanted a commerce power for Congress, he thought that a navigation act was better than nothing, and he so advised the General Court. On 28 June, after little more than three weeks of debate, the General Court passed an act "for the encouragement of Navigation & Commerce" which prohibited export trade in

British ships or any other foreign ships after August. It was understood that the restrictions would be lifted when foreign nations relaxed their restrictions against the United States. In addition, a duty was levied on foreign goods carried in American ships and foreign merchants were to pay a double duty on goods they carried themselves. At roughly the same time the General Court also levied 10 to 22½ percent duties on imported goods which were also manufactured in Massachusetts.[20]

Massachusetts's navigation act, in accord with the strategy which produced it, was "intended as a temporary expedient . . . in confidence that the other States would respectively enact a similar one." At about the same time that Massachusetts acted New Hampshire and Rhode Island passed similar legislation.[21] Connecticut was a problem. In May 1785 that state framed a navigation act which exempted from duties all foreign goods imported by the citizens of Connecticut and levied duties on foreign goods imported from other states, but which did not discriminate against Great Britain. Connecticut, accused of being interested in "her own emolument *solely,* without regarding the welfare of the whole," was destroying whatever effect New England solidarity might have had against the British. The key element upon which the navigation act was based—the bond between the states in the face of an external threat—was nonexistent. Connecticut's act, which gave "preference to foreigners in prejudice to the United States," was "construed as indicating an abatement of that mutual affection . . . which subsisted among them in the time of their calamity and distress."[22]

This major flaw in Massachusetts's commercial strategy fell heavily on the merchants, but had relatively little effect on the tradesmen, who still doubted whether "our existence as a Nation depend upon Commerce." They thought agriculture and manufacturing vital to the nation and "an extensive trade as ruinous to the manner of a Republic." It was also ruinous to their own interests. "A FARMER" threatened that if any merchant's sensibilities did not prevent him from importing goods which could be made in Massachusetts "if I were not able to overhaul him I would take up my long Gun and wink at him." In August the Committee of Tradesmen formulated a letter to their fellows throughout the nation urging them to get their states to enact measures similar to those of Massachusetts. They envisioned a continental association and argued that the United States "are so extensive in their Boundaries—so various in their Climate, and so connected in their National Interest" that a system for exchanging produce for manufactured goods would cement the union and "promote the Interest of the Whole."[23]

Not only did the tradesmen assume a great deal in expecting southern planters to foresake their long-standing free trade policy, but they also underestimated mercantile displeasure with the navigation act. The Massachusetts merchants were no longer willing to be the Confederation's sacrificial lamb. They complained that foreign merchants would be increasingly reluctant to trade with the United States "while they are encumbered with such heavy imposts." They were even more upset that the navigation act had "tied our own hands" and resulted in the transfer of much of Massachusetts's "trade to other States." New York, Connecticut, New Jersey, and Pennsylvania were purportedly profiting from Massachusetts's self-sacrifice.[24]

Massachusetts's navigation act thus had resulted in the very sort of brake on foreign trade which the merchants decried and which the tradesmen advocated. By October it was the Committee of Tradesmen which branded those who would "endeavour to weaken the operation of the act . . . [as] ENEMIES TO THE MANUFACTURING INTEREST OF THIS STATE." The merchants' opposition to the navigation act was, for a time, undone by one of their own—John Adams, whose letters reciting the advantages of prohibitive measures against the British helped silence "those who are averse to the resolution" and who, it was charged, "are uniformly against every regulation of trade." The merchants, of course, did not oppose all regulations, nor did Adams support navigation acts merely to check the inclination for "foreign gewgaw." Richard Cranch correctly stated that Adams's support for a navigation act was predicated on the belief that Massachusetts's action would "compell other States to imitate it," and on the certainty that if the other states did not pass similar legislation Massachusetts would still "get so much of their Carrying Trade as will richly compensate for any present Inconvenience."[25] Adams did not intend and certainly did not want state navigation acts to curtail foreign commerce or to harm directly his own state's interests.

Although the Massachusetts navigation act remained in force, it was soon modified in response to foreign, specifically French, complaints. In mid-November the General Court removed the restrictions against all nations save Great Britain.[26] This still did not satisfy the merchants. They continued to attack the navigation act, and it was probably partly true that the act was "struck at, by the French Interest—the British Interest—and by Self Interest." Yet there was no basis for branding the merchants as pro-British. They simply had a special view of the problem and believed that Massachusetts's commerce was being exploited by its neighbors. Finally, in July 1786 the General Court revoked the navigation act.[27]

A CONVENTION OF THE STATES

The various facets of the commercial reform movement, especially the interstate and intersectional conflicts it precipitated, were not without political ramifications. Congress's failure to meet adequately a problem which affected all the states in varying ways, hardly attested to the Confederation's stability. The realization that the nation's problems might go unresolved—that reform would most likely not come from Congress —had prompted interest in the calling of a convention of the states in late 1784. There seemed, to some, no other way to make the "great and effectual repairs" required to keep the Confederation operating. Richard Henry Lee noted that when told that Congress could recommend changes in the Articles of Confederation "the friends to convention answer—it has been already done in some instances, but in vain." Nevertheless, by late December conversation about a convention ceased. Apparently the desire to keep reform within Congress, the beginning of the drive for a commerce amendment, and efforts to finally settle the troublesome matter of the western lands overcame the still limited appeal of extracongressional reform.[28]

While conditions may not have been right in 1784, an external solution grew more appealing and more defensible as the nation's problems multiplied. Moreover, there was already an inkling of the rationalization which eventually permitted the progression from the Annapolis Convention to the Philadelphia Convention and major revision of the Confederation. Mann Page tried to ease Richard Henry Lee's fear of a convention by assuring him that there was no danger "of making the Experiment as we are not obliged to part with the old Confederation till the new is adopted."[29] What Page overlooked, but which most federalists did not, was the degree to which even admitting the need for extracongressional action would stimulate proposals for reform which might go beyond the spirit of the Confederation. They still feared nationalist policies and believed that a convention would reawaken the nationalist movement and open the door to unrestricted reforms.

While less visible and influential after 1783, nationalist politicians had not given up hope for restructuring the Confederation. Some, like Gouverneur Morris and John Jay, believed that as "national spirit is the natural result of national experience" that commercial distress would bind the states together, weaken objections to political centralism, and stimulate interest in their solutions to the nation's problems. They surmised that a commerce power would broaden congressional influence and make it easier for other reforms to follow.[30] Charles Thomson even advised against demanding passage of the impost because it might "awaken jealousy" and prevent giving Congress "the power of regulating commerce . . . [which would] give weight to the federal council and dignity to the nation." He reasoned that if Congress were given commercial powers "the minds of the people will be better disposed for granting other necessary powers."[31]

Thomson, Morris, Jay, and some of the nationalists who agreed with them were wrong in assuming that commercial problems would stiffen the bonds of union. Apart from underestimating the effects of sectional conflict, they did not take into account that many politicians who supported commercial reform did not want additional changes in the Articles of Confederation. In fact, it was a fear of central government which induced many northerners who worked to give Congress greater commercial powers to demand that any revenues arising from commercial duties be used only by the individual states. Their support for reform did not extend beyond the relatively narrow limits of commerce. This distinction was central to another part of the story of commercial reform.[32]

A state navigation act was not the only alternative to congressional action to which Massachusetts merchants and politicians looked. Their degree of commitment to commercial centralization was very evident in Massachusetts's call for a convention of the states. In May 1785 Governor Bowdoin, in a speech to the General Court concerning the importance of commercial reform, suggested that if the members agreed with his idea to extend Congress's power by "special delegates," they should "take the necessary measures for obtaining such a convention or congress, whose agreement when confirmed by the States would ascertain those powers." Bowdoin reminded the representatives that state action, like a navigation act, was only needed until Congress had the power "to preserve the union, to manage the general concerns of it, & secure & promote its common interest." By this time it was clear that the drive in Congress for commercial reform was hopelessly stalled, and in June the General Court instructed its congressional delegates to propose "a Convention of Delegates from all the States . . . to revise the Confederation and report to Congress." Massachusetts's call to a convention was specifically intended to accomplish the commercial reorganization which the South was blocking. One writer judged that "whether the Southern States are or are not to be the dupes of New England policy, still some revolution in the American system is not very remote."[33]

The Massachusetts delegates, Rufus King, Elbridge Gerry, and Samuel Holten, refused to act on their instructions. They believed that extracongressional reform might not only take the direction which the Massachusetts General Court intended. Pointing to recently proposed plans which "would inevitably have changed our Republican Governments, into baleful Aristocracies," they warned that a call to a convention would "produce thro-out the Union, an exertion of the friends of Aristocracy, to send Members who would promote a change of Government." Ideology was not the only reason they objected to a convention. Their fear of a major revision of the Articles of Confederation also reflected a concern with sectionalism. Their analysis of the situation and the possible dangers was remarkably similar to William Gordon's warning in 1782 that the New England states would be the principal sufferers if the Confederation were centralized. There was nothing new about the fear that nationalists and southerners might ally against New England either in 1782 or 1785.[34]

The question of the balance of political power between the states and Congress was inextricably tied to the question of sectional power. The commerce fight merely reemphasized that congressional authority could be used to further sectional ends. King, Gerry, and Holten certainly had a keen awareness of the intricacies of sectional conflict by September 1785. They might even have been more aware of it than some of their colleagues in Massachusetts. In response to King's query Nathan Dane admitted that perhaps the Massachusetts representatives had not "sufficiently considered the interests and motives of the different States, of landed and commercial men, of Republican and Aristocratical Politicians."[35] The delegates were, moreover, not alone in realizing the continued danger of nationalism, that liberty could be lost "by the artifices of a few designing men, and a general inattention of the many." No matter how anxious the Massachusetts federalists were for commercial reform, they opposed "a general Revision of the Confederation." It did not take long for the General Court to heed the warning. In late November it revoked the instructions.[36]

SECTIONAL DISCORD

The failure of the states to solve the problem of commerce threw the matter squarely before Congress. For a time hope for reform lingered, on the not unrealistic assumption that the worsening commercial situation might induce the various opponents to relax their objections for the good of the whole. In late November Elbridge Gerry reported that Congress was freer from domestic and foreign influence than it had ever been. The only factions, he asserted, were "produced by clashing of interest" and among these he saw a "general Disposition to reconcile." Those conflicts of interest, however, were not so easily resolved. The continual conflicts among the states, their unwillingness to keep from doing "little things to gain advantage over their neighbors," and their fear of trusting "one another under qualified powers" raised questions about the very foundation of the Union—questions which, it began to appear, the system could not answer.[37] Moreover, the fact that the Confederation was taking on the appearance of a loose conglomeration of self-interested states without "accord, without plan, without a uniform system," reinforced Great Britain's commercial strategy, which some already thought resulted "as much from the hope of effecting a breach in our Confederacy as of monopolizing our trade."[38]

Sectional conflict was still the major barrier to commercial reform. Even the British reportedly proceeded on the assumption that "the Southern States will never interest themselves in a case where the Northern are principal sufferers." Thomas Jefferson pointed out that as long as the sections were unable to compromise and the regulation of commerce remained "in the hands of thirteen Legislatures, they need not fear a union in their proceedings." It was up to the United States, he thought, to "shew whether they are true prophets." To all appearances they were. The probability of a commercial treaty, upon which northerners had pinned their hopes since 1783, seemed more remote than ever.[39]

Southerners, or at least those like Richard Henry Lee who strongly opposed commercial reform, remained convinced that Congress had all the authority it needed to formulate commercial treaties. Yet, that restricted power was still not enough for the merchants, for it prevented Congress from making "specific and effective stipulation for reciprocating commercial advantages with the other party."[40] John Adams even wrote to his old friend, Richard Henry Lee, advocating a prohibition on the importation of British goods and, more important, a prohibition on the exportation of American goods in "British vessels." Adams's pronouncement that "our Ships and Mariners will be Castles & Garrisons to us The mutual dependence of the States upon one another will be a strong cement to our union in interest & affection" had no effect on Lee. Adams's castles and garrisons, with which all of the states could theoretically repel the British, would have to have been manned by New Englanders. The southerners simply did not believe that their interests would really be defended. For Lee "the Spirit of Commerce" was and would always remain "the Spirit of Avarice."[41]

There was simply no escaping Stephen Higginson's assessment that the insurmountable differences "between the Northern and Southern productions and circumstances relative to commerce" prevented the southern states from being "the Carriers of their own produce . . . the northern states now are and ever will be the great Navigators." The southern planters, still governed by the need "to exchange their products for the greatest quantity of foreign goods," were willing, said Nathan Dane, to have the northern merchants be "their carriers *submodo,*" but they did not want them "to have it in their power to monopolize at will." The question was simply one of power. In 1776 Edward Rutledge had objected to the northern states' power in the Articles of Confederation and had declared an intention to "Keep the Staff in our own Hands." Southerners envisaged a similar sectional domination if commercial centralization occurred. One New Englander aptly noted that "the balla. between them & us [in commerce] . . . is against them and therefore they wish to have the staff in their own hands."[42]

Certainly by the late summer of 1785 many influential northerners, especially those interested in commerce, were terribly frustrated. Pleas for assistance and rational analyses of the problem had failed to produce any modification in the southern position. Not only did most southern delegates refuse to give Congress a power to regulate trade, but they also, it was said, "throw cold Water on all such Ideas." From a northern perspective, then, southern opposition demanded a tactical change. Even James Madison concluded that New England was being driven "to some irregular experiments."[43]

Some observers were not surprised by the deadening effects of sectional conflict upon a Union which had always had a "great tendency toward dissolution." The commerce fight widened the rift between the sections to such a degree that there seemed to be a chance that the disparity in commercial goals would soon separate "the Northern from the Southern States."[44] Indeed, an agitated Rufus King suggested that in the event the southern states continued to block commercial reform the eight northern states were "*competent* to form, & in the event must form, a sub-confederation." John Adams assured King that if the northern states "pursue the Plan you mention, and the other five should only lay on heavy duties upon British Tonnage & prohibit British ships from importing any thing but the production of Great Britain" that the British would be forced to come to terms. This, essentially, was all that King wanted. He did not necessarily want to destroy the Union. He simply believed that the southern states might be moved to agree to commercial reform if they found "a decided disposition in the Eastern States to combine for their own security."[45]

Although the threat of subconfederation was probably all that was intended, at the most some sort of northern commercial alliance, the suggestion of such a radical alternative evidenced the temperature to which sectional animosity was rising. While subconfederation may not have been really feasible, it had been proposed at various times since 1775. The talk intensified and the number of proposals increased in relation to heightened sectional tensions after 1785. It has been asserted that these proposals were generated by the supporters of strong central government—by those men who came to be known as Federalists after 1787. But not all political behavior in the 1770s and 1780s can be traced to the particular ideologies of the two major factions. Although the conflict between federalists and nationalists was an integral part of revolutionary politics, it can hardly describe the entire scope of political behavior. It is even more invalid to attempt to describe political behavior before 1787 in terms of post-1787 behavior. Disunion sentiments were primarily motivated by a frustration born out of the attempt to operate a polarized Congress in a sectionally torn nation. The apparent inability and unwillingness of the delegates to disregard their various sectional interests and solve some pressing problems reinforced the long-standing belief that a Union of such varied and distinct interests could not long endure. Although it is difficult to integrate sectional conflict and to explain the role of sectional pressures in the politics of a nation which shortly created a powerful central government, the disunion proposals and the pressures which produced them have an important place in the closing years of the Confederation. Sectional conflict was one of the primary reasons for the Confederation's demise.

Those New Englanders interested in commercial reform, from whom many of the proposals came, were generally opponents of strong central government motivated by powerful sectional commitments. Looking down upon the southerners as men whose "minds and constitutions want the energy and habits of attention and perseverance of the Northern States" who would not agree to an evidently much-needed commercial reform, subconfederation seemed a likely means for the New Englanders to get rid of their opponents, or at least to scare them. Continued southern recalcitrance in early 1786 pushed Benjamin Lincoln to the conclusion that the Union would be more easily governed and more assured of permanence if "the United States extend from east to west, instead of their standing, as they now do from North to South." With little holding the sections together the situation got progressively worse. While disunion was never attempted,the South was, in 1786, faced with a threat of sectional dismemberment leading to a perpetual second-class status in the nation. Moreover, disunion itself continued to be offered as an alternative to the Confederation.[46]

Although by early 1786 the fact that a real problem of commerce existed was no longer a matter of debate, there was still considerable disagreement on what to do.[47] There continued to be some feeling that the southern states might yet give in—that "the Northern and Southern States are fast approaching a similarity in manner." Georgia and South Carolina's passage of the commerce act of 1784 had been the cause of some optimism. It was predicted that South Carolina, more or less governed by the Charleston merchants, would soon lend its support to the northern bloc. Further hope was generated by reports that the British were responsible for inciting antinorthern feeling in the southern states by spreading the "alarm among the planters, that a navigation act would lower the price, and advance the freight of bulky articles."[48]

But southerners did not need to be convinced of that by the British. Even the conflict between northern merchants and tradesmen did not lessen their fears. Merchants wanted to control foreign trade and thereby become the South's sole carrier, and tradesmen wanted to limit foreign importation and thereby become the South's sole supplier of manufactured goods. Either way the southern planters would have been put at a disadvantage. Unlike these southern planters whose interests demanded a free trade, the protariff forces believed, much like the merchants though from a different perspective, that "trade like an helpless infant needs parental care." Merchants and tradesmen were, moreover, bound to each other more so than either was bound to the South. In fact, in New York City the two mercantile groups cooperated in trying to revive the economy.[49]

The southern bloc did not crack, and even though the commerce act of 1784 was finally passed by the states, it was so qualified and amended that it was useless. Moreover, the push for a commerce amendment, for a far broader commerce power, made the limited thrust of the 1784 action far less important to northerners. Although by 1786 all the southern states save North Carolina had passed the commerce act, it is important to recognize that this had little relation to their resolute opposition to a commerce amendment. They were willing to have restricted commercial reform, but their solution did not meet northern mercantile needs. With almost no chance for any action in Congress the discussion of commerce was dropped in May because of the planned meeting of the Annapolis Convention.[50]

By the time the Annapolis Convention met in September 1786 the nation was even more sectionally rent. The demand for commercial reform did not stop in the face of southern resistance. In fact, some northerners were growing more and more resentful that America's "disjointed system" was permitting the British to "pocket all the advantages of the american Economy without a Treaty." It seemed clear to them that if the United States could not secure a commercial treaty the Orders in Council would remain in force and they would be driven to trade in British ships or suffer an even worse commercial imbalance.[51] The desire for commercial respectability, and commercial treaties, was so strong that it precipitated a northern plan which sent shock waves through the nation.

7

The Mississippi Conflict

AT ALMOST the precise moment it appeared that Congress's lack of commerce powers would surely prevent the formulation of commercial treaties with any foreign power, a Spanish envoy arrived in America with the authority to negotiate and complete a treaty. Spain, however, set a condition for commercial accord which was totally unacceptable to the South—renunciation of America's claim to the free navigation of the Mississippi River. Although the fight in Congress over the terms of the proposed Spanish treaty in the summer of 1786 synthesized the various strands of sectional conflict which had plagued the nation since the beginning of the Revolution, the use of the Mississippi River had not always been a sectionally charged issue. Even while trying desperately to secure foreign assistance in the early war years, the Lee-Adams junto had consistently defended America's right to navigate the Mississippi in the face of strong Spanish and French pressure. In the darkest hours of the war, pressed by the British army and French demands, America had only narrowly escaped losing the Mississippi. Yet it had been a southern capitulation which had resulted in Congress's relinquishment of the claim to the Mississippi in early 1781.

After the victory at Yorktown had diminished the need for additional foreign assistance, Congress had quickly reaffirmed the claim to the free navigation of the Mississippi River. Although the French were powerless to prevent or undermine Great Britain's acknowledgment of America's right of free navigation, the victory proved to be a hollow one. During the war the Spanish had assumed de facto control of the Mississippi, and they did not recognize Britain's legitimization of America's claim. They were determined to maintain an exclusive control over the river and the territory adjacent to it. For a number of reasons, not the least of which was the threat of foreign interference in America's affairs, there was good ground for the belief in 1783 that a confrontation between Spain and America was inevitable.[1]

By the time negotiations with Spain began in late 1785, unified support for retention of the Mississippi River was no longer a certainty as the smoldering flames of sectional conflict put the question in a new light. By 1786 the North and the South were locked in combat which, in terms of commitment, antagonism, and implacability, far exceeded anything that had preceded. Despite the apparent sudden outbreak of barely controlled sectional hostility, the worsening intersectional relations had evolved over time in response to mutual threats and fears. The sectional lines had not always been as rigid as they were in 1786. Not all northerners had thought that it was worth losing certain benefits to stop western expansion by closing the Mississippi, and not all southerners had agreed that retention of it was vital to their interests. Some very influential Virginians had believed that navigating the inland rivers would more effectively expand the southern staple-bound merchant-dependent economy and insure that the western territories would remain firmly tied to the South than would an open Mississippi River.

Almost as soon as the war ended interest had revived in improving the navigation of the inland rivers. The most visible and often discussed scheme was the attempt in Virginia to improve the navigation of the Potomac River. The Potomac, however, was only one of the available water routes to the West, and the Virginians were not the only group eagerly eyeing the backcountry trade. Philadelphia and Baltimore merchants, who already controlled much of that trade, were just as anxious to protect and expand their own economic spheres. In fact, Virginia was the last state to swing into action. The Philadelphia merchant community intended to capture the commerce of the Susquehanna River Valley from Baltimore. In September 1783 the Pennsylvania Assembly appointed a committee to investigate and report on the advisability of constructing roads between the Susquehanna and the Schuylkill. Within a short time the plan was extended to include a navigation of the Susquehanna itself. The Baltimoreans were equally active. In late 1783 the Maryland legislature gave the Susquehanna Canal Company authority to navigate the Susquehanna from the boundary of Maryland to the Chesapeake. The Baltimore merchant community was filled with the vision of Maryland becoming "the first and richest of all the United States, and this Town, probably the Emporeum of North America."[2]

The rising competition for the backcountry trade spurred some Virginians to action. In February 1784 Thomas Jefferson advised James Madison that they had no time to lose in opening the Potomac navigation, because "if we do not push the matter immediately they [Pennsylvania] will be beforehand with us & get possession of the commerce." He suggested that "the superintendance of it [the navigation scheme] would be a noble amusement in his retirement" for George Washington. Madison shared Jefferson's concern about the importance of the backcountry trade. He pointed out, however, that Virginia, as a consequence of Lord Baltimore's charter of 1632 and its own constitution, had no express right to navigate the Potomac. Rather than seizing the Potomac or demanding recognition of what was at best a questionable right, Madison proposed that Virginia persuade Maryland to appoint commissioners to preserve "a harmony and efficacy in the regulation of both sides [of the Potomac]." The residue of ill-feeling precipitated by Maryland and Virginia's long-standing conflict over the latter's western lands threatened the likelihood of interstate cooperation. But Congress's acceptance of Virginia's new cession in March 1784 brightened the chances for such cooperation. Madison, in fact, relied on "the good humor into which the cession of the back lands must have put Maryland" to bring the Potomac navigation project to a successful end.[3]

Jefferson, meanwhile, informed Washington of the growing interest in improving the navigation of the Potomac. In early March he presented Washington with an analysis of the connection between commerce, the Mississippi navigation, the Spanish threat to the West, and the Potomac navigation which was to guide the Potomac interest through late 1785. Jefferson argued that because of the growth and importance of commerce in the world, the South had "to share in as large a portion as we can of this modern source of wealth and power." He suggested that the only way to do this, and at the same time disarm Spanish policy, was to establish lines of communication to the untapped resources in the West by "opening the upper waters of the Ohio and Patowmac." Jefferson foresaw an entirely self-sufficient, self-contained, and independent Virginia commerce which, he believed, would undoubtedly reshape the course of regional, sectional, and even national development. His visionary fancy extended far beyond the Potomac River Valley to a system of navigable rivers and man-made canals from the Ohio as far south as North Carolina which would "spread the field of our commerce westwardly and southwardly beyond anything ever yet done by man."[4]

Washington needed little persuasion to lend his name and energies to a project which he had advocated as early as 1775. He was unwilling, however, to let Jefferson's buoyant optimism go unchecked. Washington was certain that Virginia would meet some strong opposition to its effort to expand its own economic horizons. He reminded Jefferson that plans to navigate the Potomac River might have begun in 1775 "had it not been for . . . the opposition which was given (according to report) by the Baltimore merchants." They were, he said, alarmed by the prospect of "a water transportation to George Town of the produce which usually came to their market."[5] Nothing had changed by 1784. It was still highly unlikely that the Baltimore merchants would stand idly by while a few Virginia and Maryland planters cut them out of the backcountry trade. This was especially true because the Potomac navigation was part of a still wider effort to free Virginia from the Baltimore merchants.[6]

The key to this strategy was pinned on enhancing the economic power of the burgeoning port of Alexandria, "because it is a rival in the very bottom of Baltimore."[7] In the spring of 1784 James Madison led a move in the Virginia House of Burgesses to restrict that state's commerce to the ports of Alexandria and Norfolk in order to enable the Virginians to organize their internal commerce and get their goods to port and thence to market without interference from the Baltimore merchants. Madison's effort fell short of its mark. The House added three ports to the original two, and this partial centralization, it was feared, would simply collect "the produce of this state in particular ports, and thereby throw it more particularly into the vortex of Baltimore."[8]

Some Virginians looked to other means to enhance their commercial strength at the expense of Baltimore. The competition for supremacy in the Potomac River Valley had already played a major role in the capital fight. It was assumed that Maryland offered Annapolis as a site for the federal residence in early 1783, backing out of the informal agreement with Virginia to submit a joint site for a capital city, "to preserve the whole benefit to themselves, of which Virginia at George Town would have participated." Even after it became obvious that the northern states opposed the selection of any southern site, Jefferson was certain that the slightest hope for a location at Annapolis would drive Maryland to "sacrifice a certainty for George T." Under no circumstances were the Virginians prepared to support "Annapolis or any other situation North of Patowmack which would attract the trade of Chesapeak."[9]

Although the dual-residence compromise was acceptable to the Virginians because the selection of a Potomac site promised that the nation might eventually have a single capital city in the South, a temporary residence in Annapolis was not. They feared that having Congress in Annapolis would increase Baltimore's commercial influence, whereas "a position at the head of the Potomack tends to check the growth of Baltimore as what she now gains from that quarter wod. be diverted to Alexandria as the seat of Congress." Joseph Jones even thought that having the federal residence on the Potomac could succeed where the port bill had failed. Noting how beneficial an effect Congress's residence had had on Philadelphia's commerce, Jones argued that a location at George Town would alleviate Virginia's most pressing problem—the lack of a single commercial entrepôt. Nevertheless, he was forced to admit that this would "hurt the trade of Baltimore." Jones was, therefore, certain that Maryland would never permit Virginia to complete its plan to navigate the Potomac "so long as they have any hope of keeping Congress at Annapolis." Virginia, he reasoned, had no alternative but "to lighten the influence of Annapolis and increase that of the head of the Potomack."[10]

Congress's speedy adjournment from Annapolis in mid-1784 and the selection of New York City in late 1784 as Congress's temporary residence were quite compatible with Virginia's economic goals. But the decision to construct only one capital city on the Delaware forced a reassessment. The Virginians wanted to eliminate the danger of a growth of Baltimore's influence, but they did not want to harm themselves. They therefore led the successful effort to expunge the appropriation for the construction of a capital city. By late 1785 a federal residence in Annapolis was no longer a danger, a capital city on the Delaware was not going to be constructed, and Congress was safely situated in a city which had hopes but no real chance of keeping Congress. In addition, ongoing plans to navigate the Potomac River and western expansion suggested that the nation would eventually have a single southern capital on the Potomac.

By mid-1784 the Virginia leaders decided to sidestep Baltimore's expected opposition by appealing to the Maryland planters, who had as much to gain from getting free of Baltimore's clutches as they did. In August an appeal for interstate cooperation addressed "To the inhabitants of POTOMACK RIVER in MARYLAND AND VIRGINIA" set plans in motion. Less than a month later there was a meeting in Alexandria attended by men "who lived contiguous to Potomack, and wish to see an attempt made to open and extend the navigation of that river."[11] In late December Maryland and Virginia were considering proposals to let the project proceed, and a meeting in Annapolis attended by Thomas Stone, Samuel Hughes, Charles Carroll of Carrollton, Horatio Gates, and George Washington laid the foundation for the incorporation of a private company.[12]

In late December Virginia's House of Burgesses appointed commissioners to treat with Maryland and Pennsylvania on the question of inland navigation. The enthusiasm with which the Potomac supporters greeted this measure was warranted.[13] Within a short time Maryland appointed Thomas Stone, Daniel St. Thomas Jenifer, Thomas Johnson, and Samuel Chase to settle the jurisdiction of the Chesapeake and Potomac navigations. They met in March 1785 at Mt. Vernon with

George Mason and Alexander Henderson and cleared the way for the Potomac Company to begin operation.[14] A very brisk sale of shares in the company indicated the relative health of the project.[15] The sale of shares did not necessarily mean, however, that the project would succeed, and it certainly did not suggest that the Baltimore or Philadelphia merchants were willing to admit defeat. On the contrary, the Philadelphia, Baltimore, and Potomac interests continued to jockey for position in the race for commercial expansion. Despite the attempts to illustrate the advantages to be derived by "the Middle States" from an improved navigation of the Potomac River, it was evident that the Baltimore and Philadelphia merchants had a great deal to lose. Washington, for one, was still afraid that "if the Baltimore interest can give its effectual opposition," Pennsylvania might not permit the Potomac Company to build the necessary communication roads between the Chesapeake and the Delaware.[16]

Washington even tried to persuade Robert Morris to lend his support to the Potomac Company by assuring him that "the mercantile interest of Baltimore" had been less than honest in treating "the extension of the navigation of the Potomac as a chimerical plan." The Potomac Company's initial successes did not elicit the support for which Washington hoped. Some Virginians further harmed the possibility of interstate cooperation by gloating about the success of a project which the Philadelphians had almost self-righteously declared "would never be more than a matter of amusement."[17] Although the Virginians certainly had good reason to be gratified by the speed with which they had reached their goal, the realization that the Potomac navigation was more than a matter of amusement spurred Pennsylvania and Maryland to get on with their own projects. With Virginia now clearly leading the pack, it was up to its competitors to make up for lost time. The Philadelphians were, as Washington himself soon learned, very interested in taking advantage of their own opportunities in the West. In June 1785 the Pennsylvania Assembly appointed commissioners to examine and undertake an improvement of the navigation of the Susquehanna River. Before the end of the year Maryland invited Pennsylvania and Delaware to a commercial convention designed to smooth interstate relations and advance prospects for opening the Susquehanna. The conflict between these disparate interests continued to disrupt Chesapeake politics until the Annapolis Convention met in September 1786.[18] Yet, almost imperceptibly, the conflict between Maryland and Virginia was giving way to a much more dangerous conflict between the North and the South. By the time the Annapolis Convention met the fight over the navigation of the Mississippi River had drastically changed the nature and face of congressional politics.

WESTERN EXPANSION

While the various internal improvements projects were diverting some attention away from the Mississippi navigation, the conflict between the United States and Spain was slowly coming to a head. In early June 1784 a committee composed of Samuel Hardy and James Monroe of Virginia and Edward Hand of Pennsylvania advised Congress that America's foreign ministers should be instructed "not to relinquish or cede" the right to a free navigation of the Mississippi in whatever negotiations they might enter into with Spain. Within a few months it was clear that the Spanish were still determined to obtain "the exclusive navigation of the Mississippi." François Barbé-Marbois, acting at the request of Francisco Redon, agent of the Spanish court, sent Congress a letter which set forth Spain's steadfast position on the Mississippi River. But even Barbé-Marbois realized that Congress, and particularly the southerners, would resist Spain.[19] Congress began discussion of the Spanish demands in late December amid southern cries of "national outrage." Under no circumstances were they willing to give up the right to navigate the Mississippi River.[20]

But other matters got in the way, and Congress was slow in appointing a minister to negotiate with Spain. It was, moreover, becoming clear, especially to those whose interests were not directly connected to the Mississippi navigation, that nothing short of a war which America was ill-prepared to fight would induce Spain to drop its demand to control the Mississippi River.[21]

While Congress was occupied with the commercial reform movement, the Spanish took the initiative. Less than seven months after they informed America's foreign ministers that a representative would be empowered to negotiate a commercial treaty and settle the boundary and Mississippi disputes, Diego de Gardoqui arrived in America. By July 1785 he was in New York City awaiting Congress's action. More than a month later Congress hurriedly appointed John Jay to negotiate with Gardoqui. Although Jay was bound by firm instructions "to stipulate the right of the United States to their territorial bounds, and the free navigation of the Mississippi from the source to the ocean," he had some very definite ideas about commerce and the western lands which were to make him most receptive to Gardoqui's position.[22]

There was still a great deal of support for retention of the Mississippi River in 1785. It was certainly true, as one French minister noted, that "those who profit by this navigation are not inclined to relinquish it." Spanish control of the Mississippi River was anathema to the settlers in the West, especially those in Kentucky, who depended on it to get their goods to foreign markets, and to the southerners who looked westward with visions of sectional expansion.[23] There were some other considerations which, for a time, also disposed some northerners to support a free navigation of the Mississippi River. It was, for example, feared that closure of the Mississippi would deprive the United States of a very rich fur trade. The prospects of speculation in land also seemed to require an open Mississippi as it was deemed by some essential "to enhance the value of the Lands on the NW side of the Ohio."[24] Even more compelling was the relationship of the western lands to the federal debt. New Englanders still believed that the revenue resulting from the sale of western lands might be used to pay off the federal debt without resorting to commercial taxes which would lighten their own pockets. In addition, northern and southern federalists alike expected that if such revenues could fill the federal coffers, there would no longer be the danger that centralizing revenue programs, like the impost, could be used to restructure the Confederation.[25]

There was, however, much more at stake than profits, revenue, or American integrity. Gardoqui was certain that, like the British and French before him, he could use America's sectional diversity, that the chance for a commercial treaty, coupled with the opportunity of preventing further western migration, was enough to secure northern support for occlusion of the Mississippi River. The spiraling sectional hostilities by late 1785 made his task much easier.[26] Although Elbridge Gerry and Richard Henry Lee agreed in the summer of 1785 that the revenue from the sale of the western lands was vital to the Confederation's future, the South's refusal to support commercial reform had a dramatic impact on northern attitudes toward the Mississippi.[27]

In March 1785 the Massachusetts General Court instructed its delegates to defend America's claim to the free navigation of the Mississippi. But less than a year later the Massachusetts delegates were strong advocates of occlusion in order to secure a treaty. Completion of a Spanish treaty promised to fulfill northern desires by giving the United States a degree of commercial stature and independence without requiring the commercial legislation which southern opposition precluded. Commercial accord with Spain might also have disposed other nations, especially Great Britain, to rethink their restrictive policies.[28] These commercial considerations had grave import for the Mississippi negotiations. Richard Henry Lee, for one, was very worried that Spain's "very tempting commercial offers" and "large commercial benefits" might induce the northerners to give up the Mississippi River.[29]

Commerce was not the only reason that northerners came to support occlusion. Equally, if not more, important was the relationship of the

Mississippi River to the western lands and to the nation's future sectional identity. In 1783 reports about large numbers of settlers home-
steading in the backcountry "without any title" had raised the danger
that the western lands might never "be improved to public advantage."
The probable loss of so important a national resource to an unrestricted
and even anarchical western settlement prompted Congress's request
for Virginia to renew the cession of its western lands.[30]

Almost immediately after Congress accepted Virginia's new cession
in March 1784, Congress began to develop policies for regulating the
sale and disposal of the national domain. In the land ordinances of 1784
and 1785 Congress established strict guidelines for the measured settlement and growth of the West. The national domain was divided into ten
districts; the settlers were given the right of self-determination, with
congressional guidance; and provisions were made for the territories to
be admitted to the Union. For purposes of settlement the land was
divided into townships of which parcels were to be sold by federal
commissioners. In theory by May 1785 the United States had a well-
planned system for managing the enlarged national domain.[31]

The intricate solution to the problem of the western lands did not
remain in effect long. Land speculators, who it was said "expect fine
picking," soon got into the act and before too long the land ordinances
ceased to have any real meaning.[32] Although land grabbing helped
destroy the nation's first attempt to deal with territorial expansion,
northerners and southerners had conflicting views about the advisability of increasing the number of states in the Union.

Southerners had special concerns about the "rage for emigration"
and an unordered growth of the West.[33] The goal of the land ordinances,
as perceived by their architect Thomas Jefferson, was to guarantee a
controlled western expansion leading to an enlarged Union. It behooved
the South, especially from the point of view of its probable rising
influence in the nation, to make sure that there were precise guidelines
for settlement, that land speculators be prevented from raping the
western lands, and that the new territories remain bound to the Confederation. On the other hand, the prospect of an expanding South was
coldly received in a North involved in an unsuccessful and frustrating
test of sectional power. The South's refusal to aid northern interests
opened many northerners' eyes to the fact that the Mississippi River
was much more than a gateway to untapped national resources. They
began to realize that it was also a key to western expansion and a future
southern domination of the Union.

Many northerners believed that depriving the West of a necessary
commercial outlet would enhance the value of their own landholdings

and stop the flow of settlers who had been migrating to the Trans-Allegheny since the 1770s. It was, for example, reported that in 1784 Massachusetts alone lost some 5,000 inhabitants to the West. While this might be an exaggeration, still a settler lost to the North was a settler gained by the South. John Jay, in whose hands rested the Mississippi's future, decried the "rage for emigrating."[34] But this exclamation, un-like the southerners', did not suggest a desire for ordered rather than unordered western expansion. William Grayson was unimpressed by the passage of the land ordinances. He pointed out that while some norther-ners wanted the western lands sold in such a manner as to benefit their own citizens "others are apprehensive of the consequences which may result from the new states taking their positions in the Confederacy. They perhaps wish that this event may be delayed as long as pos-sible."[35] Support for occlusion and even the disunion sentiments which came out of the North in 1785 and 1786 reflected a desire to insure a sectional balance which would favor commercial interests. One way to do this was to close the Mississippi River.

What concerned some southerners, and why for them the Mississippi River was so important, was the belief that without federal control or some sort of common bond there was nothing to guarantee western loyal-ties. In 1779 Charles Carroll of Carrollton had pointed out that the people in Kentucky "will always be somewhat different from that of old Virga[.] Slavery must prevail in the latter for some years to come; on the west side of the mountains there will be but few; if any Negroes." He pre-dicted that the two regions would never remain united because of "the Allegani mountains . . . [whose] dictates in spight of the vanity, avarice, & folly of many must be obeyed at last." The course of events until 1785 seemed to substantiate his view. In mid-1785 Thomas Jeffer-son admitted that the recent separation of the state of Franklin from North Carolina had increased his "Anxieties for Virginia." An open Mississippi seemed the surest way to prevent economic necessity, un-checked by any commonality of interest, from driving the West to ally with Spain, or any power which held the Mississippi.[36]

Nevertheless, this southern concern about the statehood movement, the desire to keep the West tied to the Union, was not reflected in uni-form support for an open Mississippi. One of the motivating forces behind the effort to navigate the Potomac River was the professed desire to bridge the gap between old and new Virginia—to "bind the rising world . . . to our interests" and to cement "the Eastern and Western Territory together."[37] This seemed a particularly worthwhile goal and a necessary safeguard if the Spanish succeeded in keeping American shipping from the Mississippi River.[38] But the most active supporters of the Potomac navigation did not see it as a hedge against occlusion. They wanted the Mississippi River closed and believed, like many northerners, that the westerners' "mercantile Connections could be of no Use to the Old States" and that they would leave the Union at the first opportunity "if the obstructions between the two countries remained, and the navigation of the Mississippi should be free." They were, in any event, certain that when the Mississippi River did become important to American interests the weight of population would decide the issue in America's favor.[39]

James Madison thought this analysis based "on both very narrow and very delusive foundations" which did not take into account that occlusion would cost the nation that "which is to be sold for the benefit of the common Treasury." Madison, still the committed nationalist, was even more worried about the possible fallout from an occlusion move. He realized that many southerners did not agree with the Potomac interest, and he correctly assumed that increased intersectional hostility, which would necessarily follow occlusion, might block any attempt to strengthen Congress.[40] In the long run an improved navigation of the Potomac River might have lessened the importance of the Mississippi River. In late 1785, however, and certainly by 1786, many southerners were reluctant to wait until a measured expansion to the westward would give them indisputable control of the Mississippi River. There was no telling what the northern states would do, in the interim, to protect their own base of power.

It was, moreover, certain that the westerners would not permit occlusion to go unopposed. Even before news of the preliminary treaty had reached America in 1783 an anxious George Mason predicted that omission of the right to the free navigation of the Mississippi would "occasion another War in less than Seven Years: the Inhabitants think they have a natural Right to the free (tho' not exclusive) Navigation of that River." Whether Great Britain or Spain controlled it, the potential for conflict was the same.[41] In 1784 and 1785 westerners began to force the issue. By early 1785 it seemed they might "kick up a Dust" if Congress did not resist Spain.[42] The westerners were unprepared to wait until the sheer bulk of population decided the matter, and they certainly had no desire to become the commercial and political appendages of the east coast states. Between January and July the newspapers were filled with news about the Mississippi crisis and predictions of an impending clash between America and Spain. With increasing reports of Spanish seizures of American vessels on the Mississippi, cries were raised against those "piratical robbers," and garrisons in the West began to be fortified.[43]

For a time, western demands had little impact on those men who still wanted to close the Mississippi and buy time for the Potomac navigation. Within months, though, the Potomac interest joined in the southern defense of the right to the free navigation of the Mississippi River. The reason for this change can be easily seen in the experience of James Monroe. Monroe, through late 1785, had also believed that an open Mississippi would enable the western states to outnumber the present states in the Union. He did not see the issue as a North-South conflict and still strongly supported commercial reform, believing, from "confidential communications," that the New Englanders were acting "ingenuously."[44] He soon had reason to question this trust.

In early September 1785 Monroe left Congress on a tour of the backcountry which carried him through Kentucky.[45] He returned to Congress a changed man and informed Jefferson that his experiences in the backlands had impressed him "with a conviction of the impolicy of our measures respecting it." Monroe now believed that the number of states to be carved out of the national domain ought to be decreased to enable them better to reach the requisite population levels to enter the Union. What he had seen, especially in Kentucky, convinced him that if Spain controlled the Mississippi the westerners would be induced, by expedience if nothing else, to ally with Spain. In a reversal of his earlier position he warned that if the Mississippi were closed "we separate those people I mean all those *westward* of the *mountains* from the federal *Government*."[46]

When closure of the Mississippi River came under discussion in Congress in 1786 Monroe was more convinced than ever that the Mississippi had to remain open. In July he reported that a proposal to divide the national domain into not less than three nor more than five states had "open'd the eyes of a part of the Union so as to enable them to view the subject in a different light from what they have heretofore done." The northerners, he said, wanted to rescind all previous land regulations and increase the number of inhabitants required for new states to be admitted to the Union to "one 13th part of the free inhabitants of the U.S." This, he believed, "evinces plainly the policy of these men to be to keep them out of the Confederacy." He was no less certain that occlusion, ostensibly only the price for obtaining a commercial treaty, was actually designed "to break up . . . the settlements on the western waters, prevent any in future, and thereby keep the States southward as they are now." It had become clear, in light of stirrings in the West and northern hostility, that the Mississippi navigation was important to the South and that the Potomac interest had been premature, short-sighted, and terribly naive in trusting that an improved navigation of the Potomac would remove the need for the Mississippi River. It was also inescapably clear that the northern states wanted to limit the future growth of the southern states.[47]

Northerners made no secret of their belief that emigrants to the West would be "lost to the Confederacy." In and out of Congress they openly declared "their desire if possible to prevent emmigration." Their real meaning was clear. They feared a shifting of the sectional balance in the nation.[48] But southern policy was not merely defensive. Guillaume Otto, an astute observer of the American scene, believed that southerners wanted an open Mississippi not only to keep what they had, but also to protect their future, to draw "thither by degrees the inhabitants of New England, whose ungrateful soil only too much favors emigration." Northerners and southerners alike understood that the western territories "will gradually form themselves into separate governments; they will have their representatives in congress, and will augment greatly the mass of the southern states." The issue was not American or Spanish, but southern, control of the West. The northern states were so implacable in their demand for occlusion and the conflict was so basic to the very foundation of the Union that Guillaume Otto thought it "may be the germ of a future separation of the southern states."[49]

SECTIONAL CONFRONTATION

Because of their conflicting instructions, John Jay and Diego de Gardoqui were unable to resolve anything at their initial meetings. When the time came for concessions, it was Jay who willingly bowed to Spanish demands. Monroe later noted that soon after he returned to Congress Jay, evidently believing him still to be pronorthern, informed him that the only way to reach an accord with Spain was to drop America's claim to the free navigation of the Mississippi. According to Monroe, Jay had previously approached other delegates with the outlines of a plan.[50]

After having prepared the groundwork, Jay began the attempt to have his instructions revised on 28 February 1786 in a report on the case of the Spanish seizure of an American vessel on the Mississippi. Jay reported that the king of Spain was determined "to exclude all Nations from the navigation of that part of the Mississippi which runs between his territories." He revealed that his negotiations with Gardoqui were stalled because of their conflicting instructions and, urging against armed conflict, defended the efficacy of compromise by using the Potomac interest's own arguments. He argued that because the Confederation would grow stronger and the land adjacent to the Mississippi would eventually be peopled with large numbers of Americans little would be lost by giving up the use of the river for the present. Within a few months, after receiving a letter from a now exceedingly hopeful Gardoqui which glowingly described the advantages of a Spanish treaty, Jay was prepared to demand a revision of his instructions. He sent Congress a letter, read on 31 May, in which he again pointed out that he and Gardoqui could not negotiate unless the demand for the Mississippi navigation was relaxed. He suggested that all future negotiations be carried on in secret and requested that Congress "appoint a committee empowered to instruct and direct me on every point and subject relative to the proposed treaty with Spain."[51]

Some southerners were not taken in by Jay's ploy to have himself relieved "from the instructions respecting the Mississippi and to get a Committee to cover the measure." Monroe was sure that Gardoqui's real mission was not to formulate a commercial treaty, but to get Jay to agree to cede the Mississippi, and he was "perfectly satisfied that *the latter required no arguments to bring him into the same sentiment.*" After Jay's letter was read the southerners declared that the creation of a committee to direct Jay was "without the power of Congress," because nine states were needed to formulate instructions relative to treaty negotiations and a committee could not be created which possessed such a power.[52]

Notwithstanding this objection Jay's request was referred to a three-man committee consisting of Rufus King, Charles Pettit, and Monroe. The latter had no illusions about his colleagues' feelings or the effect the committee's composition would have on southern hopes. Monroe viewed the Massachusetts delegates, with the possible exception of Nathaniel Gorham, as enemies and accused King of being "associated in this business" because his recent marriage to John Alsop's daughter interested him in turning "the commerce of the Western country down" the Hudson instead of the Mississippi. Pettit, who he said supported occlusion because of his state's displeasure with Virginia's financial policies, was of even more concern to Monroe than King and Massachusetts because of Pennsylvania's "influence with *Delaware* and *Jersey.*" Southern prospects for a successful defense of the Mississippi navigation were very dim.[53]

Monroe was unable to overcome King and Pettit. Although Jay's report to the three-man committee in early June contained no new information, it referred the matter to the committee of the whole and ordered Jay to appear before Congress. In his address on 3 August Jay continued to balance the Mississippi navigation against the chance for a commercial treaty and the opportunity to have "a very convenient neighbour, or a very troublesome one." Jay, after reaffirming his opposition to "every idea of our relinquishing our right to navigate it," offered Congress a way out. He suggested that instead of giving up the right Congress could simply agree to "forbear to use the navigation" for the duration of the proposed treaty. The southerners accepted neither his solution to the dilemma nor his arguments in defense of it.[54]

The committee of the whole considered Jay's report on 10 August and immediately postponed discussion. Monroe did not think that postponement evidenced "that the majority are ag'nst. Jay's propositions." Quite to the contrary he had "satisfactory documents to believe that 7. States are for it." Monroe chafed at Jay's self-righteous attitude as a man faced with an irreconcilable problem trying to serve America's best interests. He accused Jay of negotiating "expressly for the purpose of defeating the object of his instructions" and charged that the northern states were so desirous of completing a commercial treaty and blocking southern expansion that they completely supported Jay's scheme and would "risque the preservation of the confederacy on it." In fact the Massachusetts delegates, who according to Monroe were Jay's "instruments on the floor," had already moved in committee "to repeal his ultimata with the view of suffering him to proceed at his pleasure." Monroe was determined to "throw every possible obstacle in the way of the measure."[55]

The southerners at first offered a compromise. They were willing to enter into a commercial treaty if New Orleans remained open to American shipping. Despite Madison's warning that after making this concession Monroe and his supporters would "have to combat under the disadvantage of having foresaken your first ground," the southerners moved the proposal, and it was rejected.[56] The attempt to block occlusion did not stop because of this setback. The southerners wanted to revoke Jay's instructions, to shift the site of negotiations to Madrid, and to empower Adams and Jefferson to negotiate with the Spanish through the good offices of the French. Some of them evidently approached Guillaume Otto in mid-August, for he informed the Count de Vergennes that the southern states had formed "a league to break off completely every negotiation with Mr. Gardoqui" and to place the negotiations "in the hands of his Majesty." Otto, not wishing to support the losing side, thought that the southerners "had vainly flattered themselves that they could detach Pennsylvania and New Jersey from the league of the North."[57] The northern delegates had, in the meantime, satisfactorily stifled the demand for external assistance.[58]

Congress finally began to consider a resolution to revise Jay's instructions on 28 August. The next four days saw a series of straight sectional
votes. The southerners, fighting a losing battle, kept enunciating their
position over and over again. They maintained that Jay's assessment of
the situation was wrong, that Spain needed American commerce more
than America needed Spanish commerce. They argued that occlusion of
the Mississippi River was not only unnecessary, but also dangerous as it
would "fix the weight of population on one side of the continent only."
They declared that Congress had no right to dismember existing states,
that occlusion was "inadmissable upon the principle of right, and independent of right, upon the highest principles of national
experience."The southerners argued that they alone had the right to
decide a question which threatened them with territorial dismemberment. They even tried to get northern support for retention of New
Orleans as an open port and again suggested that Jay's commission be
revoked and that Jefferson be given control of future negotiations with
Spain. Moreover, the southerners consistently maintained, even until
the final vote on Jay's new instructions, that it was inadmissible for
seven states to revise treaty instructions. None of their motions passed.
Finally, on 31 August Jay's instructions were completed. Jay was to
"propose, and if possible obtain" the use of the Mississippi River from
thirty-one degrees north latitude to New Orleans, but if this failed he
could "consent to an article or articles stipulating . . . a forebearance of
the use of the said river Mississippi for a period not exceeding twenty
years."[59]

Because according to the Articles of Confederation nine states were
needed to ratify a treaty, the South had been out-voted only for the
moment, not defeated. Jay now had a free hand in the negotiations, but,
as Otto pointed out, because his instructions were not "constitutional he
cannot conclude a treaty without encountering bitter reproaches from
the five southern states." Monroe, for one, did not believe that Jay
would complete a treaty. By late September he had learned nothing
other than that Jay's compatriots "affirm he will proceed." Monroe's
initial feeling was correct.[60] In early October Jay informed Gardoqui
that he was now able to "receive Propositions relative to certain Matters
of Difference between our Countries." A commercial treaty would have
neatly avoided the problem of southern refusal to give Congress a power
of commerce, but only if it could be ratified. Since the southern states
could prevent ratification, Jay was ultimately forced to admit that it was
useless to formulate a treaty which those states would violently oppose.
He did not proceed with the negotiations, and the unsettled status of the
Mississippi River was left for a new government to decide.[61]

A SOUTHERN DEFENSE

The Mississippi issue, which epitomized the nation's sectional dissimilarity, raised questions about the nature of the union which influenced congressional politics and reshaped the conflict between federalists and nationalists. Soon after the Mississippi votes were concluded Henry Lee surmised that if the plans for improving the navigation of the Potomac River progressed it would be "another strong evidence that difficulty vanish as they are approached, and will be a strong argument among the politicians to favor of the Spanish treaty and the occlusion of the Mississippi." Lee guessed wrong and misjudged the central theme of the Mississippi conflict and probable southern reaction. The continued control of and trade with the western territories was only part of the issue. Even if the Potomac navigation could have been completed in time enough to stabilize east-west relations, the fact still remained that for most southerners the attempt to occlude the Mississippi revealed a larger northern scheme to seize control of the nation. The seven northern states' refusal, in late September, to remove "the injunction of secrecy" from the Spanish negotiations confirmed the southern view that "the Ballance of Power is in the Eastern States, & they appear determined to keep it in that direction." By October even Henry Lee was forced to admit that "the decided difference which prevailed in Congress . . . [was] generally understood in every part of the union."[62]

Northern superiority was reason enough for southerners to be upset and angry. The response to the prospect of occlusion in the West, however, gave them even more reason to redouble their efforts to defeat northern, and especially, New England policies. There were rumors, which reached Jefferson in Europe, that if the Mississippi River were closed "the Eastern and Western parts" of the Union would divide.[63] This did not only affect southerners. A convention of settlers in western Pennsylvania voiced its objection to occlusion and pledged support for the southern states against "the Eastern and some of the Middle States." Pennsylvania could ill afford to ignore this serious threat. Western Pennsylvania could very easily demand the independence for which its southern neighbors had been striving for years. When Robert Morris and the Republicans regained control of the Pennsylvania Assembly, they quickly aligned with the southern states and disclaimed support for occlusion.[64]

The pressure on Virginia, which had opposed occlusion, was even more severe. The Kentuckians conveyed to Richmond their "horror [at] the Idea of their being . . . sacrificed, & their Interests sold by those whom they have considered as their brethren, friends, and fellow citizens.'' The Virginians immediately set about trying to allay those fears. The legislature sent Congress a memorial attacking occlusion and instructed its delegates to oppose "any efforts to barter or surrender free & common use of the River."[65] The Virginians had their own scores to settle too. Henry Lee, who had never really concealed his Potomac interest leanings, was dropped from the congressional delegation in December because of "his supposed heterodoxy touching the Mississippi."[66] Lee eventually cleared his name and was reinstated. Yet the attempt to ferret out northern sympathizers is indicative of the vehement reaction to occlusion and was symptomatic of the impotence many southerners felt. Although getting rid of, or attacking, Lee might have assuaged some pent-up frustrations, it did not speak to the real problem. The South was not defeated because of any internal wavering, but because of the sectional configuration in Congress.

The northern states, particularly New England, won a very costly pyrrhic victory in August 1786. Even before the voting ended some southerners actively began seeking a rapprochement with the middle states. The alliance between nationalists and southerners, which many New Englanders had so long feared, became a reality. In the meantime, a few influential nationalist politicians had continued to ready themselves for a final effort to create a strong central government. They passed one hurdle at the Annapolis Convention, where delegates from four middle states and Virginia set the nation on the road to Philadelphia.

8

The Annapolis Convention

DURING THE entire revolutionary era there were only two extra-congressional assemblies to which representatives from all the states were invited. One was the Philadelphia Convention, the other the Annapolis Convention. Although it has long symbolized the beginning of a turning point in the American Revolution, the Annapolis Convention has generally been viewed as only a prelude to the drama in Philadelphia. It is just as important to understand the steps which led to the Annapolis Convention as it is to elucidate the origins of its more celebrated lineal descendant. It is very likely that comprehensive constitutional reform might never have begun had the Annapolis delegates not started the nation on the meandering road to Philadelphia. If this road had a specific and identifiable starting point, it was certainly in the mercantile reform movement. While many states considered the two major alternatives, state navigation acts or sanctioning federal legislation, the stalemate in Virginia between the supporters and opponents of commercial reform gave rise to a compromise measure—a commercial convention which changed the course of the American Revolution.

Soon after the Virginia House of Burgesses convened in October 1785 it appointed a committee to consider formulating a state navigation act. Less than two weeks later another, more hotly contested, avenue of discussion was opened when a bill came out of committee calling for the delegates in Congress to be instructed "to give the assent of the state to a general regulation of the commerce of the United States, under certain qualifications." A committee was immediately appointed to formulate the instructions.[1]

Madison was the admitted leader of the proreform faction and was probably responsible for the referral of the question of federal commercial reform to the House. In early May William Grayson had sent him a copy of the proposed commerce amendment along with information about the grim prospects of passage. Madison's ideologically based desire to strengthen Congress and his interest in fashioning a healthier Virginia economy distinguished him from his more cautious colleagues who, like Richard Henry Lee in Congress, feared that strengthening Congress's commerce powers would also strengthen the already dominant northern merchants. Madison believed that the British challenge could be met and the economy righted only "by a harmony in the measures of the States" with the most efficient means to enable Congress to direct the nation's commerce. If that was not possible, if the states would not sacrifice their individual prerogatives, he wanted Congress "otherwise constituted; let their numbers be increased, let them be chosen oftener, and let their period of service be shortened, if any better medium than Congress can be proposed . . . let it be substituted; or lastly let no regulation of trade adopted by Congress be in force untill it shall have been ratified by a certain proportion of the States."[2]

For Madison, commercial reform was a perfect place to begin the lengthy process of strengthening the central government. But he was essentially looking for a constitutional solution to a fundamentally sectional problem. Although certainly significant, a fear of Congress misusing its authority was not really central to the problem of commercial reform. Even after he was given a detailed account of the sectional nature of the commerce fight, Madison's certainty that the nation's commercial ills resulted from a defect in the Articles of Confederation convinced him that any action other than amending the Constitution would simply perpetuate Congress's sisyphean struggle to keep the Union from sinking "by standing constantly at the pump, not by stopping the leaks which have endangered her."[3]

In early November petitions poured into the House from merchants throughout the state. The question was whether the representatives would support an amplification of Congress's commerce powers or look to state action for relief.[4] A majority of them seemed amenable to the former, but "under certain qualifications," which Madison feared would limit Congress's ability to set meaningful policies. There was, however, considerable opposition to a commerce amendment.[5] The instructions to the delegates which the House began to consider on 14 November were simply intended to demonstrate Virginia's support for temporary and limited commercial regulations. In addition to preventing Congress from imposing commercial duties on the individual states and requiring that two-thirds of the states be needed to pass said commerce act, the House, on 30 November, limited the grant to a thirteen-year duration. Madison later noted that limiting the commerce power's "duration to a short term has ultimately disappointed our efforts." The Madison wing, desperately trying to give some semblance of continuity to the proposed commerce power, moved that it terminate after the term ended "unless continued by a like proportion of votes within one year immediately preceeding the expiration." The motion was overwhelmingly defeated.[6]

Madison was resigned to defeat, and rather than adopt "a temporary measure which may stand in the way of a permanent one," he was prepared "to trust to further experience, and even distress" to produce the requisite and fitting extension of Congress's power. On 1 December he and his supporters, choosing "to do nothing than to adopt it in that form," moved that the previously passed resolution "does not, from a mistake, contain the sense of the majority of this House that voted for the said Resolution." The House recalled the measure from the Senate, and a coalition of proponents and opponents of unrestricted commercial reform revoked the instructions.[7]

With the time for adjournment fast approaching and "the apprehensions, in some minds, of an abuse of power," it seemed almost certain that no action would be taken. The belief, however, that commercial reform was necessary for the nation and threatening to "the States having a surplus" had earlier prompted Joseph Jones to suggest a middle-of-the-road alternative. He advised Madison that "a Convention of Deputies from the several States for the purpose of forming Commercial regulations similar to the British Nav: act . . . wod. be the most likely mode to obtain success to the measure."[8] Jones's suggestion lay dormant until early December when the Mt. Vernon delegates, George Mason and Alexander Henderson, informed the House of Maryland's desire to meet again with representatives from Virginia and its intention to call another meeting to which representatives from Pennsylvania and Delaware would be invited.[9] The possibility that Maryland, Pennsylvania, and Delaware, all interested in improving the Susquehanna navigation, would advance measures contrary to Virginia's interests might, then, have stimulated interest in federal commercial reform. David Stuart pointed out that if the Virginia legislature took any action on commerce "it may be ascribed to a letter from the legislature of Maryland, requesting an appointment of commissioners by each state to fix on a similarity of restrictions."[10]

Five days after discussion of the Mt. Vernon resolves, John Tyler moved for a "meeting of Politico-Commercial Commissioners from all the States for the purpose of digesting and reporting the requisite augmentation of the power of Congress over trade." Madison was very cool to the idea. He still favored a commerce amendment. Nevertheless, he had no illusions about the representatives supporting "a perpetual grant" and thought it unfortunately more probable that a convention, having "fewer enemies," would instead be attempted. He noted that the idea "seems naturally to grow out of the proposed appointment of Comsrs for Virga. & Maryd. concocted at Mount Vernon."[11] In the meantime, the House had been considering implementing unilateral trade restrictions. On 13 January 1786, but a few days before scheduled adjournment, the House determined that there was insufficient time to discuss adequately a navigation act and tabled the matter.[12]

Just when it seemed that nothing would be done John Tyler resubmitted his convention proposal. The House, with surprisingly little controversy, resolved that it and Maryland make "a joint application to congress" for support in navigating the Potomac River, that the two governments appoint commissioners to confer "on such subjects as may concern the commercial interests of both States within the powers of the respective States," and that this resolution be communicated to the other states in the Union "that they may be requested to nominate Commissioners for the purposes expressed." The Senate quickly approved the resolutions, and on 21 January Edmund Randolph, James Madison, Walter Jones, St. George Tucker, and Meriwether Smith were appointed to meet in convention with commissioners from the other states "to take into consideration the trade of the United States; to examine the relative situations and trade of the said States; and to consider how far an uniform system in their commercial regulations may be necessary to their common interest and their permanent harmony."[13]

The attempt to understand Virginia's action has been unnecessarily complicated by the effort to relate what the delegates did at Annapolis to Virginia's invitation. The proposal for a commercial convention was no more than an eleventh-hour compromise engineered by the more cautious and fearful members of the Virginia legislature and designed to respond to the nation's commercial problems without sanctioning too comprehensive an extension of Congress's powers. Although John Tyler proposed the measure, it has often been asserted, on no more evidence than old histories of Virginia which relied on Madison's later version of the story, that Tyler acted in behalf of Madison and his proreform faction.[14]

Some forty years after the fact Madison told Noah Webster that the Annapolis Convention resulted from "effort made by myself to convince the legislature of the necessity of investing Congress with such [commercial] powers." He maintained that the actual proposal "was introduced by another member [Tyler], more likely to have the ear of the legislature on the occasion than one whose long and late service in Congress, might subject him [Madison] to the suspicion of a bias in favor of that body."[15]

At the time, however, Madison was very upset that after the failure to establish a navigation act the legislature had dismissed "the original propositions for a general plan" in favor of a method which was "liable to objections and will probably miscarry."[16] The selection of Annapolis as the site of the convention did not diminish Madison's doubt that it was intended to further commercial reform. Choosing Annapolis because it was "most central and farther [removed] from the suspicion, which Phila. or N. York might have excited, of congressional or mercantile influence" seemed very strange for a meeting supposedly intended to solve problems which so vitally affected merchants and the balance of power in the Confederation and whose suggestions were to be sent to Congress. The hardening of the sectional lines in Congress raised doubts about the convention from a totally different perspective. Joseph Jones, who had originally suggested the idea of a commercial convention and who had voted against an unlimited grant of power to Congress, was soon sorry that a convention had been substituted for direct congressional action. Jones might have feared, as other southerners did within a few months, that northerners might control the convention and possibly do more damage to southern interests than would passage of a commerce amendment.[17]

Part of the difficulty in trying to get a clear picture of the Annapolis Convention lies in the complexity of the political scene in 1786. The wide variety of issues which affected the nation, the sections, and the states makes it difficult to synthesize the various parts of a very intricate story into a comprehensible whole. Although Madison, and some other nationalists, realized that a convention limited to commercial concerns could point the way to more comprehensive constitutional reform and seized upon a golden opportunity at the Annapolis Convention, the prospect did not appear to them until well after the call for a commercial convention. It is tempting, in fact too tempting, to perceive state responses to Virginia's invitation within the context of nationalist politics and the later significance of the Annapolis Convention. Although ideology was important, it was only one of the stimuli affecting the states. The continuing federalist-nationalist conflict, the worsening sectional situation, and the pull of subsectional and state interests interacted to form the unsettled preconvention political environment. Maryland's refusal to appoint delegates to a convention to be held in its capital city was a case in point.

RESPONSE IN THE STATES

Even before Virginia issued its call for the Annapolis Convention plans were underway in Maryland to coordinate opposition to the Potomac navigation. The relative success of the Potomac Company had not quieted the acquisitive and jealous Baltimoreans. On 20 February 1786 the Maryland House of Delegates discussed a proposal from Pennsylvania to open "a navigable communication between Chesapeake and Delaware Bays, and for an effectual improvement of the Susquehanna." After very little debate the House and Senate concurred on the importance of following up the proposal, and the tristate convention was born. The following day Samuel Chase, Samuel Hughes, Peregrine Leatherbury, William Smith (Baltimore-Town), and William Hemsley were appointed to meet with delegates from Pennsylvania and Delaware. After dallying for almost two years the Susquehanna interest was finally attempting to catch up with the Potomac Company.[18]

The Susquehanna and Potomac supporters within the Maryland legislature did not get into any discernible conflict until receipt of the invitation to the Annapolis Convention. On 8 March the House requested the Senate's speedy concurrence in appointing delegates to the convention. The Senate requested additional time to give the matter closer attention. Three days later it refused to take any action. The Senate defended its refusal to appoint delegates to the Annapolis Convention on purely ideological grounds, arguing that measures had already been taken to strengthen Congress, namely the unpassed commerce act of 1784 and the impost of 1783, and that any sign that Congress needed external assistance to solve the nation's problems would lessen America's standing and reputation in foreign eyes. The most dramatic reason the Senate gave for not appointing delegates, and the one which has usually been accepted as the sole reason for Maryland's nonappointment, was a fear that the Annapolis Convention "may produce other meetings, which may have consequences which cannot be foreseen. Innovations in government, when not absolutely necessary, are dangerous, particularly to republics, generally too fond of novelties, and subject to change." The following day the Senate resolved to authorize the Mt. Vernon delegates to again meet with delegates from Virginia, to proceed with the tristate convention, and to inform Virginia that Maryland would not attend the Annapolis Convention but would have its delegates meet with Virginia's in early September. The House assented to the first resolution, but refused to accept the other two.[19]

While a lack of evidence prevents careful analysis, Maryland's refusal to appoint delegates raises some interesting questions. Although the

Senate's professed reason for refusing to appoint delegates to the Annapolis Convention gains credibility in light of what later occurred, it is debatable whether a fear of constitutional excess was a primary reason or merely a convenient justification for the action. Because the decision not to appoint was dictated by only part of the legislature, there is reason to doubt that the Senate's defense was the sole motivation for the action it took. The House's retaliatory refusal to continue to support the tristate convention suggests that there might have been other elements than ideology or Confederation politics at play. Because of its timing, purpose, and audience, the Annapolis Convention promised, and seemed intended, to undercut or even supersede Maryland's tristate convention. The tristate delegates would, at the least, have been constrained to develop their own commercial arrangements, given the Annapolis Convention's broader mandate, including discussion of the efficacy of adopting a uniform system in interstate commercial relations.

Underlying the decision not to appoint delegates, coloring Maryland politics in general, was a clash between the Baltimore pro-Susquehanna interest and the Potomac interest. Although it might certainly be true that some senators were concerned about a rush to revise the Articles of Confederation, the two branches of the legislature were not so dramatically different, socially, economically, or ideologically, as to suggest that one would be more worried than the other about the Articles of Confederation. Some very influential House leaders, however, including William Paca, Thomas Stone, and Samuel Chase were either directly involved in or supported the Potomac Company. They threatened Baltimore's position in the Potomac River Valley, which might have been strengthened at the tristate convention, and they were also deeply involved in a movement for debtor relief and paper money. The question, then, is to what extent these conflicts affected Senate-House relations and Maryland politics and to what extent these issues colored Maryland's consideration of the Annapolis Convention. While the importance of state politics in determining Maryland's refusal to appoint delegates to the Annapolis Convention requires further study, the response in other states reinforces the notion that there might have been more at stake and at issue in Maryland than ideology.[20]

The situation in Pennsylvania and Delaware seems to bear this out. Although there was a history of fierce factional conflict in Pennsylvania, there was none of the wrangling which characterized Maryland's reaction. On 23 February the Pennsylvania Supreme Executive Council "warmly recommended" the Annapolis Convention to the Assembly as the only means to "remove the many evils by which the trade of

America has been so long and exceedingly oppressed." Within a month
it resolved to appoint five delegates to the Annapolis Convention and a
short time later agreed to appoint delegates to attend the tristate convention. On 5 April the Assembly appointed Francis Hopkinson, John
Ewing, David Rittenhouse, Robert Milligan, and George Lattimer delegates to the tristate convention and six days later chose Robert Morris,
George Clymer, John Armstrong, Jr., Thomas FitzSimons, and Tench
Coxe to attend the Annapolis Convention.[21] In mid-June, with even less
time devoted to the matter, Delaware appointed Gunning Bedford,
William Killen, and John Jones to attend the tristate convention and sent
George Read, Jacob Broom, John Dickinson, Richard Basset, and Gun-
ning Bedford to Annapolis.[22]

The conflict-free appointment of delegates in Pennsylvania and Delaware need not suggest a victory for nationalism, just as the nonappointment in Maryland need not suggest a victory for federalism. By
early 1786 the political scene, more than ever before, was colored by
sectionalism and not ideology. Nationalist talk and activity, apart from
some conjecture that the Annapolis Convention could serve as a potentially useful but second-rate substitute for more meaningful action,
concerned either stimulating constitutional reform in Congress or calling a general convention of the states. Surely the Pennsylvania Constitutionalists were no less afraid of a major revision of the Articles of
Confederation than the more conservative Maryland senators. That so
many influential nationalists were appointed in Pennsylvania and Delaware may simply reflect the obvious—that at least in early 1786 the
Annapolis Convention had a low profile and was considered fairly
insignificant. In late 1788 a Republican Assembly appointed Tench Coxe
to serve in the last four months of the Confederation Congress. The
Constitutionalists/Antifederalists attacked this action. In response,
however, it was pointed out that "No such objection was made to his
taking his seat in the convention at Annapolis. To this infinitely higher
and more honorable trust, he was appointed by the *present Antifederal
Party*."[23]

It is important to bear in mind that the various state legislatures were
dealing with an unknown. Aside from some limited New England conventions in 1780, there had never been a meeting of state representatives
outside of Congress. There was, with a few notable exceptions, surprisingly little controversy about and almost no public debate on the
merits or dangers of a commercial convention. In the first place, there
was little reason to expect that an issue which had stalemated Congress
could be successfully handled. In the second place, there was a safeguard that no matter what the delegates did in Annapolis, Congress was
not obliged to pay them any heed or sanction their behavior. Having

been instructed to confine their attention to commercial problems, there seemed scant likelihood that the delegates would be able to do anything extraneous, let alone justify it, if they did.

The appointments in two states changed that and paved the way for what happened in Annapolis. The two states were New York and New Jersey—New York because of Alexander Hamilton and New Jersey because of the instructions to its delegates. A New York legislature which was just as state-minded as the Constitutionalist-controlled Pennsylvania Assembly sent a very similar sort of delegation to the Annapolis Convention. Governor Clinton submitted Virginia's invitation to the legislature on 16 March. After almost two months, during which time the legislature was discussing the problem of commerce and struggling over passage of the impost, five delegates were appointed to attend the Annapolis Convention—Robert R. Livingston, James Duane, Alexander Hamilton, Robert C. Livingston, and Egbert Benson, who happened to be the godfather of John Jay's daughter. It was later noted that after the Clintonian legislature refused to ratify the impost William Duer, a long-time associate of Robert Morris, pressed for the appointment of delegates to the Annapolis Convention. As was the case with all but one of the complying states, New York duplicated Virginia's original resolution and instructed the delegates only to "take into consideration the Trade and Commerce of the United States."[24]

Although the majority of the representatives probably had no interest in the Annapolis Convention other than as a way to stabilize the nation's commerce, Alexander Hamilton had his own very special ideas. Hamilton had long advocated using an independent convention to revise the Articles of Confederation. According to Robert Troup, he did not believe that the Clintonians would support federal measures, such as an impost or commerce power, which might prevent them from continuing to gouge their neighbors with state tariffs. If Troup is to be believed, Hamilton had no "partiality for a commercial convention, otherwise than as a stepping stone to a general convention to form a general Constitution." Although it is dangerous to accept these remembrances as fact while discounting Madison's, it remains that Hamilton had been talking about that type of convention since 1780. Egbert Benson later admitted that he himself had been undecided about whether or not to attend the convention until he had a conversation with John Sloss Hobart, his colleague on the Supreme Court, "the Convention the subject, [which] terminated in a Conclusion that the present Opportunity was not to be lost for obtaining a Convention to revise the whole of the Articles of Confederation as a Mode or System of Government."[25]

New Jersey's unique response to Virginia's invitation was not a consequence of pronationalist sympathies. Although a degree of external influence helped direct the legislature, its action was simply a result of the state's ineffectual and seemingly never-ending attempt to loose the constricting grip of Philadelphia and New York City on its economy. New Jersey, sorely pressed in trying to raise both federal and state revenues from its own commerce, wanted Congress to control the western lands for purposes of revenue and supported a federally controlled impost, hoping that it, in conjunction with a congressional power to regulate trade, would prevent especially New York from continuing to emburden its commerce with duties and tariffs. With apparently no choice available but to rely on its own resources, the legislature had passed the impost in December 1783, but instead of passing the supplemental revenue it resolved to raise additional revenues within the state to pay off the interest on the federal debt owed to its own citizens. In December 1784 the legislature had ordered the state treasurer to meet no further congressional requisitions until all the states passed the impost and until Congress formulated a more equitable means of raising additional federal revenues than further taxes on commerce.

New Jersey's plan was put to the test when Congress, in the requisition of 1785, called upon it to raise three million dollars, of which two-thirds was to be used to discharge the interest on the domestic debt. Besides not directly benefiting New Jersey's citizens, who were in theory being taken care of by their own government, the requisition threatened to further upset the state's financial stability. The legislature was additionally rankled by New York's refusal to pass the impost. On 20 February 1786 it determined, with only three negative votes, not to pay its share of the requisition until the impost was passed and until all state imposts and tariffs were revoked.[26] Despite New Jersey's justifiable grounds, its unilateral action threatened Congress's authority. There was even some talk about armed conflict between New Jersey and New York. Congress, apprehending a dangerous situation, quickly appointed Charles Pinckney, Nathaniel Gorham, and William Grayson to go to New Jersey and address the legislature on "the fatal consequences that must result from their refusal to comply with the Requisition of September 1785."[27]

On 13 March, the day after the New Jersey legislature tabled discussion on the appointment of delegates to the Annapolis Convention, Pinckney appeared before it. He chided the legislature for its action and emphasized that maintenance of the Union demanded strict compliance with congressional dictates. He coupled his request for revocation of the February act, however, with the suggestion of a possible way out of the dilemma. He remarked that if New Jersey thought itself "unequally situated," or felt it did not "participate in those common benefits which the general government is expected to dispense to its members—if she thinks with me, that its powers are inadequate to the ends for which it was instituted, and that they should be increased—there can be no doubt of the conduct she ought to pursue. She ought immediately to instruct her delegates in congress, to urge the calling of a general convention of the states, for the purposes of revising and amending the federal system."[28]

Pinckney convinced the legislature of the connection between New Jersey's commercial and financial difficulties and the basic structure of the Confederation. The legislature rescinded its antirequisition act on 17 March, but reaffirmed its demand for passage of the impost and for giving Congress the power to regulate trade. Although the legislature did not instruct its delegates to propose a convention of the states, on 20 March it appointed William Churchill Houston, James Schuurman, and Abraham Clark delegates to the Annapolis Convention "to take into consideration the Trade of the United States . . . to consider how far an uniform system in their Commercial Regulations and *other important Matters* may be necessary to their common interest & permanent Harmony" (italics mine). These instructions, which were the most open-ended passed by any state, enabled the delegates assembled in Annapolis to overstep the convention's original bounds.[29]

ALTERNATIVES FOR REFORM

The Annapolis Convention achieved special significance after an abortive effort finally to call a general convention of the states. Pinckney's address to the New Jersey legislature may very well have been part of this drive. In early March, shortly before going to New Jersey with Pinckney and Grayson, Nathaniel Gorham told Caleb Davis about a plan in Congress to have a convention "consider whether they will establish a federal government with powers adequate to the necessities & happiness of the Union." Within the month some anonymous critics in Virginia prayed for the day "when we shall see a NATIONAL CONVENTION sit, composed of the best and ablest men in the Union, a majority of whom shall be invested with the power of altering it." There was also a call for a "national Convention" from Massachusetts.[30]

By this time, however, the beginning of the Mississippi conflict began to sour some southerners on the idea of a general convention. They, like the Massachusetts delegates in 1785, were worried that the sectional forces operative in Congress would be equally evident in a convention. William Grayson believed that it was "better to bear those ills we have than to fly to others we know not of." Grayson was certain that the New Englanders, only interested in commercial reform, would use a convention to secure that end no matter what the cost to the South. For James Madison, to whom Grayson addressed his comments, restructuring the Confederation was still a high priority. Although he had been disappointed by Virginia's failure to sanction commercial reform, which might have led to further constitutional changes, he nevertheless conceded that the Annapolis Convention was "bettter than nothing, and as a recommendation of additional powers to Congress is within the purview of the Commissioners it may possibly lead to better consequences than at first occur."[31]

Although Madison remained dubious about the Annapolis Convention, he was intrigued by the possibility that it might stimulate constitutional reform. He even advised James Monroe in mid-March that as "we have both ignorance and iniquity to combat, we must defeat the designs of the latter by humouring the prejudices of the former. The efforts to bring about a correction through the medium of Congress miscarried. Let a convention, then, be tried." But he was talking about the Annapolis Convention, which he now believed could be a cautious first step in revising the Articles of Confederation by testing the political climate and by preparing "the public mind . . . for further remedies." Grayson's disheartening warning, however, suggested that sectional conflict might prevent the constitutional reform for which Madison hoped. He was very concerned that the threat of occlusion was "putting arms into the hands of the enemies to every amendment to our federal system" and, left only with the option of the Annapolis Convention, unwillingly concluded that the time was simply not right for a general convention.[32]

For a time, however, it still seemed that, despite increasing sectional hostility, reform could be stimulated within Congress. On 3 May Charles Pinckney moved that Congress appoint a committee either to consider amending the Articles of Confederation or to call a general convention of the states. The latter, he believed, was the "only true and radical remedy for our defects." Few of his colleagues agreed with him and instead of calling a convention Congress appointed a "Grand Committee on Federal Powers" to prepare amendments to the Articles of Confederation.[33] To those anxious for change the Annapolis Convention seemed, more so than in early 1786, to be a serendipitous opportunity to bypass Congress and set the reform movement in progress. It appeared that it could even serve a similar purpose as a general convention if it could "do more, if it comprehended more Objects." After the appointment of the "Grand Committee" Benjamin Rush was optimistic about the Annapolis Convention "as an opinion seems to have pervaded all classes of people that an increase of power in Congress is absolutely necessary for our safety and independence.[34]

Although this might have been true, to a degree, sectional conflict complicated the situation and played a dramatic role in deciding the question of constitutional reform in Congress. On 28 May, a few days before the Mississippi issue reached the floor of Congress, Grayson assured Madison that proper amendments would never be agreed upon because "the eastern people mean nothing more than to carry the commercial point." He predicted that Pinckney would "be astounded when he meets with a proposition to prevent the states from importing any more of the seed of Cain . . . [and New York and Pennsylvania would] feel themselves indisposed when they hear it proposed that it shall become a national compact that the sessions [of Congress] shall always be held in the centre of the empire [on the Potomac]." Grayson's understanding of the sectional forces in Congress and not ideological objections convinced him that there could not be "a reformation on proper principles" and that "things had better remain as they are then not to probe them to the bottom." George Washington had the very same conclusion about a general convention. Although he believed that without extensive reforms "the fabric will fall," he did not think conditions were "ripe for such an event" as a convention.[35]

On 7 August the "Grand Committee" reported seven amendments to the Articles of Confederation, among which were a commerce power and a federal revenue. The Mississippi conflict immediately made its presence felt. It appeared to Henry Lee that if a treaty were made which benefited one section at the expense of another "the great object viz bracing the federal government may be thwarted, and thus in pursuing a lesser, we loose a greater Good." On the same day that the Massachusetts delegates moved to give John Jay a free hand in the negotiations with Gardoqui, Charles Pinckney tried to point out the consequences of closing the Mississippi River. He declared that entering into an inequitable commercial treaty was not the way to achieve commercial respectability and warned that occlusion would end all hope for reformation of the Articles of Confederation. Pinckney's restrained, almost genial, attempt to bridge the widening sectional gap contrasted with William Grayson's threat that if the Mississippi were closed "to obtain trivial commercial advantages for their brethren in the East," the

southerners "would never grant those powers which were acknowledged to be essential to the existence of the Union." The pull of sectional interest was by this time too strong to be overcome by logic,
self-restraint, or even threat. The report of the "Grand Committee" was
tabled. There it lay for the duration of the Confederation period.[36]

Even had they passed, the amendments would not have fully satisfied
nationalist critics. There was no reference to giving Congress supreme
authority over the states. Yet passage of the amendments, even in
Congress, might have demonstrated the Confederation's ability to respond to stress. Many federalists had met nationalist critiques of the
Confederation with an assertion that whatever problems the nation
faced they could be easily corrected—that the United States was a new
nation and "fast recovering from the fatigue of Warr . . . like a young
Man who by sleep shakes off his Weariness." Even during the height of
the Mississippi conflict James Monroe still believed the Confederation,
"with a few alternatives, the best that can be devised." The tabling of
the amendment proposals proved to be a critical setback. It maintained a
stressful situation which further validated nationalist predictions about
the consequences of weak central government. Moreover, the closure of
Congress as an avenue for reform left certain nationalists with no alternative but to rely on the Annapolis Convention.[37]

SECTIONAL TENSIONS IN PRECONVENTION POLITICS

New England, which ought to have had the most interest in amplifying
Congress's commerce power, was very guarded about Virginia's call to
a convention. Only Rhode Island and Massachusetts appointed delegates. Some very important politicians in the latter state argued against
the action, its delegation was constantly changing personnel, and no
delegates from either of the two states ever arrived in Annapolis.
Connecticut did not appoint any delegates, owing, thought James Madison, to its recent troubles with radical local "Conventions." New
Hampshire, apparently very concerned about "the want of a general
system of Commerce," was reported to have appointed a delegation in
early April. But by August there were still calls for an appointment of
delegates from New Hampshire, and none ever appeared in
Annapolis.[38] The response in Massachusetts was even more mixed.
After two appeals by Governor Bowdoin, who had personally advocated calling a convention of the states in 1785, the General Court
appointed Caleb Davis, Benjamin Goodhue, Tristram Dalton, and John
Coffin Jones in March. Within less than two months they had all re-

signed. In June, again at Bowdoin's urging, the legislature appointed
Francis Dana, Elbridge Gerry, Stephen Higginson, and George Cabot.
Gerry declined the appointment within the week, but in July Higginson
reported that he and John Lowell, Theophilus Parsons, James Sullivan,
Dana, Cabot, and Gerry were to attend the convention. A different
delegation set out for Annapolis in early September.[39]

This unstable atmosphere may have resulted from the clash between a
desire for commercial reform and a fear of the convention. Nathaniel
Gorham, who would rather have had a general convention, was worried
about Massachusetts's effect on the Annapolis Convention. He
acknowledged that "we have Men among us who have sufficient Commercial Knowledge," but pointed out that they were "some what antifederal in their opinions." Gorham wanted to "send Men of good
Federal ideas," otherwise they "may overthrow the whole plan." The
promise of commercial reform was a strong inducement in favor of the
meeting. Jabez Bowen, for example, believed that the New England
states could not afford to let the Annapolis Convention "pass unnoticed
by any means. if we can Secure the carrying trade of the Southern
States, there will always be incouragement for the Building of vessels in
the Northern States."[40]

To some other New Englanders the Annapolis Convention threatened
to actualize the very fears which had caused the Massachusetts delegates to oppose the calling of a convention of the states in September
1785. Rufus King and John Adams, both of whom were among the
strongest supporters of commercial reform, were in agreement that
reformation of the Articles of Confederation, no matter how necessary,
should take place only in Congress. King thought that the merchants
throughout the nation were of a common mind in uniformly opposing a
general convention. His uncertainty that the Annapolis Convention
would effect "those measures essentially necessary for the prosperity
and safety of the states" was predicated on the belief that the plan for a
commercial convention "did not come from the persons favorable to a
commercial system common to all the States, but from those, who in
opposition to such a general system, have advocated the particular
regulation of individual states." While King questioned the ambiguous
origin of the convention, Stephen Higginson wondered about its probable effects. He believed that the appointees "from New York, Pennsylvania, and Virginia, and the source from whence the proposition was
made" proved beyond a doubt that "political Objects are intended to be
combined with the commercial." He doubted whether Madison, Hamilton, Morris, FitzSimons, and Duane, all "esteemed great
Aristocrats . . . know or care much about commercial Objects." Those

aristocrats, against whom King, Gerry, and Holten had railed in 1785, only wanted to restructure the confederation.[41]

By August the Mississippi conflict threatened the Annapolis Convention just as it affected reform within Congress. Although there was still some support for "a plenipotentiary Convention," James Madison feared that increasing sectional tensions might now short-circuit any attempt at constitutional reform. The southern reaction was the most dramatic and, in the long run, the most significant. Earlier in the year some Virginians, already worried about the unfavorable sectional balance in Congress, had taken Maryland's defection very hard. Madison was outraged at the "mistaken notion" with which Daniel Carroll had attempted to justify his state's refusal to appoint delegates. Edmund Randolph cryptically noted that Maryland's absence would create "a dreadful chasm . . . a chasm more injurious to us, than any other of the delegates." Maryland's refusal to appoint delegates threatened to throw the weight of influence to the northern states and seemed to confirm a long-standing fear that the northern states would and could, with little difficulty, secure support in southern commercial centers like Baltimore and Charleston.[42]

Maryland's defection proved even more serious after rumors that some frustrated northerners had met in New York City to plan a sub-confederation. James Monroe wanted to make sure that if the Union did split into two confederacies that "Pena. if not Jersey should be included in ours."[43] He wanted to take immediate action to crack the northern bloc and asked Madison to persuade James Wilson and Arthur St. Clair to support the South's antiocclusion stance. Madison could not reach them, but he learned that Wilson was aware that closure of the Mississippi "tends to defeat the object of the meeting at Annapolis, from which he has great expectations." This was not enough for Monroe, who now believed that Massachusetts had passed its navigation act only to induce the southern states to prohibit "foreign Vessels from coming to our ports, which means the Vessels from the Eastern States may obtain high Freights and keep down the price of produce." He even wanted "the admission of a few additional states into the confederacy in the southern scale" before risking commercial reform. Monroe, positive that "the Eastern men" intended to use the Annapolis Convention for their own purposes, advised Madison to do all he could to get Pennsylvania and New Jersey to reverse their positions on the Mississippi navigation. He also suggested that if, as "the ablest men" now believed, the Confederation required major reforms, the southern states had to "act with great circumspection and to be prepar'd for every possible event—to stand well with the Middle States especially."[44] They did.

A GENERAL CONVENTION OF THE STATES

By 1 September Egbert Benson and Alexander Hamilton were in Newark on their way to Annapolis. After stopping in Philadelphia, they continued their journey and reached Annapolis on 8 September. On 3 September James Read, in Philadelphia, informed his brother George that he had tried, as requested, to obtain information about Pennsylvania's delegation. He had talked with Mrs. FitzSimons and learned that neither her husband nor Robert Morris would attend. Her belief that Coxe, Clymer, and Armstrong would be going to Annapolis was verified in the prints. Read also heard "in the coffee-house that there were two gentlemen from New Jersey, on their way," but he could not find out their names.[45] The Delaware delegates were also on their way to Annapolis. On 8 September Madison reported that upon his arrival he had "found two comsrs. only [probably from New Jersey]. A few more have since come in, but the prospects of a sufficient no. to make the meeting respectable is not flattering." Thomas Cushing and Francis Dana had apparently left Boston for Annapolis on the 21st, with Higginson and Gerry expected to follow. On 10 September, however, Cushing, Dana, and Samuel Breck wrote to Benson and Hamilton from New York City and requested them "to communicate to the Convention if it should be opened before we arrive, that we shall set off from this Place to morrow to join them." They also mentioned that the Rhode Island delegates "may be expected soon after us."[46]

Although the Massachusetts and Rhode Island delegates never completed their journeys, they might have believed that the convention would follow standard practice and wait for late arrivals, as Congress had to do to get a quorum and as the Philadelphia Convention later did, or simply disband. The delegates who did arrive in Annapolis did neither. On 9 September one of the delegates, probably Abraham Clark, reported that only New York, New Jersey, Delaware, and Virginia were in attendance. He noted that "we wait with impatience for the more distant states, as without a deputation from seven at least, it seems improper to enter on the main business." One writer feared that the delegates might not want to get on with the main business anyway. He cautioned them "not to exceed the bounds of their commissions, and not to inter-meddle into any thing that may, in the smallest degree, interfere with the rights of individual states; their business is to form such a code of commercial regulations as will prove beneficial to the United States."[47] The delegates believed otherwise.

The convention opened on 11 September and appointed Benson, Clark, Coxe, Read, and Randolph to prepare a report. Madison reported that unless other delegations arrived quickly "it is proposed to break up the Meeting, with a recommendation of another time & place, & an *intimation* of the expediency of extending the plan to other defects of the Confederation." Years later he revealed that this proposal came from Abraham Clark, whose state had instructed him to consider other problems and which still desired reformation of the Articles of Confederation. Three days later the delegates adopted an address and adjourned. The commissioners began their report by stating that the nonattendance of delegations from New Hampshire, Massachusetts, Rhode Island, and North Carolina had prevented them from carrying out their instructions "to take into consideration the trade and Commerce of the United States." The commissioners, though, submitted that New Jersey's notion "of extending the powers of their Deputies . . . was an improvement on the original plan, and will deserve to be incorporated into that of a future convention." They contended that as a power over commerce was so comprehensive that it would necessitate "a correspondent adjustment of other parts of the Foederal System," it was logical for the states to appoint delegates to meet at another convention to be held in Philadelphia "the second Monday in May next, to devise such further provisions as shall appear to them necessary to render the constitution of the Foederal Government adequate to the exigencies of the Union."[48]

Notwithstanding New Jersey's instructions, the Annapolis delegates did exceed their authority in calling another convention and some of them defended their behavior in strikingly similar ways. On 17 September Rufus King relayed the information that Egbert Benson and Alexander Hamilton had told him that the delegates had decided to call for a second convention because not enough states had sent delegations, because "the authorities of the Delegates assembled were so essentially different," and because Virginia's original proposition was "so far short of the Reform which is necessary." Tench Coxe gave the same accounting of the meeting in his report to Benjamin Franklin and the Pennsylvania Council. A few weeks later St. George Tucker admitted to Monroe that he and the other delegates had "certainly exceeded our powers in this address." Tucker, again blaming sparse attendance as the primary reason for the delegates' actions, pointed out that they had also wanted to prevent foreigners "from Recieving the same impression about the disjointed Counsels of the States as we ourselves felt." He reasoned that "it was better to do something extraneous, than to let it be discovered that the plan of the Convention had altogether miscarried." Tucker said that the commissioners had desperately tried to give their report "that consistency which it now appears to possess," but admitted that "perhaps the veil under which the Concealment is made is too thin to beguile even the common observor."[49]

Guillaume Otto was one observer who was not beguiled. He charged that the address was purposely obscure and filled with "circumlocutions and ambiguous phrases" in order to prove that commercial reformation could not be attempted "without at the same time touching upon further objects." Otto accused a class of men in America who were possessed of property, who were creditors, and who were fearful of the people, with moving the nation toward a new central government. He argued that "circumstances ruinous to the commerce of America" had furnished these men with the opportunity to chart a new course for the nation without issuing a call for "a new organization of the federal government" which would have raised too strong an opposition. Otto charged that they had not wanted the Annapolis Convention to accomplish its appointed task because it "was only intended to prepare a question much more important than that of commerce." This plan was so well managed, he argued, that the Massachusetts and Rhode Island delegates had "tarried several days in New York, in order to retard their arrival." Almost two years later Richard Henry Lee also charged that the idea of a convention was proposed at a time when the nation was desirous of some sort of constitutional reform. But because "the idea of destroying ultimately, the state governments, and forming one consolidated system, could not have been admitted," the Annapolis Convention was limited to commercial considerations. This prospect, "pleasing to the commercial towns" and of no concern to the landed people, allowed a meeting to take place at which "a few men from the middle states . . . hastily proposed a convention to be held in May."[50]

It is primarily charges like these which have shrouded the Annapolis Convention in an aura of conspiratorial mystery exaggerated by a paucity of contemporary correspondence. Various conclusions can be drawn from the information which does exist. There is no doubt that some persons saw the Annapolis Convention as the last hope to reform the Articles of Confederation. Despite the delegates' assertions to the contrary in the address and in their private correspondence, their instructions, with the exception of New Jersey's, were not materially different. Although they maintained that commercial reformation would necessitate a more fundamental readjustment of the Articles of Confederation, the New England federalists, who had led the mercantile reform movement, continued to support giving Congress only the power to regulate trade. Guillaume Otto's assertion that an interstate mercantile faction engineered the call to a general convention is incorrect insofar as he included the New England merchants. As late as August it was reported that all the Massachusetts delegates had again declined their appointments. When questioned by Washington, Henry Knox ascribed New England nonattendance at the Annapolis Convention to "torpidity in New Hampshire; faction, and heat about their paper money in Rhode Island; and jealousy in Connecticut." He also noted that the continuing unsettled situation in Massachusetts, the beginning of civil disturbance, prevented the delegates from arriving on time.[51]

Rather than remaining in New York as part of a plan, the Annapolis delegates might have been convinced by their colleagues in Congress not to take part in a convention which threatened to advance the nationalist cause. There is also a possibility that the Annapolis delegates believed that their not showing up would have kept the convention from obtaining a sufficient number of states to convene. Thomas Cushing, who opposed the Massachusetts mercantile faction, and Francis Dana were certainly not nationalists. Although they wrote to Hamilton and Benson requesting a delay, the reaction of some New Englanders to the call for a general convention evidences, at the least, a strong opposition to extracongressional reform. In October Rufus King, in an address to the Massachusetts House of Delegates, argued that the states had formed the Confederation and that a convention would be independent of and superior to them. He maintained that only Congress was "the proper body to propose alterations" in the Articles of Confederation. Less than a month later Nathan Dane echoed King in staunchly defending the Articles of Confederation and warned that "the first principles of government are to be touched with great care and attention."[52] Many New England delegates opposed referral of the Annapolis Convention's report to a congressional committee and continued thereafter to oppose extracongressional reform.[53]

The Annapolis Convention's call for a more comprehensive convention to reform the Articles of Confederation came at a critical and opportune moment. By the end of 1786 there was little doubt that the Confederation was in need of some sort of repair. When Thomas Jefferson learned of the Annapolis Convention's abortive meeting, he remarked that "if it should produce a full meeting in May and a broader reformation, it will still be well." The question was whether or not an independent convention was the proper means to reform the Confederation and how far that reform should go. Some men looked to a convention to which the state legislatures would appoint delegates; others wanted state conventions to appoint delegates to a sort of constitutional convention; others wanted the amendment process to remain in Congress; and still others opposed any extensive reformation of the Articles of Confederation.[54]

By early 1787 there were nationalists who had a clear notion of how to use an independent convention. Since 1783 they had been readjusting their ideological defense for the existence and necessity of a strong central government; the vissicitudes of the Union from 1785 to 1787 played right into their hands. The sectional statemate in Congress, the rift between New England and the South, the failure to reform the Articles of Confederation within Congress, the inability of federalists to mend fences and make the Confederation a more effective system—all reinforced increasingly sophisticated arguments about the basic and irreparable defects in the federal constitution.

9

A Hoop to the Barrel

DESPITE THE number and variety of issues which precipitated interstate and intersectional conflicts after 1783, the dispute between nationalists and federalists concerning the nature and role of central government remained an integral part of revolutionary politics. Nationalists continued to point out the dangers inherent in a governmental system which had power located in the extremities. They argued that without sufficient centralized power the United States would remain "a union without bonds of union, like a cask without hoops," forever battered by the unyielding "preference to local and inferior considerations."[1] Although their complaints and political theories remained basically unchanged, nationalists were unable to defend the need for centralized power with the same arguments they had used during the war. They needed a more sophisticated rationale to render Congress immune from a periodic rise and fall of authority which occurred in tune with the nation's vicissitudes. While agreeing that government had to "be watched over with a wakeful and distinguishing eye," critics of decentralized government were quick to point out that this was "far different from that excess of jealousy, which from a mistaken fear of abuse, withholds the necessary power." This question of necessity, of the critical importance of centralized authority, was one of the foundations upon which nationalist theorists based their postwar tactical shift.[2]

With this shift nationalists attempted to overcome the powerful objections to political centralism and to defuse the fear that excess was inherent in centralized power. They tried to show that there was far more to fear from the unavoidable consequences of a central government that was too weak and warned that America would one day face the "discord, confusion, and never ceasing wars, which has been the inevitable lot of separate Sovereignties and neighboring States." If conditions were allowed to so deteriorate, nationalists maintained, order would finally be restored by instituting measures "not only unconstitutional but repugnant to & destructive of the Principles of Political Freedom." Centralized authority was, then, held out as the only way to avoid that future crisis and the resultant destruction of republicanism. In answer to the stock federalist charge that central government and tyranny went hand-in-hand, John Dickinson asserted that only with the safeguard of a powerful central government could the Revolution be maintained and "liberty . . . thereby better secured."[3]

The concept of limited liberty, within the confines of the rule of law, was quite different from the obeisance to state sovereignty which nationalist malcontents said "threw the whole power in the hands of the people" in 1776 and left human frailty and selfishness "to act with a force, but feebly restrained by the weak barrier of a nominal *union*." They believed that limiting Congress's power not only increased the likelihood of interstate conflicts, but also left nothing to guard against the people, who were "not able to govern themselves," confusing "Liberty and licentiousness."[4] One way to remedy the states' inability to "secure the life, liberty and property of individuals against the lawless invasions of private incendiaries" was to create "a constitution, whereby the whole nation may be united in one government." Some nationalists did support a unitary central government, a very radical departure from the Confederation's "combined sovereignty," for it, more than any other alternative, promised the ultimate in control and security.[5]

Other nationalists realized that it was doubtful whether they would be able to promote such drastic change. Rather than testing a basic tenet of revolutionary ideology, essentially eradicating state governments, they had another notion of how to structure a central government. Whereas the states reluctantly and jealously doled out insufficient powers to Congress because of the fear of abuse, giving greater powers to a central government instituted to stabilize society could be more easily defended. In 1785 Noah Webster struck a neat compromise between unitary central government and federation which promised the utmost in effectiveness, while remaining within the broad outlines of revolutionary ideology. He asserted that as towns and cities were in general matters "mere subjects of the State . . . [so] let the several states, as to their own police, be sovereign and independent, but as to the common concerns of all, let them be mere subjects of the federal head." In defense, he continued to hammer home the by now familiar argument that in a government formed by the people "tyranny can never be established," but in a nation without centralized authority "such power will inevitably create itself."[6]

Implicit in this apology for centralized power, which required further development, was the idea of a central government which, like the state governments, derived its authority from the consent of the people. At various times nationalists had defended their reforms by appealing to the people as "the sovereign as well as the subject" with a nascent understanding that one way to circumvent the states in reforming the federal constitution was to partake of the sovereign power of the people. A few thinkers realized the tactical advantage, and even necessity, of integrating the drive for constitutional reform at the federal level with the standard revolutionary concept that "all power is derived from the people at Large."[7] With this as a theoretical base it seemed logical to assume that a popularly established central government could be defended as being no more dangerous than the state governments. Even within the existing political system some scribes declared Congress to be "a deliberative assembly of *one Nation*" responsible to and, in fact, "the same Body as the People." The idea of popular sovereignty was to provide the reason and justification for the establishment of a national government which was considerably more powerful than anything which could have been established earlier and certainly more powerful, in terms of its effect on the people, than even Parliament had been. The people still had every reason to be jealous of their liberty, but in portraying central government as the protector and direct agent of the people, nationalists were on much safer ground by 1786 and 1787 than they had been in 1780 in distinguishing "between manly jealousy and mean suspicion."[8]

The restructuring of the Confederation in 1787 was not the result of a slow acceptance of nationalism's new concepts. Many of its leading proponents had, themselves, always realized that theory without empirical support was incapable of evoking change; that "necessity alone can work a reform." This was even truer in peacetime in a "Democratical" nation whose leaders "must always *feel* before they can *see*."[9] Nevertheless, men like Robert Morris, James Mercer, and Gouverneur Morris were certain that the Confederation's defects would inevitably lead to a "Sense of Want" which would "stimulate the States . . . [to construct] a good American Establishment," that those men "among the *more elevated Ranks* [who loved] . . ."peace quiet Establishments and permanent security" would one day see the error of "trusting Power to improper Hands."[10]

The states' apparent lack of concern with the welfare of the Union, demonstrated at times by Congress's inability to secure a consistent quorum, seemed by 1785 and 1786 to portend the "severe sufferings and sad experience" needed to stimulate reform.[11] For some, the choice which nationalists wanted the political leaders to make—between preventative reforms to limit state sovereignty, or "the dissolution of our Political Union"—was already at hand. But the progression from difficulties to reforms was not that simple or direct.[12] Although conflicting state and especially sectional interests weakened the Confederation and reinforced nationalist views, they also remained powerful obstacles to reform. Nationalists had been quite correct in 1783 in predicting that peace, the removal of an external threat, would wither the bonds of union.

The inability of the states and sections to agree on commercial reform, western land policy, or a location for the capital demonstrated the destructive effects on the Union of the states' apparently uncontrollable "Interests or Passions." Congress, which some men freely ridiculed as a "company of old Indian Sachems (who have no real authority)," had become little more than a battlefield. But the nation's very real problems did not seem able to stimulate remedial action or force interest to give way to necessity. It appeared that something more was needed to overcome the pull of special interests and break down the non-ideological barriers to reform. It is important to remember that ideological conflict had very little to do with the Confederation's growing weakness. Federalists did not uniformly and dogmatically oppose specific revisions in the Articles of Confederation—they merely opposed wholesale restructuring of the Confederation. Although federalists and nationalists disagreed violently on the sorts of measures needed to stabilize the nation, very few politicians believed that action was not needed. Some men, and not only nationalists, waited impatiently for "some imminent danger pressing hard upon us, to make us feel our need of union." As Gideon punished the men of Succoth for failing to aid him in fighting the Midinianites, so Jeremy Belknap believed that "we must strove to our duty, and be taught by the briars and thorns, as Gideon taught the men of Succoth."[13] The question was, once taught, how far the reformers would go in revising the Articles of Confederation.

In 1786 Daniel Shays played the part of Gideon, as Massachusetts and much of the nation was rocked by an outbreak of civil disturbances, by the "intoxicating Draughts of Liberty run mad." Rumors about plans "to Annihilate Govts." and "all debts" and even to have "a new division of property" scared political leaders throughout the nation.[14] The feared "levelling principle," intended to give the people a voice in the political process and a share of the economic benefits of society, seemed to reach epidemic proportions in an already dispirited nation aflame with "a Rage for paper Money." There was a convention movement in New Hampshire, a popular uprising in Connecticut, reports of insurgency in Vermont, and debtor rioting in Maryland.[15] The dissidents in Rhode Island even gained control of the government. Almost immediately after taking office they passed debtor-relief legislation which helped spread the alarm about "the Political Storm" in that state.[16]

The civil disturbances were the Confederation's and federalism's supreme test; the proof, as it were, of repeated warnings that without strong central government there was no real "security against the most extensive of all EVILS, anarchy" and "rather worse than anarchy . . . a pure democracy."[17] Federalists took it for a political maxim that civil liberty was not a by-product of, or dependent upon, a government of laws (as nationalists believed), "but a power existing in the people at large, at any time, for any cause, or for no cause, but their own sovereign pleasure, to alter or annihilate both the mode and essence of any former government, and adopt a new one in its stead." In 1778 they relied "upon the Principles and manner of the People" to maintain order and in 1785 still rebuked the notion that "our happiness depends more on the form of a union than in frugality, the love of your country, and attention to the social virtues." It was this dependence for structure and stability upon self-restraint instead of authority which nationalists critiqued after 1783. Their advantage ultimately lay in the fact that many federalists, their revolutionary ideals notwithstanding, had their own interests to protect. Even Richard Henry Lee, who in less than two years was leading the fight against ratification of a new constitution, admitted that "Publick Liberty" and "*popular government*" could not be maintained "without *virtue* in the people."[18]

Despite federalism's identification with republicanism and federation, it was not democracy, and its leaders were by no means of the people. Men like Elbridge Gerry, Richard Henry Lee, Alexander Hamilton, and James Madison had far more in common with each other than with rebellious debtor farmers in western Massachusetts. There was a line which federalists would and could not cross, and the civil disturbances forced many of them to make a hard choice. Federalism, erected on a basic assumption about and belief in the people, was unable to withstand the crushing reality of social upheaval. Even after the initial crisis passed federalism was unable to regain its earlier strength in combating nationalism. The civil disturbances, which for a time had every appearance of being systemic, forced political leaders, with federalists prominent among them, to choose between their previously untested ideals and political stability. Many of them, concerned about their position in society, were driven to the conclusion that in 1776 they had foolishly sacrificed "National Faith & National Honour to an overstrained Zeal for Liberty & Love of the People."[19]

Some cynics were dubious about the origins of the unrest and pointed an accusing finger at the supporters of a "special Convention." Although the charge of conspiracy is impossible to document, it is certain that some politicians welcomed the stimulus to political change. Stephen Higginson, whose politics had changed since 1783, looked forward to the Philadelphia Convention and wrote from Massachusetts that "by next Summer we shall be here prepared for any thing that is wise and fitting."[20] For a time, vestigial federalist paranoia had little effect on men looking for "almost any change that may promise them quiet and security." Even some "old Whigs" reportedly wanted "a general government of unity . . . as they consider these seperate Sovereignties as insupportable and quite incompatible with a general government."[21] Increased support for rule by "the few" for "government high handed and efficient to one of laxity and anarchy"; infatuation with the idea of a monarchy "in some leading minds"; and renewed interest in the Society of the Cincinnati evidenced the anxiety produced by the disturbances and reflected a quite pervasive desire for order.[22]

The pressure for political change was great and the fear was real, and in many cases lingered, but the civil disturbances and the reaction to them did not make up the whole of the quickly changing preconvention political scene. Little more than two months after the Mississippi conflict, William Grayson conjectured that the New England states would doubtless relax their pro-occlusion stance in order to direct their own and Congress's energies to meeting the crisis in the states. His analysis might have been valid within the unsettled context of late 1786; by early 1787, however, the disturbances no longer inspired the dread that they had a few months earlier. "The fire" which Stephen Higginson and others hoped would lead to constitutional reform began to dampen. He advised Henry Knox to build support for the Philadelphia Convention and "an efficient General Government" by drawing "strong Arguments from the insurrection in this State [Massachusetts]." Knox admitted the logic of this approach, but he was having difficulty in convincing leaders who were beginning to "speak of the disorder of Massachusetts as produced by local causes." If Massachusetts's experience could no longer be generalized, if the nation was not faced with imminent destruction, then the old conflicts and differences could continue to impede the chances for constitutional reform. By early February Shays's Rebellion was over, the disturbances in the other states had either not reached a comparable level or had also been controlled, and a fear of "the growing power of Congress" was still very much in evidence.[23]

Federalist ideology, stabilizing after the immediate shock of the disturbances, doubtless accounted for much of that fear. The question of sectional equilibrium in Congress and the continuing effects of sectional conflict are, however, equally important in explaining especially New England's reluctance in early 1787 to support or attend a general convention or to tamper with the Articles of Confederation. Despite the questions which had been raised about the Confederation, there was, by early 1787, certainly less need for strong central government to assist the states in quelling internal uprisings. Moreover, many New Englanders still worried about the possibility that southerners and middle states nationalists might conspire in a convention to their disadvantage. While New England was dragging its feet, with men like Rufus King and Nathan Dane arguing against extracongressional reform, the sectional alignment in Congress shifted and intensified the now isolated New Englanders' concerns about nationalists, southerners, and an independent general convention.

OBSTACLES TO REFORM

The southern states were only slightly more internally stable than the northern states in 1786 and 1787. Even before the disturbances in New England, South Carolina was rocked by similar forces. In mid-1785 the underrepresented westerners acted out their frustrations. There were riots in Camden, exclamations that "THE EMPIRE OF LAWS IS SUBVERTED," and reports about "Anarchy at present prevailing in the State." Many South Carolina leaders had as little assurance as the northerners that they would be able to continue to use state authority to contain political dissidence.[24] Although most of the other southern states were relatively free of that sort of debtor unrest, they did have similar societal imbalances and a real potential for trouble. Henry Lee thus anxiously reported that Shays's Rebellion "portend[ed] extensive national calamity—the contagion will spread and may reach Virginia." It did, but from a different source. By December 1786 George Washington predicted that Virginia's stability could "give energy to the foederal System . . . if the unlucky stirring of the dispute respecting the navigation of the Mississippi does not become a leaven that will ferment and sour the mind of it."[25]

The political fallout from the Mississippi conflict did not end with the tabling of the amendment proposals in August 1786. After he returned from the Annapolis Convention to an angry Virginia, Madison was more concerned than ever that the triumph of "temporary and partial interests" would decrease Congress's prestige and "interfere with the policy of amending the Confederacy." By the end of the year Patrick Henry, "hitherto the Champion of the federal cause," was said to oppose constitutional reform because of the "sacrifice of the Mississippi." He even refused to go to Philadelphia because of his violent opposition to occlusion.[26] More serious problems than one man's defection also arose. The threat of a backcountry mobilizaton and its probable effects on internal harmony and the strengthening of the Confederation, which had so scared southern nationalists in 1786, seemed to be becoming a reality. There were disturbances in Northumberland County in Pennsylvania and in the Wyoming territory, and there was a revolt in western North Carolina.[27]

In early 1787 there were pronouncements from Pittsburgh, Kentucky, and western North Carolina that closure of the Mississippi River would "be the Means of a Revolution and a separation," that the people would "look upon themselves released from all federal obligations"[28] Grayson and Madison even saw a pattern—a relationship between the disturbances in the northern backcountry and the separation movement in the southern. They believed that Great Britain and Vermont were instigating the troubles in order to carve a new nation out of the western territories. Rather than submit to a domination by the older states, the westerners were reportedly thinking of aligning with the British. Until a short time before the Philadelphia Convention met there was still some concern that closure of the Mississippi would precipitate a western revolt.[29]

While separation was not a new threat, it had a similar effect on many southern leaders as the debtor rioting did on northern leaders, but with a marked difference. It made strong central government more attractive, but it also reconfirmed southern antagonism toward the northerners. Many southerners believed, if for no other reason than to mollify the westerners, that they had to rescind John Jay's Mississippi instructions. They could not accomplish this without New Jersey and Pennsylvania. By the end of 1786 southern efforts paid off as New Jersey, concerned about losing benefits in the federal domain, instructed its delegates to uphold America's right to the free navigation of the Mississippi River.[30]

After Robert Morris and the Republicans swept to power, Pennsylvania became interested in reversing its stance. In February 1787 North Carolina joined New Jersey and Virginia in passing antiocclusion instructions. There was even a possibility that Rhode Island would join the antiocclusion movement. Rhode Island, evidencing the same concerns it had had when opposing passage of the first impost, was, with New Jersey, worried that occlusion would hurt it as a landless commerce-dependent state. James Madison optimistically reported that Rhode Island "begins to see the policy of some States in her neighborhood in excluding the federal territory from the Market at which they offer their own [lands]. N. Jersey has entered fully into this view of the matter, and feel no small indignation at it." While Massachusetts and New York had sectional reasons for promoting occlusion, they also had land claims which would have leaped in value if the Mississippi were closed.[31]

Southern resentments, especially against New York and Massachusetts, led to another development which confirmed the sectional realignment in Congress and underscored the new cooperation between the middle states, nationalists, and many southern delegates. Although it has been ignored in terms of preconvention politics, an attempt to return Congress to Philadelphia put New England on the defensive and more than balanced the anxiety-generated procentralism reaction which had resulted from the civil disturbances. While there had been little choice in 1784, according to James Madison a New York residence had "been for a considerable time a thorn in the middle of many of the southern members." He was certain, though, that the New England delegates would never agree to a change "whilst they remain so much gratified in its temporary residence." But by early 1787 the southern states could count on middle state support. Moreover, they had a new score to settle which bound them together. William Blount thus informed his brother that having sold their tobacco he was going to remain in New York to await an expected vote on the residence—"to do this Act I owe myself, the Yankees and the State of New York." His reason for wanting to get Congress to Philadelphia was to "thereby pay Sundry Stat[es] their Incivility which lay east of the North."[32]

In early February Nathaniel Mitchell, trying to speed Delaware's arrival in Congress because the South Carolina delegation's term was expiring, told Governor Collins that the southern states were "ripe for a removal of Congress to Philadelphia . . . the first time they all agreed upon this subject since their coming to New-York." The same day he informed Gunning Bedford, one of the Delaware delegates, that the matter could easily be settled in "one or two days" and assured Bedford that he would "be received with open Arms by all the Southern States."[33] The New England delegates hoped to avoid a confrontation by having Congress adjourn immediately after sanctioning the Philadelphia Convention. The pro-Philadelphia forces, predominantly southern and confident of victory, wanted to push the matter. They believed, and not without some justification, that New York's refusal to pass the impost did not recommend it as a worthwhile site for Congress.[34]

The only thing that stood in the way of a removal was the absence of a delegation from either Delaware or Maryland. Although nothing had happened by March, a southern victory seemed likely. Arthur St. Clair, for example, was so confident of a removal that he began to inquire about securing temporary lodgings in Philadelphia. Other Pennslyvanians were just as confident.[35] But enmity alone could not carry the day. By the end of the month the imminent departure from Congress of William Bingham and William Irvine of Pennsylvania, the expiration of South Carolina's appointment, the continued absence of a Maryland delegation, and the expected adjournment of Congress made a removal increasingly doubtful.[36]

As the time for adjournment drew closer the southerners had no choice but to make the attempt. On 10 April Dyre Kearney of Delaware and William Blount of North Carolina finally moved for adjournment to Philadelphia. James Varnum's motion to substitute Newport for Philadelphia was overwhelmingly defeated. Another inconclusive vote for adjournment to an unnamed city preceded a vote on whether or not to retain Philadelphia in the original motion for adjournment. Surprisingly, the Rhode Island delegates, who might very well have been acting out of opposition to occlusion, voted to let Philadelphia stand. Congress then adjourned for the day, with this test vote apparently foreshadowing a Philadelphia removal the following day. Rufus King, however, who told Elbridge Gerry of the appearance of the "injurious influence of 1783," and the other Massachusetts delegates, according to Madison, prevailed upon Peleg Arnold to change his vote.[37] The motion was thus defeated by the barest of margins. The closeness of the vote, in fact the defeat of the proposal "by half a vote," suggested that Congress might still return to Philadelphia.[38]

While the attempt to remove Congress was taking place, the southern delegates had been anxious to get John Jay to report to Congress concerning his negotiations with Gardoqui. In early March it appeared that they would be unable to secure Jay's appearance, because they couldn't "*risk a refusal* and they cannot resort to the present thin Congress with any hope of success." James Madison, determined to get the facts, took it upon himself to visit Gardoqui. He discovered that the negotiations were closed, however, and was extremely angry that a member of Congress had to learn the information from a foreign minister. The arrival of the Delaware delegation and the support of New Jersey and Pennsylvania soon made it possible to call Jay to account. On 4 April Congress ordered him to provide it with information concerning "the State of his Negotiations." Jay reported two days after the defeated motion for a Philadelphia removal. Although Jay had already decided not to proceed with what would have been pointless negotiations, the news that he had agreed to America's forebearance of the right to navigate the Mississippi inflamed southern resentments.[39]

Although there was no longer a real threat of occlusion in a Spanish treaty, sectional conflict remained heated. On 10 May Kearney and Samuel Meredith of Pennsylvania again moved for a removal of Congress. After a series of conflicting motions removal was narrowly defeated. John Jay, for one, was still very worried about the "party" which supported removal and which did not contain a "single Member from either of the eastern States." New England and New York's narrow escape hardly reflected an ease in sectional tension. The following day the southerners attempted to formally rescind Jay's Mississippi instructions.[40] While sectionalism was shaping politics in Congress, however, the stage was being set for political change outside of Congress.

IMPETUS FOR CHANGE

By early 1787 there was a growing belief that there might finally be the establishment of a strong central government in the independent convention which some nationalists had long advocated.[41] Yet there was still considerable opposition to giving up "the smallest attribute of independent [state] Sovereignty." While establishing more governmental controls was one way to deal with uncooperative states and a troublesome populace, there was a contrary view that this might result in even more serious upheavals, because the people "are an ass that will not travel with a greater load than what he is pleased himself to take up."[42] In addition to uncertainties about the kind and degree of reforms needed, it was unclear whether an independent convention could assume Congress's right to propose changes in the Articles of Confederation. Madison noted that some political leaders opposed the convention as "an extra constitutional measure, and that their objections would be removed or lessened by a sanction from Cong's. to it." On 20 February the New York delegation, acting on its legislature's instructions, introduced a resolution calling for such a sanction. The following day the proposal carried, but over the objections of the New England delegates, who, reportedly, only voted for it when "they saw it would be carried without them."[43]

The New Englanders' trepidation was so great that it appeared that "the Convention will be but partial in point of representation," that the New England states would stay away from it like they had stayed away from the Annapolis Convention. In early January Rufus King alluded to the appointment of "Mifflin, the two Morris', Fitzsimmons," in much the same way that Stephen Higginson had referred to the appointment of "aristocrats" to the Annapolis Convention. Yet King had learned a lesson and realized that it was very likely more dangerous not to attend the convention. He warned that "the times are becoming critical" and that "a movement of this nature ought to be carefully observed by every member of the community." He was determined not to let nationalists and southerners conspire and scheme among themselves. Shortly before Congress took the convention proposal under consideration, King admitted that the appointment of numerous and enlightened men was necessary to "establish a more permanent and vigorous government." Noting that Pennsylvania and New Jersey were now under "a southern influence" and that all the states south of New York had already appointed delegates, however, King agreed "to the measure from an Idea of Prudence, or for the purpose of watching, than from any expectation that much Good will flow from it." It was, then, to New England's advantage to oppose congressional sanction and prevent the convention from having too much power and thereby block anything being done in the convention detrimental to New England's interests. Despite King's well-conceived rationale vis-à-vis the convention, it was still questionable in March whether or not the New England states would all attend.[44]

Because of the powerful ideological and even more forceful sectional barriers to major revision of the Articles of Confederation, it is quite possible that nothing of consequence would have happened in Philadelphia had not many New Englanders' (and probably most federalists') continued faith in the Articles of Confederation, and their ability to maintain control in the states, been shattered when a final chapter of Shays's Rebellion was written in the Massachusetts state election in the late spring of 1787. By early March 1787 Stephen Higginson realized that Shays's Rebellion no longer excited the fears it had earlier. But he was still certain that "National Government must arise out of necessity alone, and be the effect of confusion," and intended to "give way to dire necessity, and with vigilance turn every event to a good purpose." Washington agreed that the nation "had yet to *feel* and *see* a little more before it [reformation] can be accomplished."[45] The nation did soon see and feel when in the largest voter turnout of the 1780s a reform faction headed by John Hancock swept into power in Massachusetts. The governing elite was finally being called to account. In a typical preelection diatribe "BRUTUS" warned against an alliance of the military and monied interests in Massachusetts and equated a vote for Hancock with a vote against the rich. In early 1787, having controlled a popular uprising and faced with a new sectional threat, most Massachusetts politicians had more to lose than to gain from a convention. In addition to distrusting nationalists and southerners, they had every reason to believe that state governments, and theirs in particular, were secure enough to handle civil unrest. Defeat at the polls destroyed their confidence.[46]

Citizens in and out of Massachusetts expected that because this "Revolution" changed the administration that "Measures will be changed also so far as to accord with the Vox Populia." There were reports that "the insurgents of Massachusetts had got full posssession of the government constitutionally; they talk of a depreciating paper and other villainous acts."[47] There were other signs that the various popular movements had not peaked. Rhode Island continued to be a thorn in the nation's side. The dreaded paper money party's refusal to attend the Philadelphia Convention led some observers to exclaim that "the current Madness in that State has not yet completed its course," and others to suggest that Rhode Island be "dropped out of the union, or apportioned to different states."[48]

There was also the continued danger of pockets of more violent resistance. In March Governor Bowdoin had requested federal assistance to prevent any Massachusetts insurgents from spreading to neighboring states. By May new disturbances in Sharon, Connecticut, allegedly instigated by Shaysites, suggested that the dissidents did not only intend to press their demands within the political process.[49] The Massachusetts state election, the continuing effects of political dissidence in Rhode Island, and the threat of new uprisings combined to show many New Englanders, among them some previously strong defenders of the Articles of Confederation, that something had to be done, that their control of state governments was not strong enough to protect them from the people. In early May Bowdoin, fearing a new reign of terror in Massachusetts, suggested that "the preventing of insurrections would be a proper subject for the consideration of the federal Convention." Henry Knox, trying to get New Hampshire's delegation to leave for Philadelphia, told James Sullivan that the convention was "the only means of avoiding the most flagitious evils that ever afflicted three millions of freemen." In January he had had difficulty in equating Massachusetts's experience with the situation in other states; he had a much more receptive audience by May.[50]

William Grayson, who was as wary of their designs as the New Englanders were of the southerners', even asserted that some easterners were "for placing Congress *in loco* of the King of G.B." He accused them of wanting a central government composed of an upper and a lower house and an executive in order "to prostrate all the state legislatures."[51] Some New Englanders did have this radical a change in mind. One frustrated politico remarked that if a loss of property and the destruction of society were "the Effects of Popular Government grant me a Monarchal One." Indeed, the threat of social revolution was the driving force behind the writing of a new federal constitution in Philadelphia. Elbridge Gerry, a committed federalist and later an opponent of the Constitution, went to Philadelphia convinced that "unless a system of government is adopted by compact, force, I expect will plant the standard; for such an anarchy as now exists cannot long last." This feeling was not confined to New England. George Mason, also a future opponent of the Constitution who was certain that the republicans now came from "the southern & Middle States, & the Anti-Republicans from the Eastern," wrote that "the expectations and hopes of all the union centre in this convention. God grant that we mat be able to concert effectual means of preserving our country from the evils which threaten us." It appeared, even more so than in 1786, that if the Articles of Confederation were not reformed in time that the lack of centralized authority would inevitably lead to "despotism, arbitrary monarchy, aristocracy, or what is still worse, an oligarchy." Most politicians knew their history well enough to assume that the United States would surely duplicate the experience of other nations which had been confronted with a similar breakdown of order.[52]

TOWARD A NATIONAL GOVERNMENT

The convention seemed to be the only means at hand "to remove the defects of the Confederation, produce a vigorous and energetic continental government, which will crush and destroy faction, subdue insurrections, revive the public and private credit, disappoint our transatlantic enemies and their lurking Emissaries among us, and finally (to use an Indian Phrase) endure 'while the sun shines, and the river flow.' " The unstable situation in many of the states satisfactorily demonstrated to some that "the Political existence of the United States, perhaps depends on the results of the deliberations of the Convention which is to meet at Philadelphia next month, for the purpose of forming a national government."[53] But the Philadelphia Convention was not designed to form a national government. In fact, although many nationalists were pleased that Congress had legitimatized the convention in February, some were concerned that Congress had expressly sanctioned the convention for the purpose of proposing changes in the Articles of Confederation.[54] They wanted to use the convention as a means to scrap the Articles and "consolidate the Several Governments into one general and efficient," or, at the least, to "arm the federal head with a negative *in all cases whatsoever* on the local legislatures." George Washington did not want the delegates to go to the convention "under fetters" and to adopt "temporizing expedients, but [to] probe the defects of the Constitution to the bottom, and provide radical cures; whether they are agreed to or not."[55]

James Madison was equally clear about the proper actions for the convention. He thought it would be better "to work the valuable articles [of the Articles of Confederation] into the new System, instead of engrafting the latter on the former." Rather than going as far as some other nationalists in advocating a unitary national government, Madison said that he sought "the middle ground, which may at once support a due supremacy of the national authority, and not exclude the local authorities wherever they can be subordinately used." The goal was the same. The central government was, in either case, to be supreme.[56]

The dilemma was how to overcome the states in constructing a political system which restricted their sovereignty. John Jay declared that if "it is intended that this convention shall not ordain but only recommend; if so there is danger that their recommendations will produce endless discussion, perhaps jealousies and party heats." He suggested that instead of calling a convention to point out defects or to propose changes in the Articles of Confederation, Congress ought to declare that "the present Federal Government is inadequate" and call for "state conventions . . . with the sole and express power of appointing deputies to a general convention." Jay wanted no alteration of the Constitution attempted, and believed that none would be worth the effort, "unless deducible from the only source of just authority—the People." Jay, like many nationalists, was worried that the convention, as empowered, would only "tend to approximate the public Mind to the changes which ought to take place."[57]

Although Jay and other nationalists knew what they wanted a convention to do, few men believed that the Philadelphia Convention could circumvent the states, or that it had the power to establish a supreme government. Henry Knox, for instance, suggested that the convention, once assembled, should "request that State Conventions might be assembled for the sole purpose of chusing delegates to a continental convention in order to consider and decide upon a general government." This would, he thought, "to all intents and purposes, be a government derived from the people, and assented to them as much as they assented to the confederation." While either Jay's or Knox's proposal would have forced the nation to decide whether or not to write a totally new constitution, there was a risk that if Congress and the states were presented with a choice, a constitutional convention might not be accepted.[58]

Stephen Higginson's concern about state interference in the reform process drove him to another conclusion. He believed that man's natural jealousy of those in power, who attempted to extend their powers, would raise insurmountable objections to any reform attempted by Congress and even obviated making the attempt. For this reason he supported "a special Convention," but he did not want to approach Congress or the states after having gotten the opportunity to use one. Instead of concentrating on the calling of another convention to write a new constitution, Higginson looked to a popular ratification to insure the new government's sovereignty. He proposed "to have Special Conventions appointed" in the states which would vote on the Philadelphia Convention's report: "if nine of those State Conventions shall report in favor of the system, Congress shall be authorized thereupon, to declare it to be the federal Constitution of Government, and the States shall be compellable to conform to and govern themselves by it." Madison totally agreed that a new constitution had to be ratified "by the people themselves in the several States [in order to] render it clearly paramount in their Legislative authorities." While the people in the states were to have the power to uphold or reject whatever proposals came out of Philadelphia, Congress and the state governments were effectively to be bypassed.[59]

For most politicians the Philadelphia Convention was only a method to propose changes in the Articles of Confederation. It was, in this regard, no different from the many other proposals for a convention of the states during the revolutionary era. It is partly for this reason that the preconvention atmosphere was remarkably devoid of the sort of visceral ideological conflict which had, for example, characterized the impost fight. The lack of intense ideological conflict did not necessarily reflect support for the convening of a constitutional convention or the establishment of a national government. It simply attested to the acceptance of a convention as an alternative to the amendment process of the Articles of Confederation. Moreover, the expectation that Congress would retain its authority, that the Articles of Confederation would remain in operation, that the Philadelphia delegates were bound by sufficiently clear instructions, can also help explain the relative lack of controversy.[60] There was also a realization among many politicians that some reforms were needed. The contrast between 1787 and 1783, when federalists prevented a heavy-handed attempt to restructure the Confederation, is indicative of the changes in the political climate.

Still, the fairly impressive reasons supporting constitutional reforms, of one sort or another, cannot be taken as a whole to demonstrate a wide-ranging support for nationalism. Temperate and measured reform of the Confederation was quite different from a nationalist blueprint for change. For this and other reasons the convention was hardly assured of success. Some viewed it as "a very doubtful Measure at best" which would, in the end, be immobilized by the same irreconcilable differences which had plagued the nation and which had ended any hope for reform within Congress. Conflicting ideologies and antithetical state and sectional interests portended sparse attendance, deadlock, and even early dissolution. There was still good reason to believe that the nation's "distresses are not sufficiently great to produce decisive alterations."[61]

Despite the potential for conflict rather than cooperation and inaction rather than reform, there was a major difference between May 1787 and August 1786. While solutions to the nation's problems may still have been in doubt and while many divergent interests still had a lot at stake, conditions in the nation at least insured that the convention would meet. Samuel Holden Parsons was not alone in realizing that the extraordinary pressures in 1787 were similar to those forces which had produced a union in 1776 and reforms in 1781. He was certain that "no future Convention can be in circumstances to devise or effect the necessary reforms so effectually as the present."[62] Nationalists were not about to let this, probably their last, opportunity slip away. While most delegates went to Philadelphia expecting to hash out solutions to the problems of the Articles of Confederation, a number of influential leaders went with the express purpose of writing a new constitution.

Epilogue

THE ESTABLISHMENT of a national government in 1788, like the creation of a union and the formulation of the Articles of Confederation, reflected the inhibiting effects of centralizing pressures. Throughout the revolutionary era fluctuating centrifugal and centripetal forces altered the locus of political power, but without ever squelching fundamental differences between sections.

As we have seen above, from 1776 to 1778 the pressing need to present a common and united front to the British muted the divisiveness of basic ideological and sectional differences. Even so the debate over the Articles of Confederation and other clashes evidenced the strength of sectional commitments. Heavy military pressure on the southern states by 1779 simply exaggerated the deep-seated intersectional mistrust which debilitated the Lee-Adams junto. The middle state nationalists used the same war-induced anxiety which necessitated the establishment of a union in their efforts to strengthen Congress. In 1781 they made major modifications in Congress's authority and laid the groundwork for further amplifications.

Southern support for nationalist policies was more indicative of the effect of the war on politics than of a commonality of interests. Nationalists like James Madison and Joseph Jones distrusted northern designs at the very time they were trying to strengthen Congress. Although not all southerners were drawn to nationalism because of specific pressures, when the war drew to a close nationalist strength began to decay. By mid-1783 a southern shift to New England sparked a federalist resurgence. Despite such successes for the revitalized Lee-Adams junto as crippling Robert Morris, establishing a Board of Treasury, delaying passage of the impost, attacking the Society of the Cincinnati, breaking the French and middle state merchants' grip on the economy, and keeping Congress out of Philadelphia, their coalition was

165

flawed by the same unresolved sectional conflict which had been their undoing in 1779.

Before long federalist lines broke in the face of a series of increasingly violent and connected sectional clashes. From 1784 through 1787 the struggle over such issues as the location of a capital, commercial reform, federal revenue, western lands, and the Mississippi navigation widened the breach between the sections to such a degree that it impaired Congress's effectiveness and raised serious questions about the viability of the Confederation. By the time the Philadelphia Convention met, a crisis of authority within the states and the inability of Congress to solve the nation's problems created a political climate favorable to constitutional reform.

Several states, however, had qualms about changes in the Articles of Confederation which would result in supreme central government. Although the New York delegates moved for the congressional sanction which probably helped insure that the Philadelphia Convention would convene, New York was not pronationalist. The resolution to sanction the convention resulted more from the politicking of anti-Clintonians than from a state commitment to constitutional reform. New York's Clintonian principles of "a state impost, no direct taxation," and opposition to any federal reforms which "may destroy our own influence and cast a shade over that plentitude of power which we now enjoy" were very evident in the appointment of delegates to the Philadelphia Convention. Some even felt that the appointment of Abraham Yates and John Lansing, Jr. was designed to control Alexander Hamilton and "to impede any measures that might be proposed." Hamilton meanwhile tried unsuccessfully to secure the appointment of two additional delegates from among the nationalists Egbert Benson, James Duane, John Jay, and Robert R. Livingston.[1]

Other federalists were just as wary of a general convention. Indeed, some of the doubts about reforms being decided upon either in or out of a convention stemmed from the belief that "the present popular opinion is that we should be very jealous of conferring power on any man or body of men." Richard Henry Lee, concerned about the direction proreform sentiments might take, reminded George Mason that when the Articles of Confederation were first submitted to the states there were complaints "of the too great, not the defective powers of Congress." Although most federalists supported reformation of the Articles of Confederation by May 1787, they were still unwilling to cross the line which led to supreme central government. They recognized an implicit danger that "from the unexpected evils we had experienced from the democratic principles of our government, we should be apt to turn to opposite extremes . . . in endeavouring to steer too far from Schylla, we might be drawn into the vortex of Charybdis."[2]

These sorts of ideological concerns were more than balanced by some very serious sectional questions. Issues like commerce, revenue, and the slave trade were just as important to some as constitutional change.[3] Sectionalism's influence went far beyond specific demands and concerns. James Madison was very surprised that support for disunion "after long confinement to individual speculations & private circles, is beginning to shew itself in the Newspapers." One writer suggested that the nation would be better off if the delegates "distribute[d] the States into three Republics," rather than trying to amend the unworkable Articles of Confederation or erecting "one general government." There were even rumors that if the convention were able to accomplish anything that two, three, or even four confederacies would and should be established. The continued interest in disunion reflected a belief that sectional splits in the nation were simply too ingrained to be erased permanently, that a political arrangement which corresponded to the nation's natural and unavoidable sectional limits could more effectively and realistically deal with sectionalism than strained compromises designed to perpetuate an unnatural organization. Many of the old sectionally charged issues were rehashed in the convention as the delegates fought over the problems of commerce, representation, and revenue.[4]

The delegates at Philadelphia, however, had special concerns which were, in the end, more powerful than their sectional interests. The need to centralize government in order to stabilize control over the states and the people took precedence over their separate interests. Despite their economic, sectional, and ideological differences the men we call our Founding Fathers, the men who made the Revolution, sat in Congress, and wrote two federal constitutions, had one thing in common—they were leaders. Whether because of wealth, education, achievement, or social position, they were different from the majority of those who peopled the United States. That we know who they were and what they did separates them from their now nameless countrymen.

Although the decision to abandon the Articles of Confederation in June 1787 and the subsequent transformation of the Philadelphia Convention into a constitutional convention were high-handed and without precedent, the important point is that those actions were eminently defensible. The relatively easy change in the convention's focus and then, against what in early 1787 would have seemed insurmountable odds, ratification of a new constitution did not demonstrate the existence of a major ideological consensus. They cannot even be used as proof that most politicians had ceased to support the Confederation.

The formulation of a new constitution reflected not so much an overwhelming support for national government as it did the effects of a set of circumstances which placed the elite, federalist and nationalist, northern and southern, in essentially the same position it had been in in 1776. But some federalists did put up a fight. Throughout the revolutionary era they had defended themselves and the nation from the specter of tyrannical central government. Although James Warren, among others, decried the "Imbecility and Inattention" which helped the Confederation "fall into ruin," it remained that federalists were unable to modify the political system until extraordinary conditions obviated measured and limited constitutional reforms.[5] Their shortsightedness, given the advantage of hindsight, lay in their initial agreement to have a general convention at which some nationalists were able to present a body of thought which formed the outline of a new type of central government as well as a ready defense for that government.

A number of federalists quickly realized their error in agreeing to a general convention and recognized the dangers of what had been wrought. Men like Richard Henry Lee, Abraham Yates, George Clinton, Elbridge Gerry, George Bryan, John Nicholson, and George Mason, forced to labor under the confusing banner of antifederalism, tried to prevent the ratification of a constitution which erected "a National Government instead of a Federal Union of Sovereign States." Abraham Yates complained that the Philadelphia delegates "paid no more regard to their orders and credentials than Caesar when he passed the Rubicon." George Bryan charged that "the anti-constitutional or Aristocratic Party" had controlled the convention. He even argued that the delegates had been appointed "without much Expectation of any thing very important being done by them till towards the close . . . when Surmises were spread from other Quarters that Something injurious to the Liberties of the People was about to be produced."[6]

Although the Constitution went too far to suit most federalists, it promised to give the nation a degree of stability, order, and longevity which it had not had under the Articles of Confederation. The Constitution's opponents were hampered in their attempt to make substantive changes in it because they had previously supported constitutional reforms. A warning James Madison had given to James Monroe with respect to southern concessions during the Mississippi controversy had, as it turned out, prophetic meaning for federalists—they too had "to combat under the disadvantage of having foresaken . . . [the] first ground."[7] Nationalists had been describing the failings of the Articles of

Confederation since 1780, and by 1787 their arguments had been, in a sense, empirically validated. The Constitution's opponents, trapped by their own espousal of the need for a more effective central government, albeit within the confines of the Articles of Confederation, could only react awkwardly and defensively to the nationalists. They could not retreat, as they previously had, to the security of the Articles.

Even more important than the nation's general malaise and the difficulty in distinguishing between degrees of reform in weakening opposition to the Constitution were the continuing implications of the Shaysite political victory in Massachusetts. During the debates in the Massachusetts ratifying convention the argument was made that "a coercive power over the whole, searching through all parts of the system, is necessary to the preservation of the greatest happiness of the whole people . . . To avoid the greatest and to choose the least of two evils, is all that we can do." Even Rufus King, the aristocrats' enemy in 1785 and 1786, now attacked the Confederation as "a mere Federal government of states. Those, therefore, that assemble under it have no power to make laws to apply to the individuals of the States confederated; and the attempts to make laws for collective societies, necessarily leave a discretion to comply with them or not." This was a hard argument to counter. Although many federalists were outraged by the formulation of a constitution which "had few federal features," they had a difficult choice to make and faced an almost insoluble dilemma. As Elbridge Gerry viewed the situation, if the people adopted the Constitution "their liberties may be lost; or, should they reject it altogether anarchy may ensue."[8]

After ratification Samuel Henshaw thanked "God we have a federal government," a supreme government, when he saw the results of the state election in Massachusetts.[9] The need for this sort of buffer between the rulers and the ruled, more than any other single factor, primed the political leaders for change and, for a time, balanced the pull of sectional differences. Nevertheless, the establishment of a national government did not reshape the nation's sectional character.

While not all of the delegates at Philadelphia, or all politicians, reacted the same way to the complex pressures in 1787 and 1788, certain consistencies did emerge. Faced with a common internal threat, many of the leaders felt obliged to build upon their points of agreed interests, specifically their economic and political powers, rather than permit their conflicting interests to destroy them. But, as in 1776, compromise to meet a common danger, which spelled possible ruin for all, did not mean that sectional interests were no longer important or that the potential for sectional conflict had lessened. Each side entered the new political

arrangement with the expectation that once having erected a suitable
defense against societal decay and having solved some of the nation's
serious problems, it would be able to promote its own interests. The
leaders certainly had common interests to protect, but they also had
conflicting interests to advance. James Madison perceptively remarked
that entry into a national government was "recommended to the Eastern
States by the actual superiority of their populousness, and to the South
by their expected superiority."[10]

The establishment of a national government was atypical when compared with the rest of revolutionary political behavior. It is thus invalid
to use the very visible compromises in 1787-88 to prove that sectional
interest was less important than other considerations, that sectionalism
cannot have had a great impact on American politics. The later revolutionary period, even more so than the period when the Articles of
Confederation were written, saw a unique combination of events and
pressures raise questions which temporarily suppressed sectionalism's
pervasive influence on the political scene. It is, therefore, necessary to
recognize the revival of sectional conflict in the First Federal Congress
to understand its continuity in American politics.

As soon as Congress established a revenue, resolved the question of a
bill of rights, and clarified the judiciary and executive articles of the
Constitution, sectional conflict burst forth to such a degree that James
Madison declared on the floor of the House of Representatives that "if a
prophet had risen" in the Virginia ratifying convention and "brought the
declarations and proceedings of this day into view . . . I . . . firmly
believe Virginia might not have been part of the Union at this moment."
As debate over the location of a federal capital continued to heat up the
following day Madison, his sectionalism forcing him to alter what he had
so long stood for ideologically, argued that state governments, not the
national government, "ever possess a keener sense and capacity to take
advantage of those powers on which the protection of local rights
depend." Sectionalism, which precipitated conflicts again and again to
threaten the intersectional agreement which made the revolution of 1787
possible, necessitated hard-fought compromises in 1790, 1820, and
1850. Ultimately no amount of compromise could resolve the nation's
sectional dissimilarity. The basic conflict which had threatened the
Union for decades was finally resolved only by civil war.[11]

Notes
Index

Notes

ABBREVIATIONS USED IN THE NOTES

AAS	American Antiquarian Society, Worcester, Mass.
APS	American Philosophical Society, Philadelphia, Pa.
BL	Butler Library, Columbia University, New York, N.Y.
CHSC	Connecticut Historical Society, *Collections,* 30 vols. (Hartford, 1860-1962).
DL	The David Library of the American Revolution, Washington Crossing, Pa.
ESR	William S. Jenkins and Lillian A. Hamrick, eds., *Microfilm Collection of Early State Records* (Washington, D.C., 1950).
HL	Houghton Library, Harvard University, Cambridge, Mass.
HSP	Historical Society of Pennsylvania, Philadelphia, Pa.
JCBL	John Carter Brown Library, Brown University, Providence, R.I.
JCC	Worthington C. Ford et al., eds., *The Journals of the Continental Congress,* 34 vols. (Washington, D.C., 1931-44).
JMND	James Madison, "Notes on Debates in the Continental Congress," in *PJM,* passim.
LMCC	Edmund C. Burnett, ed., *Letters of Members of the Continental Congress,* 8 vols. (Washington, D.C., 1936).
LC	Library of Congress, Washington, D.C.
MdHS	Maryland Historical Society, Baltimore, Md.
MHS	Massachusetts Historical Society, Boston, Mass.
MHSC	Massachusetts Historical Society, *Collections,* 81 vols. (Boston, 1806-1974).
MHSP	Massachusetts Historical Society, *Proceedings,* 77 vols. (Boston, 1891-1965).
NJHS	New Jersey Historical Society, Trenton, N.J.
NYHS	New-York Historical Society, New York, N.Y.
NYHSC	New-York Historical Society, *Collections,* 85 vols. (New York, 1811-1975).
NYPL	New York Public Library, New York, N.Y.
PAH	Harold C. Syrett et al., eds., *The Papers of Alexander Hamilton,* 22 vols. to date (New York, 1961—).

173

PCC	Papers of the Continental Congress, Library of Congress, Washington, D.C.
PJM	William T. Hutchinson and Robert A. Rutland et al., eds., *The Papers of James Madison,* 9 vols. (Chicago, 1962-75).
PTJ	Julian Boyd, ed., *The Papers of Thomas Jefferson,* 17 vols. to date (Princeton, N.J., 1950—).
RIHSC	Rhode Island Historical Society, *Collections,* 34 vols. (Providence, R.I., 1827-1941).
SCHS	South Carolina Historical Society, Charleston, S.C.
UNC	University of North Carolina Library, Chapel Hill, N.C.
UVa	University of Virginia Library, Charlottesville, Va.
VHS	Virginia Historical Society, Richmond, Va.
VSL	Virginia State Library, Richmond, Va.
WGW	John C. Fitzpatrick, ed., *The Writings of George Washington,* 39 vols. (Washington, D.C., 1931-44).
WJA	Charles F. Adams, ed., *Life and Works of John Adams,* 10 vols. (Boston, 1850-56).
WML	Earl Gregg Swem Library, College of William and Mary, Williamsburg, Va.
YL	Yale University Library, New Haven, Conn.

INTRODUCTION

1 Richard B. Morris, "The Confederation Period and the American Historians," *William and Mary Quarterly,* 3d ser., 13 (1956): 139-56; Cecelia M. Kenyon, "Republicanism and Radicalism in the American Revolution: An Old Fashioned Interpretation," *William and Mary Quarterly,* 3d ser., 19 (1962): 153-82; Bernard Bailyn, "Political Experience and Enlightenment Ideas in Eighteenth Century America," *American Historical Review* 67, no. 2 (1962): 339-51; Clinton Rossiter, "The Political Theory of the American Revolution," in *Origins of American Political Thought,* ed. John P. Roche (New York, 1967), pp. 97-113; Edmund S. Morgan, *The Birth of the Republic* (Chicago, 1956); Gordon S. Wood, *The Creation of the American Republic* (Chapel Hill, N.C., 1969); Charles F. Warren, *The Making of the Constitution* (Boston, 1928); George Bancroft, *History of the Formation of the Constitution of the United States,* 2 vols. (New York, 1882).

2 Merrill Jensen, *The Founding of a Nation* (New York, 1968), *The Articles of Confederation: An Interpretation of the Social-Constitutional History of the American Revolution 1774-1781* (Madison, Wis., 1963), and *The New Nation: A History of the United States during the Confederation 1781-1789* (New York, 1965); Jackson T. Main, *The Antifederalists* (Chapel Hill, N.C., 1961); E. James Ferguson, *The Power of the Purse* (Chapel Hill, N.C., 1961), and "The Nationalists of 1781-1783 and the Economic Interpretation of the

Constitution," *Journal of American History* 56, no. 2 (1969): 241-61; J. Allen Smith, *The Spirit of American Government* (Cambridge, Mass., 1965).

3 John R. Alden, *The First South* (Baton Rouge, La., 1961), and *The South in the Revolution 1763-1789* (Baton Rouge, La., 1957); Fulmer Mood, "The Origin, Evolution, and Application of the Sectional Concept, 1750-1790," in *Regionalism in America,* ed. Merrill Jensen (Madison, Wis., 1951). Some provocative essays may be found in Staughton Lynd, *Class Conflict, Slavery and the United States Constitution* (Indianapolis, Ind., 1967).

4 See H. James Henderson, "The Structure of Politics in The Continental Congress," in *Essays on the American Revolution,* ed. Stephen Kurtz and James H. Hutson (Chapel Hill, N.C., 1973), pp. 157-96, and *Party Politics in the Continental Congress* (New York, 1974). Henderson's sound account of voting behavior in Congress is an important contribution to the historiography of the Revolution. His analysis is limited, however, by a reliance upon rather standard interpretations of many issues and by the additional support of only the most easily accessible contemporary correspondence. The evidence in his book does not support his statement that roll-call analysis must be used "in association with other sources and methods of inquiry" (p. xiv). Moreover, while he admits that the disagreement over the nature of central government affected partisan politics, Henderson emphasizes the regional basis of politics to such an extent that the equally fundamental issue of ideological conflict is shunted much too far into the background.

CHAPTER 1: THE ROOTS OF CONFLICT

1 For examples of radical thought, see Committee of Correspondence of Massachusetts to other Committees of Correspondence, 21 October 1773, in Harry A. Cushing, ed., *The Writings of Samuel Adams,* 4 vols. (New York, 1911-14), 3: 64; Virginia's instructions to its delegates, 1774, in William W. Henry, *Patrick Henry, Life, Correspondence & Speeches,* 3 vols. (New York, 1891), 1: 200. On the constitutional issues of the Revolution, see C. H. McIlwain, *The American Revolution: A Constitutional Interpretation* (New York, 1923); R. G. Adams, *Political Ideas of the American Revolution,* 3d ed. (New York, 1958); C. F. Mullet, *Fundamental Law and the American Revolution 1760-1776* (New York, 1933).

2 Joseph Trumbull to John Adams, 14 November 1775, in Adams Mss. Trust, MHS; Peter Thatcher, Oration delivered at Watertown, 5 March 1776, in Hezekiah Niles, ed., *Principles and Acts of the Revolution in America* (Baltimore, Md., 1822), p. 46. See also James Sullivan to Adams, 9 May 1776, in Adams Mss. Trust, MHS; Committee of Lancaster County to Pennsylvania Delegates, 10 March 1777, in PCC, Item 69, pp. 335-38; Thomas Burke to Gov. of North Carolina, 11 March 1777, in Thomas Burke Papers, Southern Historical Collections, UNC.

3 William Bull, Jr., to the Earl of Dartmouth, 28 November 1775, in George C. Rogers, *Evolution of a Federalist William Loughton Smith (1758-1812)*

(Columbia, S.C., 1962), p. 78; Josiah Quincy to John Adams, 25 October 1775, in Adams Mss. Trust, MHS. See also Merrill Jensen, "Democracy and the American Revolution," *Huntington Library Quarterly* 20 (1957): 321-41; Robert J. Taylor, *Western Massachusetts in the Revolution* (Providence, R.I., 1954); Elisha P. Douglass, *Rebels and Democrats* (Chapel Hill, N.C., 1955). An expression of this radical ideology may be seen in "The People the Best Governors: *A Plan of Government* founded on the Just Principles of Natural Freedom," 1776, in Frederick Chase, *History of Dartmouth College and Hanover New Hampshire up to 1815,* ed. John K. Lord, 2 vols. (Brattleboro, Vt., 1928), 1: 644, 662. One of the foundations upon which these democrats drew was James Burgh, *Political Disquisitions,* 3 vols. (Philadelphia, 1775).

4 See Samuel Adams to Richard Henry Lee, 10 April 1773, Samuel Adams to Arthur Lee, April 1774, Speech by Francis Lightfoot Lee, copy 1774 [?], in Lee Family Papers, UVA (microfilm, original at American Philosophical Society; all letters subsequently noted will refer to Lee Papers); William Lee to Richard Henry Lee, 10 September 1774, in Worthington Chauncy Ford, ed., *Letters of William Lee,* 3 vols. (Brooklyn, N.Y., 1891), 1: 90; Joseph Ward to John Adams, 23 October 1775, in Adams Mss. Trust, MHS. The following may be seen for theories about union: Max Savelle, "Nationalism and Other Loyalties in the American Revolution," *American Historical Review* 67, no. 4 (1962): 901-23; Merrill Jensen, "The Idea of a National Government during the Revolution," *Political Science Quarterly* 58 (1943): 356-79.

5 See Henderson, "The Structure of Politics," pp. 165-66. Some of these men did not come into prominence until 1781, others were on the scene in 1774.

6 John Adams to Joseph Hawley, 25 November 1775, in LMCC, 1: 259-60; Samuel Adams to James Warren, 25 September 1774, in Cushing, ed., *Writings of Samuel Adams,* 3: 156-57; Joseph Hawley to John Adams, 25 July 1774, in WJA, 9: 344-45.

7 John Adams to William Tudor, 24 September 1774, in WJA, 9: 346; Samuel Seabury, "A View of the Controversy Between Great Britain and Her Colonies," 14 December 1774, in Alpheus T. Mason, *Free Government in the Making* (New York, 1965), p. 118.

8 Thomas Mumford to Silas Deane, 22 May 1775, in CHSC, 2 (1870): 235; Edmund Pendleton to Thomas Jefferson, 1 June 1776, in David J. Mays, ed., *The Letters and Papers of Edmund Pendleton 1734-1803,* 2 vols. (Charlottesville, Va., 1967), 1: 182. See also James Allen to Ralph Izard, 29 October 1774, in Anne Izard Deas, *Correspondence of Mr. Ralph Izard* (New York, 1844), p. 28; William Lee to Francis Lightfoot Lee, 25 February 1775, in Ford, ed., *Letters of William Lee,* 1: 129; Samuel Adams to James Bowdoin, 16 November 1775, in Cushing, ed., *Writings of Samuel Adams,* 3: 241; John Adams to George Washington, 6 January 1776, in WJA, 9: 370; William Heath to Washington, 28 December 1776, in *The Heath Papers,* MHSC, 7th ser., 4 (1904): 57. There is also a great deal to be found in many letters of George Washington too numerous to cite here.

9 Silas Deane to Mrs. Deane, 3 June 1775, John Adams to Abigail Adams, 17

June 1775, in LMCC, 1: 111, 130; John Adams to Abigail Adams, 29 October 1775, in Lyman H. Butterfield, ed., *The Adams Papers,* ser. 3, *Adams Family Correspondence,* 4 vols. (Cambridge, Mass.: Harvard University Press, 1963), 1: 318. See also John Adams to James Warren, 6 July 1775, in *Warren-Adams Letters,* MHSC, 72 (1917): 25.

10　John McKesson to Gov. George Clinton, 10 June 1775, in *Public Papers of George Clinton,* 8 vols. (Albany, 1902), 1: 199-200. See also Titus Hosmer to Silas Deane, 28 May 1775, in CHSC, 2: 235; Clinton to McKesson, 15 June 1775, in LMCC, 1: 125.

11　John Adams to James Warren, 6 June 1775, in *Warren-Adams Letters,* MHSC, 72:25; Nathanael Greene to Gov. Cooke, 9 August 1775, in "Revolutionary Correspondence from 1775-1782," RIHSC, 6 (1867): 117-18. See also Eliphalet Dyer to Joseph Trumbull, 17 June 1775, in LMCC, 1: 128; Jonathan G. Rossie, "The Politics of Command: The Continental Army and Its Generals" (Ph.D. diss., University of Wisconsin, 1966), p. 29; Samuel White Patterson, *Horatio Gates: Defender of American Liberties* (New York, 1966), p. 49.

12　Virginia delegates to Patrick Henry, 16 July 1776, in PTJ, 1: 461; Nathanael Greene to Gov. Cooke, 22 July 1776, in "Revolutionary Correspondence of Governor Nicholas Cooke 1775-1781," *Proceedings of the American Antiquarian Society,* n.s., 36 (1927): 309.

13　John Haslett to Caesar Rodney, 10 October 1776, in George H. Ryden, ed., *Letters to and from Caesar Rodney 1756-1784* (Philadelphia, 1933), p. 138; Joseph Ward to John Adams, 8 August 1776, in Adams Mss. Trust, MHS. For additional complaints about the southern promotions, see Samuel Adams to Joseph Palmer, 1 April 1776, in LMCC, 1: 414; Nathanael Greene to John Adams, 14 July 1776, John Adams to Greene, 4 August 1776, in Adams Mss. Trust, MHS; William Williams to Joseph Trumbull, 7 August 1776, in LMCC, 2: 41.

14　Alexander Hamilton to John Jay, 26 November 1775, in PAH, 1: 177; James Sullivan to John Sullivan, 6 December 1775, in Otis G. Hammond, ed., *Letters and Papers of Major-General John Sullivan Continental Army,* New Hampshire Historical Society, *Collections* 13 (1939): 138. See also Samuel H. Parsons to John Adams [September 1775], in Adams Mss. Trust, MHS; William Hooper to James Iredell, 6 January 1776, in Griffith J. Mcree, *Life and Correspondence of James Iredell,* 2 vols. (New York, 1858), 1: 269.

15　For the Wooster imbroglio and the Gates-Schuyler clash, see John Adams, "Autobiography," 12 August 1776, in Lyman H. Butterfield, ed., *The Adams Papers,* ser. 1, *The Diary and Autobiography of John Adams,* 4 vols. (Cambridge, Mass.: Harvard University Press, 1961), 3: 405-6; John Hancock to the Massachusetts General Assembly, 16 May 1776, William Williams to Joseph Trumbull, 26 September 1776, in LMCC, 1: 451, 2: 104.

16　Samuel Osgood to John Adams, 4 December 1775, in Adams Mss. Trust, MHS; Thomas Paine, "Common Sense," in Moncure D. Conway, ed., *Writings of Thomas Paine,* 4 vols. (New York, 1894-96), 1: 95; John Adams to Abigail Adams, 17 May 1776, John Adams to Zabiel Adams, 21 June 1776, in Butterfield, ed., *Adams Family,* 1: 410-11, 2: 21.

17　Samuel Adams to Samuel Cooper, 30 April 1776, in Cushing, ed., *Writings of*

Samuel Adams, 3: 241; John Adams to Abigail Adams, 18 February 1776, in Butterfield, ed., *Adams Family,* 1: 348; John Adams to Horatio Gates, 23 March 1776, in LMCC, 1: 406.

18 James Sullivan to John Adams, 9 May 1776, in Adams Mss. Trust, MHS; Thomas Smith to Arthur St. Clair, 22 August 1776, in William Henry Smith, ed., *The St. Clair Papers,* 2 vols. (Cincinnati, Ohio, 1882), 1: 273. See also Edmund Pendleton to Carter Braxton, 12 March 1776, in Mays, ed., *Pendleton Papers,* 1: 177; Charles Carroll of Carrollton to Charles Carroll of Annapolis, 4 October 1776, in Carroll Papers, MdHS; Josiah Quincy to Adams, 13 June 1776, in Adams Mss. Trust, MHS.

19 Carter Braxton to Landon Carter, 17 May 1776, in LMCC, 1: 454. See also Joseph Hawley to Elbridge Gerry, 1 May 1776, in James T. Austin, *The Life of Elbridge Gerry With Contemporary Letters* (Boston, 1828), pp. 175-76; Edward Tilgham to his father, 4 February 1776, in Charles J. Stillé, *The Life and Times of John Dickinson 1732-1808, Memoirs of the Historical Society of Pennsylvania* 13 (1891): 129.

20 John Adams, "Autobiography," in Butterfield, ed., *Diary and Autobiography,* 3: 34, 335; Christopher Gadsden to Samuel Adams, 4 April 1779, Charles Town, in Richard Walsh, ed., *The Writings of Christopher Gadsden* (Columbia, S.C., 1966), p. 163.

21 Willard, Secretary of the Province, to Bollan, agent in London, 31 December 1754, in Albert B. Hart, *Commonwealth History of Massachusetts,* 5 vols. (New York, 1828), 2: 461; Edward Rutledge to John Jay, 29 June 1776, Carter Braxton to Landon Carter, 14 April 1776, Joseph Hewes to Samuel Johnston, 28 July 1776, in LMCC, 1: 517, 420-23, 2: 28. For the unabated sectional jealousies, see [Joseph Ward] to John Adams, 1 July 1776, in Adams Mss. Trust, MHS; William Williams to Joseph Trumbull, 7 October 1776, in LMCC, 2: 118; Samuel Adams to Richard Henry Lee, 15 July 1776, in Lee Papers, APS.

22 Patrick Henry to John Adams, 20 May 1776, Henry to Richard Henry Lee, 20 May 1776, in Henry, *Henry Correspondence,* 1: 413, 410; Charles Carroll of Carrollton to Charles Carroll of Annapolis, 26 June 1777, in Carroll Papers, MdHS. See also Samuel Johnston to Thomas Burke, 19 April 1777, Cornelius Harnett to Burke, 13 November 1777, in Burke Papers, UNC. For some nationalists' views of the effect of the war on the formation of the Confederation, see "An Essay in the Pennsylvania Packet," February & March 1780, in Jared Sparks, *The Life of Gouverneur Morris with Selections from His Correspondence,* 3 vols. (Boston, 1832), 1: 222; Noah Webster, *A Collection of Essays and Fugitiv Writings on Moral, Historical, Political and Literary Subjects* (Boston, 1790), p. 184.

23 Joseph Palmer to John Adams, 19 February 1776, Cotton Tufts to Adams, 24 April 1777, in Adams Mss. Trust, MHS. It is important to bear in mind that there were conflicts in the northern states between New England and middle state merchants and between farmers, artisans, and merchants and in the southern states between planters and merchants.

24 William Hooper to Joseph Hewes, 1 January 1777, in LMCC, 2: 200; Thomas

Jefferson to John Adams, 17 December 1777, in PTJ, 2: 120. See also Adams to James Warren, 19 October 1775, in LMCC, 1: 236.

25 W. H. Drayton, Speech in the South Carolina Assembly, 20 January 1778, in Niles, ed., *Principles and Acts,* p. 363.

26 John Adams to Abigail Adams, 17 May 1776, in Butterfield, ed., *Adams Family,* 1: 410-11. See also Cornelius Harnett to Thomas Burke, 16 December 1777, in Burke Papers, UNC; Jensen, *Articles of Confederation,* pp. 150-60.

27 Gov. Trumbull to George Washington, 21 February 1777, in Jared Sparks, ed., *Correspondence of the American Revolution Being Letters of Eminent Men to George Washington,* 4 vols. (Boston, 1853), 1: 343-46, hereafter cited as *Letters to Washington;* Nathan Hale and others to Congress, 7 June 1776, in PCC, Item 78, pp. 169-70. For the fear that money was being concentrated in the northern states, see Thomas Burke to ———, February 1777, in Burke Papers, UNC.

28 Philip Schuyler to Gouverneur Morris, 7 September 1777, in Sparks, *Morris,* 1: 143; John Jay to Schuyler, 21 March 1779, in LMCC, 4: 109. For additional material on the Schuyler-Gates controversy, see Charles Carroll of Carrollton to Charles Carroll of Annapolis, 24 May 1777, in Carroll Papers, MdHS; Samuel Adams to James Warren, 31 July 1777, in Cushing, ed., *Writings of Samuel Adams,* 3: 396; John Adams to Abigail Adams, 11 August 1777, in Adams Mss. Trust, MHS; Rossie, "Politics of Command," pp. 235-55. On the situation with regard to Washington, see James Lovell to Samuel Adams, 20 January [1778], in LMCC, 3: 42; William Gordon to George Washington, 5 March 1777, in "Letters of Reverand William Gordon Historian of the American Revolution 1770-1799," MHSP, 63 (1931): 335; Benjamin Harrison to Thomas Burke, 3 March 1778, in Burke Papers, UNC; Rossie, "Politics of Command," pp. 395-421; Patterson, *Horatio Gates,* pp. 200-250.

29 William Duer to Robert R. Livingston, 28 May 1777, Richard Henry Lee to Patrick Henry, [26] May 1777, in LMCC, 2: 377, 373-74.

30 Rawlin Loundes to Henry Laurens, 16 August 1778, Laurens to Loundes, 23 June 1778, in Henry Laurens Papers, SCHS. See also George H. Hammond, "The Proposed Amendments to the Articles of Confederation," *South Atlantic Quarterly* 24 (1925): 411-36.

31 Richard Henry Lee to Landon Carter, 2 June 1776, John Adams to Patrick Henry, 3 June 1776, Samuel Chase to Lee, 30 July 1776, in LMCC, 1: 469, 471, 2: 32.

32 See Ralph Izard to Thomas Lynch, 8 September 1775, in Deas, *Correspondence of Izard,* p. 121; Richard Henry Lee to Arthur Lee, 17 February 1777, in Lee Papers, UVa; James Warren to John Adams, 22 February 1777, in Adams Mss. Trust, MHS.

33 *Secret Journals of the Acts and Proceedings of Congress,* 4 vols. (Boston, 1821), 2: 7-24; John Adams to Dr. Winthrop, 23 June 1776, in Adams Mss. Trust, MHS. See also William C. Stinchcombe, *The American Revolution and the French Alliance* (Syracuse, N.Y., 1969), pp. 7-8; Vergennes to Montmorin, 16 January 1777, 30 October 1778, in Paul C. Phillips, *The West*

in the Diplomacy of the American Revolution (Urbana, Ill., 1913), pp. 76-77, 83.

34 John Dickinson to George Read, 22 January 1777, in William Thompson Read, *Life and Correspondence of George Read* (Philadelphia, 1870), p. 255.

35 John Eliot to Jeremy Belknap, 12 January 1777, in *The Belknap Papers,* MHSC, 6th ser., 4 (1891): 100-102; Stinchcombe, *French Alliance,* pp. 24-26.

36 Henry Laurens to John Lewis Gervais, 5 September 1777, in Laurens Papers, SCHS. On Deane's recall see Neil Storch, "Congressional Factionalism and Diplomacy, 1775-1783" (Ph.D. diss., University of Wisconsin, 1969).

37 Arthur Lee to Richard Henry Lee, 5 September 1777, Paris, Arthur Lee to Francis Lightfoot Lee, 7 October 1777, Paris, in Arthur Lee Papers, HL; William Lee to Richard Henry Lee, 7 October 1777, Paris, in Lee Papers, UVa; Ralph Izard to William Duer, 24 November 1777, Paris, in Deas, *Correspondence of Izard,* p. 378; Arthur Lee to Samuel Adams, 25 November 1777, Paris, in Arthur Lee Papers, HL.

38 William Lee to Richard Henry Lee, 23 March 1778, Paris, in Ford, ed., *Letters of William Lee,* 2: 407; Arthur Lee to Richard Henry Lee, 9 January 1778, Paris, in Lee Papers, UVa. See also Richard B. Morris, "Labor and Mercantilism in the Revolutionary Era," in *The Era of the American Revolution,* ed. Morris (New York, 1939), pp. 76-122; Robert A. East, *Business Enterprise in the American Revolutionary Era* (New York, 1938), pp. 136-37, 141-44, 148, 155; Clarence L. Ver Steeg, *Robert Morris: Revolutionary Financier* (Philadelphia, 1954), pp. 10-15, 18-22, 32-35.

39 Benjamin Rush to John Adams, 22 January 1778, in Adams Mss. Trust, MHS; Henry Laurens to Gov. William Livingston, 27 January 1778, in David Duncan Wallace, *Life of Henry Laurens* (New York, 1915), pp. 276-77; Christopher Gadsden to William H. Drayton, 15 August 1778, Charles Town, in Walsh, ed., *Writings of Christopher Gadsden,* p. 146. See also Stinchcombe, *French Alliance,* pp. 13-17. For an interesting comparison between the model treaty and the French alliance, see Adams to James Warren, 20 May 1783, in *Warren-Adams Letters,* MHSC, 73: 192-93.

40 Ralph Izard to John Adams, 24 September, 28 September, 8 October 1778, in Adams Mss. Trust, MHS; John Adams, "Autobiography," December 1777, in Butterfield, ed., *Diary and Autobiography,* 4: 5; Samuel Adams to James Warren, [November 1778], in LMCC, 2: 476; Arthur Lee to Samuel Adams, 1 April 1778, in Samuel Adams Papers, NYPL; Beaumarchais to Vergennes, 13 March 1778, in Storch, "Congressional Factionalism," pp. 30-32.

41 Laurens wrote his remarks on a description of a conversation between Gérard and Samuel Adams, 21 April 1779, in Laurens Papers, SCHS.

42 Arthur Lee to his brother, 31 May 1778, in Laurens Papers, SCHS; James Lovell to John Adams, 1 November 1779, in Adams Mss. Trust, MHS.

43 Henry Laurens, In Congress, 9 December 1778, in Laurens Papers, SCHS; Francis Lightfoot Lee to Richard Henry Lee, 15 and 22 December 1778, in Lee Papers, UVa; Joseph Webb to Samuel Blackley Webb, 24 January 1779, in Paul Leicester Ford, ed., *Correspondence and Journals of Samuel Black-*

ley Webb, 3 vols. (New York, 1893-94), 2: 147; Storch, "Congressional Factionalism," pp. 57-60, 78-80; Stinchcombe, *French Alliance,* p. 41.

44 Francis Lightfoot Lee to Arthur Lee, 10 December 1778, in LMCC, 2: 530; Francis Lightfoot Lee to Richard Henry Lee, 25 December 1778, in Lee Papers, UVa. See also Silas Deane to Jonathan Trumbull, 20 October 1778, in *The Trumbull Papers,* MHSC, 7th ser., 2 (1902): 291-97; Beaumarchais to Congress, 24 March 1778, Memorial on the Beaumarchais Affair, L. de Francy, 14 August 1778, in Laurens Papers, SCHS.

45 James Lovell to John Adams, 14 September 1779, in Adams Mss. Trust, MHS; Richard Henry Lee to Francis Lightfoot Lee, 26 September 1779, in Lee Papers, UVa. See also H. James Henderson, "Congressional Factionalism and the Attempt to Recall Benjamin Franklin," *William and Mary Quarterly,* 3d ser., 27 (1970): 252.

46 Titus Hosmer to Jonathan Trumbull, 31 August 1778, in *Trumbull Papers,* MHSC, 2: 266; Cyrus Griffin to Thomas Jefferson, 6 October 1778, in PTJ, 2: 216. For increasing pressure on the South, see Thomas Bee to William H. Drayton, 2 April 1779, in PCC, Item 72, p. 489; Christopher Gadsden to Samuel Adams, 4 April 1779, in Walsh, ed., *Writings of Christopher Gadsden,* pp. 161-62; Richard Henry Lee to Arthur Lee, 23 May 1779, in LMCC, 4: 227-28.

47 James Lovell to Horatio Gates, 1 March 1779, in LMCC, 4: 84; James Warren to John Adams, 13 June 1779, in Adams Mss. Trust, MHS.

48 Samuel Adams to Samuel Cooper, 29 April 1779, William H. Drayton, In Congress, Henry Laurens's notes, 8 May 1779, in LMCC, 4: 185, 201; Richard Henry Lee to William Whipple, 13 June 1779, Chantilly, in Lee Papers, UVa.

49 Charles Carroll of Carrollton to Charles Carroll of Annapolis, 8 May 1779, in Carroll Papers, MdHS; William Fleming to Thomas Jefferson, 22 June 1779, in PTJ, 3: 10; James Lovell to John Adams, 13 June 1779, in Adams Mss. Trust, MHS; Daniel St. Thomas Jenifer to Gov. Thomas Johnson, 8 June 1779, in LMCC, 4: 253. John R. Alden describes the conflict over the peace demands as solely a sectional fight. Although sectional jealousy was important, its real significance in 1779 lies in the way the French and nationalists used it. See Alden, *The First South,* pp. 54-57.

50 Daniel St. Thomas Jenifer to Charles Carroll of Carrollton, 25 July 1779, in Carroll Papers, MdHS; Storch, "Congressional Factionalism," pp. 113-16; Stinchcombe, *French Alliance,* pp. 68-72.

51 *Secret Journals,* 2: 224-32; James Lovell to John Adams, 24 August 1779, in Adams Mss. Trust, MHS. See also William Whipple to Richard Henry Lee, 23 August 1779, in Lee Papers, APS.

52 James Lovell to John Adams, 27 September 1779, in WJA, 9: 488; *Secret Journals,* 2: 249, 253-57, 565-66; Lovell to Adams, 19 October 1779, in Adams Mss. Trust, MHS. Lovell and Elbridge Gerry made it a point to almost demand Adams's acceptance of the post of commissioner; see Lovell to Adams, 28 September 1779, Elbridge Gerry to Adams, 29 September 1779, in WJA, 9: 489-90, 495.

53 Samuel Flagg Bemis, *The Diplomacy of the American Revolution* (New

York, 1935), p. 101; *Secret Journals,* 2: 261-63; Phillips, *The West,* pp. 53-55, 60-66, 115-21; Stinchcombe, *French Alliance,* pp. 73-74.

54 Silas Deane to Simeon Deane, 28 September 1779, in *The Deane Papers,* CHSC, 23 (1930): 149; William Lee to Richard Henry Lee, 14 October 1779, Frankfort, in Lee Papers, UVa.

55 Richard Henry Lee to John Adams, 8 October 1779, in Lee Papers, UVa; Adams to Henry Laurens, 25 October 1779, in WJA, 9: 504.

56 Mercy Otis Warren to John Adams, 29 July 1779, in *Warren-Adams Letters,* MHSC, 73: 114.

CHAPTER 2: THE NATIONALIST ASCENDANCY

1 Curtis P. Nettels, *The Emergence of a National Economy 1775-1815* (New York, 1965), pp. 5-14; East, *Business Enterprise,* pp. 195, 208, 227; David Ramsay, *History of the United States,* 3 vols. (Philadelphia, 1818), 3: 8; Thomas Nelson to George Washington, 28 November 1779, Nathanael Greene to Washington, 6 March 1780, in Sparks, ed., *Letters to Washington,* 3: 362, 405; Charles Carroll of Carrollton to Charles Carroll of Annapolis, 29 April 1780, in Carroll Papers, MdHS.

2 Ezekiel Cornell to Gov. Greene, 18 June 1780, in LMCC, 5: 225.

3 James Madison to Edmund Pendleton, 1 September 1780, in PJM, 2: 81-82; Pendleton to Madison, 25 September 1780, in Mays, ed., *Pendleton Papers,* 1: 310. See also Herbert B. Adams, *Maryland's Influence Upon Land Cessions to the United States,* Johns Hopkins University Studies in Historical and Political Science, vol. 3 (Baltimore, Md., 1885), pp. 23-24; Merrill Jensen, "The Cession of the Old Northwest," *Mississippi Valley Historical Review* 23 (1936): 27-48, "The Creation of the National Domain, 1781-1784," *Mississippi Valley Historical Review* 26 (1939): 323-42; Frank Green Bates, *Rhode Island and the Formation of the Union,* Columbia University Studies in History Economics and Public Law, vol. 10 (New York, 1898-99), pp. 70-71, 88.

4 John Adams to Richard Henry Lee, 15 March 1780, in Adams Mss. Trust, MHS.

5 Storch, "Congressional Factionalism," pp. 163-65; Stinchcombe, *French Alliance,* p. 151. The middle state nationalists, many of whom were land speculators, wanted some power other than the individual states to control the western lands in order to protect their claims. Because of their commercial connections with the French, it was of relatively little consequence to them if Congress or a friendly foreign power had control over the western lands—in either case they stood to benefit.

6 *Secret Journals,* 2: 323-39. See also James Lovell to Samuel Adams, 8 February 1780, Lovell to Henry Laurens, 12 February 1780, Ezekiel Cornell to Gov. Greene, 22 August 1780, in LMCC, 5: 29, 34, 343; Richard B. Morris, *The Peacemakers The Great Powers and American Independence* (New York, 1965), pp. 224-38; Phillips, *The West,* pp. 141, 164.

7 John Hanson to Charles Carroll of Carrollton, 16 October 1780, in Carroll
   Papers, MdHS; "The Plain Politician," *Maryland Gazette* (Ann.), 3 March
   1780; "The Honest Politician," *Maryland Gazette* (Ann.), 10 March 1780;
   "An Anti-Anglican," *Maryland Gazette* (Ann.), 24 March, 31 March 1780;
   article dated Amsterdam, 1 May, *Maryland Gazette* (Ann.), 11 August 1780.
8 "An Anti-Anglican," *Maryland Gazette* (Ann.), 14 April 1780. See also
   Boston, 10 April, *Pennsylvania Gazette* (Phila.), 15 April 1780; *New York
   Gazette*, 8 May 1780; Delegates of Virginia to ———, n.d., in PCC, Item 75,
   p. 348; William Gordon to John Adams, 22 July 1780, in Adams Mss. Trust,
   MHS.
9 William Lee to John Adams, 15 November 1780, Bruxelles, Adams to Lee,
   19 November 1780, Amsterdam, Lee to Adams, 29 November 1780, Bruxelles, in Adams Mss. Trust, MHS.
10 John Rutledge to delegates, 24 May 1780, Camden, in "John Rutledge
   Letters," *South Carolina Historical and Genealogical Magazine* 17 (1916):
   124-25; John Sullivan to George Washington, 12 November 1780, in Hammond, ed., *Papers of Major-General John Sullivan*, 15: 198. See also
   Nathanael Greene to the General Court of Virginia, 20 November 1780, in
   PCC, Item 78, p. 349.
11 JCC, 18: 1070-71; James Madison to Joseph Jones, 25 November 1780, in PJM,
   2: 702-4.
12 John Rutledge to delegates, 8 December 1780, in "Rutledge Letters," 18: 48;
   Edward Burd to Edward Shippen of Lancaster, 26 December 1780, in Lewis
   Burd Walker, ed., *The Burd Papers. Selections from Letters Written by
   Edward Burd 1763-1828* (Pottsville, Pa., 1899), p. 118. See also an article
   dated Boston, 21 December, in *Pennsylvania Gazette* (Phila.), 27 December
   1780.
13 James Madison to Joseph Jones, 10 October 1780, in PJM, 2: 122; Theodorick
   Bland to Gov. Jefferson, 22 November 1780, Madison to Jones, 25
   November 1780, Virginia delegates to Gov. Jefferson, 13 December 1780,
   Instructions to Virginia delegates, in LMCC, 5: 456, 457-59, 485-86, 492;
   Secret Journals, 2: 392-97.
14 Joseph Jones to Theodorick Bland, 2 January 1781, Jones to George
   Washington, 21 February 1781, in LMCC, 5: 511, 578. Alden incorrectly states
   that the conflict over the navigation of the Mississippi River extends unchanged from 1779-1789. The move to cede the Mississippi in 1780 and 1781
   was more a southern reaction to war pressures than a New England dis-
   avowal of southern interests. This makes the Mississippi conflict in 1786 all
   the more important, because it clearly demonstrates the power of postwar
   sectional jealousies. See Alden, *First South*, pp. 54-57.
15 Simeon Deane to Barnabas Deane, 21 April 1781, in *Deane Papers*, CHSC, 23:
   158; Richard Henry Lee to Virginia delegates, 12 June 1781, in Madison
   Papers, LC. For additional views of the serious situation in the southern
   states, see Charles Carroll of Annapolis to Charles Carroll of Carrollton, 13
   January 1781, in Carroll Papers, MdHS; Benjamin Harrison to ———, 13
   February 1781, in PCC, Item 78, p. 117; Nathanael Greene to Gov. William

Greene, in "Revolutionary Correspondence," RIHSC, 6: 286; Abigail Adams to John Adams, 23 April 1781, in Adams Mss. Trust, MHS; Joseph Jones to George Washington, 31 May 1781, in LMCC, 6: 106; Cotton Tufts to John Adams, 20 June 1781, in Adams Mss. Trust, MHS; Report to the General Assembly of North Carolina, 29 June 1781, in Burke Papers, UNC.

16 Létombe to Castries, 18 December 1781, in Abraham Nasatir and Gary Elwyn Monell, eds., *French Consuls in the United States: A Calendar of Their Correspondence in the Archives Nationales* (Washington, D.C., 1967), p. 17.

17 John Adams to Congress, 30 March 1780, in WJA, 9: 138. See also Adams to Vergennes, 12 February, 19 February, 25 February, 21 March, 30 March 1780, Vergennes to Adams, 24 February 1780, in Adams Mss. Trust, MHS; Adams to the President of Congress, 18 April 1780, Vergennes to Adams, 25 July 1780, in WJA, 7: 151, 235; Page Smith, *John Adams,* 2 vols. (Garden City, N.Y., 1962), 1: 459-81.

18 Smith, *John Adams,* 1: 479; Benjamin Franklin to John Adams, 8 October 1780, in WJA, 7: 314-15; Vergennes to Luzerne, 7 August 1780, in Bemis, *The Diplomacy,* p. 178. See also William Gordon to John Adams, 8-11 March 1780, in Adams Mss. Trust, MHS; Samuel Adams to James Lovell, 25 March 1780, in Cushing, ed., *Writings of Samuel Adams,* 4: 186.

19 George Mason to George Mason, Jr., 3 June 1781, in Robert A. Rutland, ed., *The Papers of George Mason,* 3 vols. (Chapel Hill, N.C.), 2: 694; Arthur Lee to John Adams, 5 June 1780, in Adams Mss. Trust, MHS; Ralph Izard to Richard Henry Lee, 15 October 1780, in Lee Papers, UVa.

20 Benjamin Rush to John Adams, 28 April 1780, in Adams Mss. Trust, MHS. See also Arthur Lee to Count Sarsfield, 24 October 1780, in LMCC, 5: 426.

21 *Secret Journals,* 2: 435. See also ibid., pp. 293-94; President of Congress to John Adams, 10 January 1781, in WJA, 7: 353; Stinchcombe, *French Alliance,* pp. 38-43, 156, 167.

22 *Secret Journals,* 2: 437-43, 463; James Lovell to John Adams, 21 June 1781, in LMCC, 6: 125. See also Arthur Lee to Francis Dana, 23 July 1782, in LMCC, 6: 389-90; Stinchcombe, *French Alliance,* pp. 173-74.

23 Arthur Lee to James Warren, 15 June 1781, in *Warren-Adams Letters,* MHSC, 73: 166-67; Alexander Shippen to Abigail Adams, 17 June 1781, in Adams Mss. Trust, MHS; Samuel Adams to Thomas McKean, 29 August 1781, in Cushing, ed., *Writings of Samuel Adams,* 4: 261; John Adams to James Searle, 26 December 1781, in Smith, *John Adams,* 1: 504.

24 James Lovell to John Adams, 21 July 1781, in WJA, 7: 453; Arthur Lee to James Warren, 27 July 1781, in *Warren-Adams Letters,* MHSC, 73: 169; Stinchcombe, *French Alliance,* pp. 171-73. For an overview see "Correspondence between John Adams and Mercy Warren Relating to Her 'HISTORY OF THE AMERICAN REVOLUTION,' July-August 1807," MHSC, 5th ser., 4 (1878): 317-491.

25 Luzerne to Vergennes, 13 May 1781, in Charles P. Whittemore, *A General of the Revolution: John Sullivan of New Hampshire* (New York, 1961), p. 177. See also John Sullivan to George Washington, 6 May 1781, in Hammond,

ed., *Papers of Major-General John Sullivan,* 15: 293; Morris, *The Peace-makers,* pp. 210-11; Stinchcombe, *French Alliance,* pp. 118-32, 163-67; Luzerne to Castries, 13 August and 25 December 1781, in Nasatir and Monell, eds., *French Consuls,* pp. 145-47.

26 Samuel Huntington to Caesar Rodney, 15 June 1780, in Sol Feinstone Collection, DL; Alexander Hamilton to Isaac Sears, 12 October 1780, in PAH, 2: 474-75.

27 Edward Rutledge to John Jay, 19 August 1776, in LMCC, 2: 56; Henry Laurens to John Adams, 4 October 1779, in Laurens Papers, SCHS; Thomas Paine, "Public Good," in Conway, ed., *Writings of Paine,* 2: 66; Nathanael Greene to Jeremiah Wadsworth, 8 May 1780, in Knollenberg Collection, Box 4, YL.

28 Franklin B. Hough, *Proceedings of a Convention of Delegates From Several of the New England States Held at Boston, August 3-9 1780* (Albany, N.Y., 1867), p. 50. See also Gov. Jonathan Trumbull to Griswold and Pitkin, 17 August 1780, in Edward E. Salisbury, "The Griswold Family of Connecticut," *Magazine of American History* 11 (1884): 224; Alexander Hamilton to James Duane, 3 September 1780, in PAH, 2: 407; John Sullivan to Meshech Weare, 2 October 1780, in LMCC, 5: 397-98. Among the delegates were Cushing, Gorham, Lowell, Root, and Langdon.

29 William Bradford, President of the Convention, to Gov. Clinton, 23 November 1780, in Sparks Collection, p. 12, HL; James Warren to Samuel Adams, 4 December 1780, in *Warren-Adams Letters,* MHSC, 73: 151. See also "The Hartford Convention in 1780," *Magazine of American History* 8 (1882): 688-98; "Extract of a letter dated Philadelphia, 2 January 1780 [1781]," in John Dickinson Papers, R. R. Logan Collection, HSP. The resolves were sent to congressional committee on 12 December; see JCC, 18: 141. Among the delegates were Cushing, John Taylor Gilman, John Sloss Hobart, Eliphalet Dyer, and Egbert Benson.

30 George Washington letter, ca. 1781, sent by Joseph Jones to James Madison [endorsed Washington], in Harry D. Gilpin, ed., *The Papers of James Madison,* 3 vols. (Washington, D.C., 1840), 1: 81; Philip Schuyler to Washington, 21 January 1781, in Sparks, ed., *Letters to Washington,* 3: 212; John Sullivan to John Wendell, 21 January 1781, in LMCC, 5: 541.

31 James Duane to George Washington, 29 January 1781, in LMCC, 5: 551; Washington letter, ca. 1781, in Gilpin, ed., *Madison Papers,* 1: 81. See also Thomas Paine, "Public Good," in Conway, ed., *Writings of Paine,* 2: 33; James Duane to Washington, 4 May 1780, in Sparks, ed., *Letters to Washington,* 2: 446; John Mathews to Washington, 30 February 1781, in McKean Papers, vol. 1, HSP; Joseph Jones to Thomas Jefferson, 16 April 1781, in PTJ, 5: 469-70.

32 Thomas Rodney, "Diary," in LMCC, 6: 7; JCC, 19: 236; James Madison to Thomas Jefferson, 16 April 1781, in PJM, 3: 72. There is some reason to believe that some New Yorkers, at least, might have hoped that the Hartford Convention would lead to a northern confederacy. The New Englanders were, by this time, dismayed by the sacrifice of their own interests for the

sake of cooperation in relation to the western lands. See "A Copy of a letter in cypher from Connecticut, received, F. 4, 1781," *Magazine of American History* 10 (1883): 410-11; Philip Schuyler to George Washington, 21 January 1781, in Sparks, ed., *Letters to Washington*, 3: 213; Schuyler to Henry Van Schaack, 13 March 1787, in Henry C. Van Schaack, *Memoirs of the Life of Henry Van Schaack* (Chicago, 1892), pp. 153-54.

33 James Varnum to Gov. Greene, 2 April 1781, in LMCC, 6: 42; JCC, 20: 469-73, 21: 894-96; Allan Nevins, *The American States During and After the Revolution 1775-1789* (New York, 1924), p. 626.

34 Samuel Chase to John Sullivan, 24 December 1776, in Hammond, ed., *The Papers of Major-General John Sullivan*, 13: 306; Benjamin Rush to Richard Henry Lee, 30 December 1776, in Lee Papers, APS. See also Jonathan Trumbull to Henry Laurens, 6 September 1779, in Laurens Papers, SCHS; Joseph Jones to James Madison, 2 October 1780, in PJM, 2: 106; Ver Steeg, *Robert Morris*, p. 58.

35 Thomas McKean to Samuel Adams, 8 July 1781, in LMCC, 6: 136; Arthur Lee to James Warren, 27 July 1781, in *Warren-Adams Letters*, MHSC, 73: 170; Adams to McKean, 29 August 1781, in Cushing, ed., *Writings of Samuel Adams*, 4: 260; Joseph Reed to Nathanael Greene, 1 November 1781, in William B. Reed, *Life and Correspondence of Joseph Reed*, 2 vols. (Philadelphia, 1947), 2: 376.

36 Jensen, *The New Nation*, p. 34; East, *Business Enterprise*, pp. 110, 116, 140-47; Alexander Hamilton to Robert Morris, 30 April 1781, in PAH, 2: 606.

37 Alexander Hamilton to James Duane, 3 September 1780, in PAH, 2: 407.

38 James Madison to Thomas Jefferson, 2 June 1780, in PJM, 2: 38; William Heath to Samuel H. Parsons, 5 January 1781, in *Heath Papers*, MHSC, 5 (1905): 150; Ezekiel Cornell to Gov. Greene, 7 January 1781, Oliver Wolcott to Gov. Trumbull, 9 January 1781, in LMCC, 5: 514, 516.

39 JCC, 19: 112; James Madison to Edmund Pendleton, 29 May 1781, in PJM, 3: 140. See also Ezekiel Cornell to Nathanael Greene, 23 January 1781, John Mathews to William Livingston, 29 January 1781, in LMCC, 5: 543, 550; Alexander Hamilton, "The Continentalist IV," in PAH, 3: 670.

40 Arthur Lee to Francis Dana, 6 July 1782, in Arthur Lee Papers, HL; Lee to Dana, 23 July 1782, in LMCC, 6: 389-90. See also Lee to James Warren, 8 April 1782, in LMCC, 6: 326; Stinchcombe, *French Alliance*, pp. 179-81.

41 Arthur Lee to Samuel Adams, 6 August 1782, Charles Thomson, "Notes of Debates," in LMCC, 6: 429, 390-91. See James Madison to Edmund Randolph, 16 July 1783, in PJM, 4: 419.

42 James Madison to Edmund Randolph, 5 August 1782, in PJM, 5: 21.

43 Charles Thomson, "Notes of Debates," in LMCC, 6: 410-11; JCC, 22: 428, 449-51. See also Bemis, *The Diplomacy*, pp. 107-8.

44 JCC, 22: 459-60. See also Charles Thomson, "Notes of Debates," in LMCC, 6: 432-38.

45 Samuel Huntington to Gov. Trumbull, 24 March 1781, in LMCC, 6: 33; JCC, 19: 295; Gov. Greene to Robert Morris, October 1781, Greene to Rhode

Island delegates, 22 December 1781, in William R. Staples, *Rhode Island in the Continental Congress* (Providence, R.I., 1870), pp. 355, 363.

46 JCC, 22: 72, 132-35, 23: 447. The letter hiring Paine is in Sparks, ed., *Letters to Washington,* 3: 495. See also Virginia delegates to Gov. Harrison, 28 May 1781, in LMCC, 6: 358.

47 James Madison to Edmund Randolph, 19 and 26 November 1782, in PJM, 5: 288-90, 325-32.

48 David Howell to Welcome Arnold, 3 August 1782, in LMCC, 6: 411; "A Countryman," *Providence Gazette,* 21 September 1782; "A Freeholder," "A Vindication of the State of Rhode Island for not having granted the 5% Duties recommended by Congress," *Providence Gazette,* 9 November 1782.

49 Rhode Island delegates to Gov. Greene, 15 October 1782, in LMCC, 6: 501. See also Harry H. Clark, ed., *Six New Letters of Thomas Paine BEING PIECES ON THE FIVE PER CENT DUTY addressed to the citizens of RHODE ISLAND* (Madison, Wis., 1939).

50 Ezra L'Hommedieu to Gov. Clinton, 9 October 1782, in LMCC, 6: 501; George Mason to Thomas Jefferson, 27 September 1781, in Rutland, ed., *Mason Papers,* 2: 697.

51 James Madison to Edmund Pendleton, 30 October 1781, in PJM, 3: 297. See also Madison to Thomas Jefferson, 15 January 1782, ibid., 4: 32-33; Jensen, "Creation," pp. 325-30.

52 Pierce Butler to James Iredell, 5 April 1782, in LMCC, 6: 327; James Madison, "Observations on Vermont and Territorial Claims," 1 May 1782, in PJM, 4: 200-202; John Taylor Gilman to Josiah Bartlett, 5 August 1782, in LMCC, 6: 413-14.

53 Drinker & James to Richard Tilgham, 30 August 1782, in Drinker Letter-book, 1772-1786, HSP. See also Ver Steeg, *Robert Morris,* p. 138; François Barbé-Marbois to Castries, 25 May, 31 July, 2 October 1782, in Nasatir and Monell, eds., *French Consuls,* pp. 150-52.

54 David Howell to Gov. Greene, 30 July 1782, in LMCC, 6: 401-2; Welcome Arnold & David Howell to Gov. Greene, 13 October 1782, in Staples, *Rhode Island,* p. 393; North Carolina delegates to Gov. Martin, 22 October 1782, in LMCC, 6: 516.

55 David Howell to Nathanael Greene, 5 November 1782, in André de Coppet Collection, Princeton University; Princeton, N.J.; Howell to Welcome Arnold, 17 November 1782, in LMCC, 6: 541; "On the 5% Impost," *Providence Gazette,* 5 April 1783.

56 JCC, 23: 798; Virginia Legislature, in PCC, Item 25, p. 373; James Madison to Edmund Pendleton, 22 January 1782 [1783], Samuel Wharton to the Delaware Council, 6 January 1783, in LMCC, 7: 21, 3.

57 George Mason to Edmund Randolph, 19 October 1782, in Rutland, ed., *Mason Papers,* 2: 751-53. See also Benjamin Harrison to George Washington, 31 March 1783, in Bancroft, *Formation of the Constitution,* 1: 301. See also Randolph to James Madison, 7 February 1783, in PJM, 6: 207-8.

CHAPTER 3: A FEDERALIST RESURGENCE

1 Benjamin Rush to Nathanael Greene, 15 April 1782, in Lyman H. Butter-
field, ed., *Letters of Benjamin Rush,* 2 vols. (Princeton, N.J., 1951), 1: 268.
See also Ver Steeg, *Robert Morris,* pp. 166-67; Ferguson, *Power of the
Purse,* pp. 142-45; JCC, 22: 115.

2 James Madison to Edmund Randolph, 2 July 1782, in PJM, 4: 387; 26 June,
Independent Gazetteer (Phila.), 14 September 1782; Ferguson, *Power of the
Purse,* pp. 149-50.

3 Charles Thomson, "Notes of Debates," in LMCC, 6: 397; Robert Morris to
Congress, 29 July 1782, in JCC, 22: 434.

4 JCC, 22: 429-49; Ver Steeg, *Robert Morris,* pp. 124-28.

5 *Independent Gazetteer* (Phila.), 7 September, 26 October 1782; Broadeus
Mitchell, *Alexander Hamilton,* 2 vols. (New York, 1957), 1: 273-74; Gaspare
J. Saladino, "The Economic Revolution in Late Eighteenth Century Con-
necticut" (Ph.D. diss., University of Wisconsin, 1964), p. 195; *Independent
Gazetteer* (Phila.), 3 December 1782; Robert L. Brunhouse, *The Counter-
Revolution in Pennsylvania 1776-1790* (Harrisburg, Pa., 1942), pp. 131-32;
JCC, 23: 545-47.

6 Benjamin Lincoln to Henry Knox, 26 August 1782, in Henry Knox Papers,
MHS; James Madison to Edmund Randolph, 24 September 1782, in PJM, 5:
159. See also Lincoln to Artemas Ward, 13 September 1782, in Artemas
Ward Papers, MHS.

7 James Madison to Edmund Randolph, 22 October 1782, in PJM, 5: 214. See
also Samuel Ogden to Henry Knox, 15 October 1782, in Knox Papers, MHS;
Ferguson, *Power of the Purse,* p. 134.

8 Memorial to Congress, n.d., in William Irvine Papers, HSP; Benjamin Lincoln to Henry Knox, 3 December 1782, in Knox Papers, MHS. See also
Samuel Osgood to Knox, 4 December 1782, in Knox Papers, MHS; Richard
H. Kohn, "The Inside History of the Newburgh Conspiracy: America and
the Coup D'Etat," *William and Mary Quarterly,* 3d ser., 27 (April 1970): 190.

9 Robert R. Livingston to John Adams, 19 December 1782, in Adams Mss.
Trust, MHS. See also JMND, in PJM, 5: 361-64; *Pennsylvania Gazette* (Phila.), 1
January 1783.

10 Alexander Hamilton to James Duane, 3 September 1780, in PAH, 2: 407;
Gouverneur Morris to Nathanael Greene, 24 December 1781, in Sparks,
Morris, 1: 240.

11 Robert R. Livingston to Benjamin Franklin, 6 January 1783, Livingston to
Lafayette, 10 January 1783, in Francis Wharton, ed., *The Revolutionary
Diplomatic Correspondence of the United States,* 6 vols. (Washington,
D.C., 1889), 6: 301; Robert Morris to Franklin, 11 January 1783, in Jared
Sparks, ed., *Diplomatic Correspondence of the American Revolution,* 12
vols. (Boston, 1829-30), 12: 310. See also Thomas Paine to Morris, 20
November 1782, in *Letters of Robert Morris,* NYHSC, 11 (1879): 484.

12 Robert Morris to Benjamin Franklin, 27 September 1782, in Wharton, ed.,
Diplomatic Correspondence, 5: 774; Morris to John Dickinson, 20 January

1783, in Society Autograph Collection, Box 21, HSP; Luzerne to Vergennes, 6 February 1783, in Bancroft, *Formation of the Constitution,* 1: 294.

13 Gouverneur Morris to Henry Knox, 7 January 1783, in Knox Papers, MHS; Knox to Morris, February 1781, in Sparks, *Morris,* 1: 256. See also James Madison to Edmund Randolph, 30 December 1782, in PJM, 5: 473; Alexander McDougal to Knox, 9 January 1783, in Knox Papers, MHS; Kohn, "New burgh Conspiracy," p. 190.

14 Gouverneur Morris to John Jay, 1 January 1783, in Sparks, *Morris,* 1: 249; Abner Nash to James Iredell, 18 January 1783, in LMCC, 7: 19.

15 JCC, 24: 290; JMND, in PJM, 6: 15-16. See also James Madison to Edmund Randolph, 7 January 1783, ibid., p. 22; John Taylor Gilman to Meshech Weare, 9 January 1783, Phillips White to Josiah Bartlett, 9 January 1783, in LMCC, 7: 11, 13.

16 JMND, in PJM, 6: 31-34. See also Joseph Jones to Benjamin Harrison, 14 January 1783, in Madison Papers, LC.

17 JCC, 24: 48-49. See also JMND, in PJM, 6: 51-53.

18 JMND, in PJM, 6: 117-23, 141-49; JCC, 24: 82-97.

19 JMND, in PJM, 6: 158-65; James McDougal and Henry Ogden to Henry Knox, 8 February 1783, in United States Revolution, vol. 1, AAS.

20 JMND, in PJM, 6: 251, 281. See also James Madison to Edmund Randolph, 4 February 1783, ibid., pp. 193-94; Brunhouse, *Counter-Revolution,* pp. 132-33.

21 Arthur Lee to Samuel Adams, 29 January 1783, in LMCC, 7: 28; JMND, in PJM, 6: 259, 261, 264-65, 273.

22 Alexander Hamilton to George Washington, 7 February 1783, in LMCC, 7: 33; Alexander McDougal to Henry Knox, 12 February 1783, in Knox Papers, MHS. See also Gouverneur Morris to Nathanael Greene, 15 February 1783, in Sparks, *Morris*, 1: 251; James Duane to Hamilton, 17 February 1783, in PAH, 3: 257; Kohn, "Newburgh Conspiracy," p. 197; C. Edward Skeen, with a Rebuttal by Richard H. Kohn, "The Newburgh Conspiracy Reconsidered," *William and Mary Quarterly,* 3d ser., 31 (April 1974): 273-98.

23 JMND, James Madison to Edmund Randolph, 25 February 1783, in PJM, 6: 365-66, 286; Moses Hazen to William A. Atlee, 23 February 1783, in Peter Force Miscellany, Box 30, LC.

24 Alexander McDougal to Henry Knox, 27 February 1783, in Knox Papers, MHS; JMND, 4 March, in PJM, 6: 308-9. See also Nathaniel Gorham to Caleb Davis, 26 February 1783, in Caleb Davis Papers, vol. 12a, MHS; Alexander Hamilton to Gov. Clinton, 24 February 1783, in PAH, 3: 269; Joseph Jones to George Washington, 27 February 1783, in Paul Leicester Ford, ed., *Letters of Joseph Jones of Virginia* (Washington, D.C., 1889), p. 97; Robert Morris to Washington, 27 February 1783, in Sparks, ed., *Diplomatic Correspondence,* 12: 328.

25 Horatio Gates to Richard Peters, 20 February 1783, Newburgh, in Feinstone Collection, DL; Henry Knox to Alexander McDougal, 21 February 1783, in Alexander McDougal Papers, NYHS; Knox to Gouverneur Morris, 21 February 1783, in Sparks, *Morris*, 1: 256.

26 James Madison to Edmund Randolph, 4 March 1783, in PJM, 6: 308-9. See
    also JCC, 24: 170; JMND, in PJM, 6: 311-14; George Washington to the Officers
    of the Army, 15 March 1783, in WGW, 26: 223; Kohn, "Newburgh Conspir-
    acy," p. 205.

27 JMND, 17 March, 22 March, in PJM, 6: 348, 375-77.

28 JCC, 24: 24; Jonathan Arnold to Welcome Arnold, 11 February 1783, in Gratz
    Collection, Box 3, HSP; JMND, in PJM, 6: 215-16.

29 JMND, 17 February, in PJM, 6: 247. See also James Madison to Edmund
    Randolph, 18 February 1783, ibid., pp. 256-57; JCC, 24: 137.

30 Hugh Williamson to ———, 17 February 1783, William Floyd to Gov.
    Clinton, 18 February 1783, in LMCC, 7: 46, 48. See also JCC, 24: 204-13; JMND,
    in PJM, 6: 351, 397-402.

31 JCC, 24: 214-22; JMND, in PJM, 6: 408, 425. For many reasons the states never
    ratified the amendment.

32 JMND, in PJM, 6: 471; Joseph Jones to George Washington, 8 May 1783, in
    Sparks, ed., Letters to Washington, 4: 334.

33 JMND, 17 March, in PJM, 6: 348. See also Jedediah Huntington to Andrew
    Huntington, 18 March 1783, John Chester to Joshua Huntington, 21 March
    1783, in Huntington Papers, CHSC, 20 (1922): 460, 171.

34 Alexander Hamilton to George Washington, 17 March 1783, in PAH, 3:
    290-93; Washington to Hamilton, 16 April 1783, in WGW, 26: 324; Arthur Lee
    to St. George Tucker, 21 July 1783, in Tucker-Coleman Collection, WML. See
    also Elias Boudinot to Lafayette, 12 April 1783 (draft), in Elias Boudinot
    Papers, LC.

35 William Gordon to Horatio Gates, 26 February 1783, in "Gordon Letters,"
    MHSP, 63: 487; Arthur Lee to Samuel Adams, 5 March 1783, in Samuel
    Adams Papers, NYPL; JMND, in PJM, 6: 304-5; Lee to John Adams, 12 August
    1784, in Adams Mss. Trust, MHS.

36 See John Cox to Charles Pettit, 1 March 1783, in Joseph Reed Papers, NYHS;
    John Armstrong, Jr., to Horatio Gates, 16 June 1783, in Burnett Collection,
    Box 8, LC; Richard Butler to John Dickinson, n.d. [early 1783], in Dickinson
    Papers, R. R. Logan Collection, HSP.

37 PAH, 3: 113. See also David Ramsay to Nathanael Greene, 10 September
    1782, in Brunhouse, "Ramsay Letters," p. 71; John Taylor Gilman to Josiah
    Bartlett, 17 September 1782, in LMCC, 6: 474; Egbert Benson to Robert R.
    Livingston, 24 November 1781 [1782], in Robert R. Livingston Papers,
    NYHS; Thomas C. Cochran, New York in the Confederation (Philadelphia,
    1932), pp. 137-38.

38 Alexander Hamilton to Gov. Clinton, 12 January 1783, in PAH, 2: 240; Henry
    Knox to Gouverneur Morris, 21 February 1783, in Sparks, Morris, 1: 256;
    Knox to Alexander McDougall, 21 February 1783, in McDougall Papers,
    NYHS; JMND, James Madison to Edmund Randolph, 4 March 1783, in PJM, 6:
    297-99, 308-9.

39 JMND, 1 April 1783, in PJM, 6: 424-25; Stephen Higginson to Henry Knox, 8
    February 1787, in J. Franklin Jameson, ed., Letters of Stephen Higginson
    1783-1804, American Historical Association, Annual Report 1 (1896): 745;

Higginson to Samuel Adams, 20 May 1783, in Misc., NYHS. For a standard interpretation of federalist willingness to support a general convention, see Henderson, *Party Politics,* p. 335.

40 George Washington to Lafayette, 25 April 1783, in Sparks Collection, HL; Circular Letter, 8 June 1783, Washington to William Gordon, 8 July 1783, in WGW, 26: 487, 27: 49. See also Lafayette to Washington, 5 February 1783, in Sparks, ed., *Letters to Washington,* 3: 545; Lafayette to Alexander Hamilton, 5 February 1783, in Wharton, ed., *Diplomatic Correspondence,* 6: 240.

41 J. G. Gebhard to George Washington, 15 September 1783, in Washington Papers, LC; Edmund Randolph to James Madison, 28 June 1783, in PJM, 7: 200; David Howell to Nicholas Brown, 30 July 1783, in Brown Papers, JCBL. See also Stephen Higginson to Arthur Lee, 27 January 1784, in MHSP, 2d ser., 8 (1893): 177.

42 PAH, 3: 420; JCC, 25: 532.

43 Joseph Reed to Nathanael Greene, 14 March 1783, in Reed, *Reed Correspondence,* 2: 395; James Warren to John Adams, 27 October 1783, in Adams Mss. Trust, MHS; Stephen Higginson to Elbridge Gerry, 5 November 1783, in Misc., NYHS. See chapter 5 for the antinationalist movement in relation to foreign policy.

44 Stephen Higginson to Elbridge Gerry, Dec./Jan. 1783-84, in Russell W. Knight Collection, MHS; Gerry to Higginson, 14 May 1784, in Burnett Collection, Box 9, LC; Gerry to Higginson, 4 March 1784, in Samuel Adams Papers, NYPL. The correspondence and items attacking the society are too numerous to cite in total. See, for example, "Cassius" [Burke], *Consideration of the Society of the Cincinnati . . .* (Charleston, S.C., 1783); Worcester, 4 March, *Pennsylvania Journal* (Phila.), 20 March 1784; Norwich, 13 May, *Newport Mercury,* 23 May 1784.

45 Samuel Adams to John Adams, 15 September 1785, in Knollenberg Collection, YL. See also Nathanael Greene to Joseph Reed, 14 May 1784, in Reed, *Reed Correspondence,* 2: 409; John Thaxter to John Adams, 1 June 1784, in Adams Mss. Trust, MHS; *Freeman's Journal* (Phila.), 5 June 1784.

46 Samuel Osgood to Stephen Higginson, 2 February 1784, in Bowdoin-Temple Letters, IV, Winthrop Papers, vol. 24, MHS. See also Higginson to Theophilus Parsons, April 1783, in Theophilus Parsons, *Memoir of Chief Justice Parsons* (Boston, 1859), pp. 478-79; Higginson to Samuel Adams, 20 May 1783, in Samuel Adams Papers, NYPL; Higginson to Arthur Lee, 27 January 1784, in MHSP, 8: 179; "CASCA," *Freeman's Journal* (Phila.), 2 June 1784.

47 David Ramsay to Benjamin Rush, 8 June 1783, in Benjamin Rush Papers, David Ramsay Letters, HSP; Alexander Gillon to Arthur Lee, 29 November 1783, in Arthur Lee Papers, HL; See also Ramsay to Theodorick Bland, 8 August 1783, in Charles Campbell, ed., *The Bland Papers Being a Selection From Manuscripts of Col. Theodorick Bland, Jr.,* 2 vols. in one (Petersburg, Va., 1843), 2: 113-15.

48 Edmund Randolph to James Madison, 15 May 1783, Edmund Pendleton to Madison, 4 May 1783, in PJM, 7: 45, 12-13.

49 Silas Deane to Simeon Deane, April 1783, in *The Deane Papers,* NYHSC, 23

(1890): 147. For Connecticut, see Lebanon, *Independent Gazetteer* (Phila.), 17 May 1783; Saladino, "The Economic Revolution," pp. 198-200; *Boston Gazette,* 10 November 1783; *Pennsylvania Gazette* (Phila.), 19 November 1783; William Ellery to John Adams, 3 December 1783, in Adams Mss. Trust, MHS. For Rhode Island, see Abiel Foster to Meshech Weare, 11 August 1783, in Meshech Weare Papers, MHS; David Howell to Carden Hazard, 26 August 1783, in LMCC, 7: 240.

50 Tristram Dalton to John Adams, 16 July 1783, in Adams Mss. Trust, MHS; Rhode Island delegates to Gov. Greene, 8 September 1783, in LMCC, 7: 288.

51 *Freeman's Journal* (Phila.), 29 October 1783. See also Abigail Adams to John Adams, 30 June 1783, in Adams Mss. Trust, MHS; James Madison to Thomas Jefferson, 11 August 1783, in PJM, 7: 269. For a defense by one of the deposed delegates, see Samuel Holten to Rev. Benjamin Wadsworth, 14 August 1783, in *The Historical Collections of the Danvers Historical Society,* 26 (1938): 92-94.

52 Stephen Higginson to Theodorick Bland, 6 October 1783, in LMCC, 7: 323; 24 September, *Boston Gazette,* 29 October, 13 October 1783. See also Robert Morris to John Adams, 27 September 1782, in Wharton, ed., *Diplomatic Correspondence,* 5:771; Adams to Morris, 11 July 1783, in Adams Mss. Trust, MHS; Adams to Morris, 9 October 1783, in Wharton, ed., *Diplomatic Correspondence,* 6: 536-37. See above note 9 for Livingston's attempt to pressure Adams.

53 Stephen Higginson to Samuel Holten, 14 October 1783, in LMCC, 7: 333; Higginson to Arthur Lee, 23 October 1783, in Dreer Collection, Members of Old Congress, HSP; Col. Hull to Henry Knox, 14 October 1783, in Knox Papers, MHS. There was widespread discussion of the passage of the impost. For the events surrounding Massachusetts's passage of the impost, see Stephen E. Patterson, "After Newburgh: The Struggle for the Impost in Massachusetts," in *The Human Dimensions of Nation Making,* ed. James K. Martin (Madison, Wis., 1976), pp. 184-217.

54 Stephen Higginson to Elbridge Gerry, Dec./Jan. 1783-84, in Knight Collection, MHS; Higginson to Arthur Lee, — November 1783, in Arthur Lee Papers, HL; Samuel Osgood to John Adams, 14 December 1783, in Adams Mss. Trust, MHS. See also Van Beck Hall, *Politics Without Parties Massachusetts 1780-1790* (Pittsburgh, Pa., 1972), pp. 162-63.

55 Stephen Higginson to Arthur Lee, — November 1783, in Arthur Lee Papers; HL; Samuel Osgood to Higginson, 2 February 1784, in Bowdoin-Temple Letters, IV, Winthrop Papers, vol. 24, MHS; Lee to Theodorick Bland, 7 April 1784, in Campbell, ed., *Bland Papers,* 2: 108. See also Lee to John Adams, 11 May 1784, in Adams Mss. Trust, MHS; JCC, 26: 356-57, 27: 437-43, 469-71.

56 Alexander Hamilton to John Jay, 25 July 1783, in PAH, 3: 416; Jeremy Belknap to Ebenezer Hazard, 3 March 1784, in *Belknap Papers,* MHSC, 5th ser., 2 (1877): 309; François Barbé-Marbois to Rayvenal, 20 November 1784, in Bancroft, *Formation of the Constitution,* 1: 398. See also articles dated London, 5 January, *Pennsylvania Journal* (Phila.), 31 March 1784; Norwich, 6 May, *New York Journal,* 27 May 1784.

57 Nathanael Greene to Joseph Reed, 23 April 1783, in Reed Papers, NYHS; Greene's *Journals*, 3 September 1783, in George Washington Greene, *The Life of Nathanael Greene*, 3 vols. (New York, 1871), 3: 525; Jedediah Huntington to Andrew Huntington, 19 September 1783, in *Huntington Papers*, CHSC, 20: 466; James Madison to Edmund Randolph, 8 September 1783, in PJM, 7: 291. See chapter 9 for nationalist reactions to this vision of anarchy and the attempt to redefine their ideology.

58 Joseph Reed to William Bradford, 2 May 1784, in Reed Papers, NYHS; "GROTIUS," *Freeman's Journal* (Phila.), 22 October 1783; "INDEPENDENS," *New Hampshire Gazette* (Ports.), 23 August 1783. See also Richard Henry Lee to Wormley Carter, 3 June 1783, in James C. Ballagh, ed., *Letters of Richard Henry Lee*, 2 vols. (New York, 1911-14), 2: 282.

59 William Gordon to Arthur Lee, 2 April 1783, in Richard Henry Lee, *Life of A. Lee LL.D.* 2 vols. (Boston, 1829), 2: 291; Samuel Adams to Elbridge Gerry, 9 September 1783, in Cushing, ed., *Writings of Samuel Adams*, 4: 286; Roger Sherman, *Remarks on a Pamphlet, Entitled, "A Dissertation on the Political Union . . . "* (New Haven, Conn., 1784), p. 10; Joseph Jones to James Madison, 14 June 1783, in PJM, 7: 143; Abraham Yates, *Political Papers Addressed to the Advocates for a Congressional Revenue in the State of New York* (New York, 1786), pp. 6, 13. See also Tristram Dalton to Gerry, 13 April 1784, in Gerry Papers, vol. 2, MHS; Samuel Adams to John Adams, 15 September 1785, in Knollenberg Collection, Box 5, YL.

60 Samuel Adams to Elbridge Gerry, 23 April 1784, in Cushing, ed., *Writings of Samuel Adams*, 4: 302; Tristram Dalton to John Adams, 5 December 1783, 6 April 1784, 21 December 1784. in Adams Mss. Trust, MHS.

61 Henry Laurens to Rev. James Hall, 20 February 1783, in Laurens Papers, SCHS; Stephen Higginson to Elbridge Gerry, 28 April 1784, in Misc., NYHS; William Gordon to Arthur Lee, 2 April 1783, in Lee, *A. Lee*, 2: 291.

62 Richard Henry Lee to William Whipple, 1 July 1783, in William Whipple Papers, Force Transcripts, LC; Stephen Higginson to Elbridge Gerry, 30 October 1783, in Misc., NYHS.

63 David Howell to Jabez Bowen, 19 April 1784, in Staples, *Rhode Island*, p. 489; William Whipple to Richard Henry Lee, 15 September 1783, in Lee Papers, APS.

64 William Grayson to ———, 11 September 1783, in Etting Collection, Members of Old Congress, vol. 1, HSP; Richard Henry Lee to Samuel Adams, 14 March 1785, in Burnett Collection, Box 10, LC; "TO THE PRINTER," *Virginia Gazette* (Rich.), 25 October 1785. See also Robert R. Livingston to George DeWitt, 25 June 1784, in George Dangerfield, *Chancellor Robert R. Livingston of New York, 1746–1813* (New York, 1960), p. 208; Horatio Gates to James Monroe, 6 February 1785, in Monroe Papers, 2d ser., LC.

65 22 July, *Maryland Gazette* (Ann.), 3 August 1786; Rufus King to Elbridge Gerry, 14 May 1786, in LMCC, 8: 360.

66 David Howell to Nicholas Brown, 30 July 1783, in Brown Papers, JCBL. In his discussion of post-1783 politics H. James Henderson concentrates on what he terms the southern ascendance. He overlooks the implications of the

antinationalist movement, which accounted for the temporary, but significant, intersectional accord evident in the attacks on Morris, the Cincinnati,
and the impost. He also makes no allowance for the dual-residence compromise (see chapter 4) and the early debates on foreign policy in 1783 (see
chapter 5), which were, in part, distinctly antinationalist efforts. The spec-
tacular, but momentary, rise of federalist fortunes in 1783 and 1784 makes
the sectional conflicts later on even more dramatic. See Henderson, "The
Structure of Politics," pp. 186-87; *Party Politics,* pp. 350-430.

67 See Arthur Lee to John Adams, 14 January 1783, in Adams Mss. Trust, MHS;
Benjamin Lincoln to James Warren, 5 April 1783, in *Warren-Adams Letters,*
MHSC, 73: 201; St. George L. Sioussat, "The North Carolina Cession of 1784
In Its Federal Aspects," Mississippi Valley Historical Association,
Proceedings 2 (1908): 39.

CHAPTER 4: THE CAPITAL FIGHT

1 Arthur Lee to Francis Dana, 6 June 1782, in LMCC, 6: 379. See also Beverly
Randolph to Joseph Reed, September 1782, in Reed Papers, NYHS.

2 William Gordon to Arthur Lee, 2 April 1783, Gordon to George Washington,
13 August 1783, Gordon to John Adams, 7 September 1782, in "Gordon
Letters," MHSP , 63: 489-90, 499, 469.

3 "Extract of a letter from a gentleman in Philadelphia, dated August 16,"
Virginia Gazette (Rich.), 6 September 1783; *Virginia Gazette* (Rich.), 14
June 1783. See also Virginia delegates to Gov. Harrison, 10 April 1783, in
LMCC, 7: 133; Joseph Jones to James Madison, 28 June 1783, in PJM, 7: 197-98;
"Extract of a letter from New Jersey to Providence," 26 April, *Providence
Gazette,* 13 September 1783; "Extract of a letter from Baltimore," 3 July,
Maryland Gazette (Ann.), 31 July 1783.

4 Oliver Ellsworth to Gov. Trumbull, 4 June 1783, in LMCC, 7: 180; James
Madison to Edmund Randolph, 10 June 1783, in PJM, 7: 134.

5 Varnum L. Collins, *The Continental Congress at Princeton* (Princeton,
N.J., 1908), p. 15; JMND, 20 June, in PJM, 7: 167-70. See also a letter from
Newburgh dated 24 June, *Newport Mercury,* 9 August 1783; Item from
Philadelphia, 28 June, *Newport Mercury,* 19 July 1783; *Maryland Gazette*
(Ann.), 10 July 1783; *Pennsylvania Journal* (Phila.), 28 June 1783;
Freeman's Journal (Phila.), 16 July 1783; Marbois to Castries, 5 July 1783, in
Nasatir and Monell, eds., *French Consuls,* p. 157. I am indebted to Kenneth
Bowling for his piecing together of the events on 21 June. He is currently
working on a major study of the federal residence.

6 "Z," *Independent Gazetteer* (Phila.), 28 June 1783; James Mercer to John F.
Mercer, 15 July 1783, in Mercer Papers, VHS. See also Luzerne to Vergen-
nes, ca. 1783, in Corresp. Pol., Etats-Unis, vol. 25, Min. Aff. Etrang. Paris,
LC; Alexander Hamilton to James Madison, 29 June 1783 (draft), Hamilton to
Madison 6 July 1783, in PJM, 7: 214-15.

7 Elias Boudinot to his brother, 23 June 1783, in Collins, *Continental Congress*, p. 27; Robert R. Livingston to James Madison, 19 July 1783, in PJM, 7: 235-36; Boudinot to the President of Delaware, 22 July 1783, in Society Autograph Collection, Box 16, HSP; *Pennsylvania Gazette* (Phila.), 6 August 1783.

8 *Pennsylvania Gazette* (Phila.), 25 July 1783; Tristram Dalton to John Adams, 16 July 1783, in Adams Mss. Trust, MHS; John Armstrong, Jr., to Horatio Gates, 26 June 1783, in LMCC, 7: 200n; "To the Militia Subalterns and Privates of the City and Liberties of Philadelphia," *Freeman's Journal* (Phila.), 16 July 1783. See also Jedediah Huntington to his brother, 3 July 1783, in *Huntington Papers*, CHSC, 20: 464.

9 David Howell to Nicholas Brown, 30 July 1783, in Brown Papers, JCBL; Stephen Higginson to Elbridge Gerry, 5 August 1783, in LMCC, 7: 252.

10 Arthur Lee to St. George Tucker, 21 July 1783, in Tucker-Coleman Collection, WML. See also JCC, 24: 424-25; James McHenry to Gov. Paca, 26 July 1783, in LMCC, 7: 235-36.

11 James Madison to Edmund Randolph, 28 July 1783, in PJM, 7:256. See also Benjamin Lincoln to Henry Knox, 22 July 1783, in Knox Papers, MHS.

12 James Madison to Edmund Randolph, 5 August 1783, John F. Mercer to Madison, 14 August 1783, in PJM, 7: 263, 277; JCC, 24: 484.

13 Theodorick Bland to George Weedon, 14 August 1783, in LMCC, 7: 264; James Madison to Edmund Randolph, 18 August 1783, in PJM, 7: 281-83; JCC, 24: 498-508.

14 Petition from Philadelphia, *Pennsylvania Gazette* (Phila.), 6 August 1783; Benjamin Rush to Elias Boudinot, 2 August 1783, in Butterfield, ed., *Rush Papers*, 1: 308; Boudinot to Robert R. Livingston, 29 August 1783, in Robert R. Livingston Papers, NYHS. See also Stephen Higginson to Samuel Adams, 21 August 1783, in LMCC, 7: 272; Arthur Lee to James Warren, 17 September 1783, in *Warren-Adams Letters*, MHSC, 73: 225; Rhode Island delegates to Gov. Greene, 8 September 1783, in LMCC, 7: 287.

15 Benjamin Huntington to Mrs. Ann Huntington, 8 September 1783, in W. D. McCracken, ed., *The Huntington Letters in the Possession of Julia Chester Wells* (New York, 1905), p. 57; Arthur Lee to James Warren, 13 August 1783, in *Warren-Adams Letters*, MHSC, 73: 220.

16 William Gordon to John Adams, 28 June 1783, in "Gordon Letters," MHSP, 63: 497.

17 John Twin to William Irvine, 5 August 1783, in Irvine Papers, HSP; James Madison to Edmund Randolph, 28 July 1783, in PJM, 7: 256-57.

18 David Ramsey to Benjamin Rush, 9 September 1783, in Rush Papers, Ramsay Letters, HSP; William Grayson to ———, 11 September 1783, in Etting Collection, Members of Old Congress, HSP.

19 Joseph Jones to James Madison, 21, 28 July, 24 August 1783, in PJM, 7:237, 252, 260. See also Benjamin Harrison to Thomas Jefferson, 21 November 1783, in PTJ, 6: 358. See chapter 7 for the Potomac Company.

20 Samuel Holten to Samuel Adams, 17 September 1783, in Independence National Park Historical Museum, National Park Service, Philadelphia, Pa.; "A Message from the President and the Supreme Executive Council to the General Assembly," *Pennsylvania Gazette* (Phila.), 27 August 1783; Gouverneur Morris to John Jay, 25 September 1783, in Henry P. Johnston, ed., *The Correspondence and Public Papers of John Jay*, 4 vols. (New York, 1890-93), 3: 87; Edmund Pendleton to Madison and Jones, 6 October 1783, in Mays, ed., *Pendleton Papers*, 2: 458: See also JCC, 25: 646-58.

21 JCC, 25: 659-60. See also Thomas Jefferson, "Analysis of Votes 7 Oct. 1783," Jefferson to Benjamin Harrison, 11 November 1783, in PTJ, 6: 365-66, 352.

22 JCC, 25: 664-76. See also James Madison to Edmund Randolph, 13 October 1783, in PJM, 7: 374, and chapter 7 on the Virginia-Maryland conflict.

23 Stephen Higginson to Arthur Lee, 23 October 1783, in Dreer Collection, Members of Old Congress, HSP; Higginson to Elbridge Gerry, 30 October 1783, in Misc., NYHS; New York delegates to Gov. Clinton, 16 October 1783, in LMCC, 7: 339. See also Rhode Island delegates to Gov. Greene, 9 October 1783, in LMCC, 7: 326; Benjamin Harrison to Virginia delegates, 25 October 1783, in PJM, 7: 386.

24 James Madison to Edmund Randolph, 13 October 1783, in PJM, 7: 374.

25 JCC, 25: 697-99; Charles Thomson to Hannah Thomson, 17 October 1783, in Miscellaneous Manuscripts, APS; George Clymer to Thomas FitzSimons, 18 October 1783, in Gratz Collection, Declaration of Independence, HSP.

26 JCC, 25: 706-15; *Independent Gazetteer* (Phila.), 1 November 1783; *Pennsylvania Gazette* (Phila.), 19 October 1783; Samuel Huntington to Gov. Trumbull, 22 October 1783, in LMCC, 7: 345-46.

27 Abiel Foster to Meshech Weare, 23 October 1783, Massachusetts delegates to the Assembly, 23 October 1783, in LMCC, 7: 348-49. See also Stephen Higginson to Elbridge Gerry, 5 November 1783, in Misc., NYHS; James Warren to John Adams, 15 November 1783, Thomas Cushing to Adams, 26 November 1783, Cotton Tufts to Adams, 5 November 1783, in Adams Mss. Trust, MHS.

28 Elias Boudinot to Robert R. Livingston, 23 October 1783, North Carolina delegates to Gov. Martin, 24 October 1783, in LMCC, 7: 347, 353-54; Joseph Jones to James Madison, 30 October 1783, in PJM, 7: 388. The struggle over the location of the federal residence, like sectional politics in general, has been a long overlooked subject. John R. Alden does not mention the influence of ideology and fails to work the capital fight in 1784 and 1785 into the broader context of sectional politics; see his *The First South*, pp. 66-69. Despite H. James Henderson's professed intention to demonstrate the sectional nature of partisan politics, he glosses over the capital fight in his *Party Politics*, pp. 339-43. Lawrence Delbert Cress has a concise informative discussion of the federal residence with an emphasis upon the years between 1783 and 1785. He does an admirable job with a complex subject, but certain gaps and his broad brush strokes often fail to show the connection between the federal residence and ideological and sectional conflict in post-1783

politics; see his "Whither Columbia? Congressional Residence and the Politics of the New Nation, 1776-1787," *William and Mary Quarterly*, 3d ser., 32 (1975): 581-600.

29 "A True American," *Maryland Journal* (Balt.), 29 July 1783; Thomas Jefferson to George Rogers Clark, 4 December 1783, in PTJ, 6: 371. This conflict over the future balance in the nation will be more fully discussed in chapter 7. Although H. James Henderson maintains that from 1784-87 the "southern delegates . . . achieved a level of cohesion sufficient to lead in the shaping of policy," the fact remains that the southern delegates, who were in any event not of a single mind, did not so much set policy as prevent northern, and in most instances majority, policies from being implemented; see Henderson's "The Structure of Politics," p. 174.

30 Edward Bancroft to ———, 8 November 1783, Philadelphia, in British Public Record Office, Foreign Office 4, vol. 3, microfilm, London; William Gordon to John Adams, 7 January 1784, in Adams Mss. Trust, MHS; Stephen Higginson to Elbridge Gerry, Dec./Jan. 1783-84, in Knight Collection, MHS.

31 Silas Deane to Beaumarchais, 2 April 1784, in *Deane Papers*, NYHSC, 23: 287. See also John Yeates to Edward Hand, 24 January 1784, in Society Autograph Collection, HSP.

32 Stephen Higginson to Arthur Lee, 27 January 1784, in MHSP, 8: 179; Higginson to Theodorick Bland, January 1784, in Burnett Collection, Box 10, LC.

33 "Thoughts upon the permanent Residence of CONGRESS," "a pennsylvanian," *Pennsylvania Gazette* (Phila.), 5 November 1783; Luzerne to Vergennes, ca. 1783, in Corresp. Pol., Etats-Unis, vol. 25, Min. Aff. Etrang. Paris, LC; Samuel Osgood to John Adams, 7 December 1783, in LMCC, 7: 328.

34 *Pennsylvania Gazette* (Phila.), 5 November 1783; *Maryland Journal* (Balt.), 14 November 1783; *Pennsylvania Packet* (Phila.), 18 November 1783; Charles Thomson to Richard Peters, 19 January 1784, in Thomson Papers, LC; Robert R. Livingston to John Jay, 25 January 1784, in Johnston, ed., *Jay Papers*, 3: 109.

35 Ebenezer Hazard to Jeremy Belknap, 16 January 1784, in *The Belknap Papers*, MHSC, 2: 300; Samuel Osgood to Stephen Higginson, 2 February 1784, in Bowdoin-Temple Letters, IV, Winthrop Papers, vol. 24, MHS; Elbridge Gerry to Higginson, 4 March 1784, in Samuel Adams Papers, NYPL.

36 Thomas Jefferson to James Madison, 20 February 1784, in PTJ, 6: 546; Madison to Jefferson, 16 April 1784, in PJM, 8: 9. See chapter 7.

37 James McHenry to William Smallwood, 16 March 1784, Samuel Dick to Thomas Sinnickson, 18 March 1784, in LMCC, 7: 439n10, 473.

38 Richard Peters to Charles Thomson, 22 February 1784, in Thomson Papers, LC; John Montgomery to Cadwallader Morris, 5 March 1784, in Strettel Manuscripts, HSP.

39 JCC, 26: 222-26, 291A-95. See also Thomas Jefferson to James Madison, 25 April 1784, in PTJ, 7: 119-21.

40 John Montgomery to Cadwallader Morris, 26 April 1784, in Strettel Mss., HSP.

41 Edmund C. Burnett, "The Committee of the States, 1784," in American

Historical Association, *Annual Report, 1913*, 2 vols. (Washington, D.C., 1915), pp. 139-58; David Howell to Jabez Bowen, 31 May 1784, in Staples, *Rhode Island*, p. 514. See also Arthur Lee to John Adams, 11 May 1784, in Adams Mss. Trust, MHS.

42 Joseph Jones to James Monroe, 29 April 1784, in Monroe Papers, LC; Virginia delegates to Gov. Harrison, 13 May 1784, in LMCC, 7: 524. See chapter 5.

43 Ephraim Paine to Robert R. Livingston, 24 May 1784, in Bancroft, *Formation of the Constitution*, 1: 364. See chapters 5 and 7.

44 Hugh Williamson to James Duane, 8 June 1784, in LMCC, 7: 547.

45 *Maryland Gazette* (Ann.), 11 June 1784; *Pennsylvania Journal* (Phila.), 9 June 1784; Philadelphia, 12 June, *Providence Gazette*, 26 June 1784; Burnett, "Committee of the States," pp. 152-58.

46 Jacob Read to George Washington, 13 August 1784, in Sparks, ed., *Letters to Washington*, 4: 77; James Sullivan to John Adams, 22 November 1784, in Adams Mss. Trust, MHS. See also Philadelphia, 1 September, Hartford, 2 September, *Providence Gazette*, 11 September 1784; *Pennsylvania Mercury* (Phila.), 3 September 1784; James Madison to Thomas Jefferson, 20 August 1784, in PJM, 8: 345.

47 Francis Dana to John Adams, 12 December 1784, in Adams Mss. Trust, MHS. See also Richard Henry Lee to Thomas Lee Shippen, 10 November 1784, in Ballagh, ed., *Lee Letters*, 2: 293; Samuel Holten to James Warren, 11 November 1784, in Samuel Holten Papers, LC; John F. Mercer to James Madison, 12 November 1784, James Monroe to Madison, 15 November 1784, in PJM, 8: 133-35, 140-42; *New York Journal*, 9 December 1784.

48 JCC, 27: 678-80; Rufus King to Daniel Dilham, 12 December 1784, in King Papers, Butler Library, Columbia University, New York, N.Y.; Richard Henry Lee to Thomas Lee Shippen, 13 December 1784, in Shippen Family Papers, HSP.

49 JCC, 27: 696-703.

50 Richard Dobbs Spaight to Edward Hand, 28 December 1784, in Hand Papers, Force Trans., LC; Joseph Jones to James Monroe, 20 January 1785, in James Monroe Papers, WML; Jones to Monroe, 19 March 1785, in Monroe Papers, LC.

51 Virginia delegates to Patrick Henry, 13 February 1785, in Executive Papers, VSL.

52 Francis Dana to John Adams, 30 January 1785, James Warren to Adams, 28 January 1785, in Adams Mss. Trust, MHS; Samuel Osgood to Elbridge Gerry, 3 January 1785, in Elbridge Gerry Papers, vol. 2, 1770-1848, MHS.

53 Francis Dana to John Adams, 30 January 1785, in Adams Mss. Trust, MHS; Cochran, *New York*, p. 143; Elbridge Gerry to Adams, 14 February 1785, in Adams Mss. Trust, MHS.

54 William Grayson to James Madison, 16 September 1785, in PJM, 8: 364.

55 Edmund Pendleton to Richard Henry Lee, 7 March 1785, in Mays, ed., *Pendleton Papers*, 2: 475; Samuel Hogden to William Short, 5 April 1785, in Dreer Collection, Members of Old Congress, HSP; JCC, 28: 231-34; Samuel

Hogden to Timothy Pickering, 13 April 1785, in Timothy Pickering Papers, MHS; Joseph Jones to James Monroe, 15 April 1785, in Monroe Papers, LC.

56 William Grayson to James Madison, 1 May 1785, in PJM, 8: 276; Grayson to George Wahington, 8 May 1785, in LMCC, 8: 119. See also JCC, 28: 212, 232-35, 264, 29: 542-43.

57 William Grayson to James Madison, 21 August 1785, in PJM, 8: 349.

58 Pierse Long to John Langdon, 21 August 1785, in Pierse Long Papers, NYHS; JCC, 29: 734.

59 Joseph Gardner to John Bayard, 11 February 1785, in Gratz Collection, Box 5, HSP; Ebenzer Hazard to Jeremy Belknap, 9 March 1785, in Hazard Letters, Belknap Papers, MHS; George Washington to William Grayson, 22 June 1785, in WGW, 28: 172-73.

60 William Grayson to James Madison, 16 September 1785, in PJM, 8: 264; Grayson to George Washington, 30 October 1785, in LMCC, 8: 225-26; Philadelphia, 30 October, *Newport Mercury*, 12 November 1785. A further conflict over the federal residence is discussed in chapter 9.

CHAPTER 5: COMMERCIAL REFORM

1 New York, 8 May, *Pennsylvania Journal* (Phila.), 15 May 1782; *Pennsylvania Journal* (Phila.), 9 June 1782; translation of a letter from Marbois to Vergennes, 13 March 1782, in Adams Mss. Trust, MHS.

2 William Gordon to John Adams, 7 September 1782, in "Gordon Letters," MHSP, 63: 468; Storch, "Congressional Factionalism," p. 214; Richard Henry Lee to William Shippen, 7 January 1783, Chantilly, in Feinstone Collection, DL.

3 John Jay to Robert R. Livingston, 18 September 1782, in Wharton, ed., *Diplomatic Correspondence*, 5: 740; JMND, 24 December, in PJM, 5: 441-43.

4 John Adams, quoting John Jay, "Journal of Peace Negotiations," 5 November 1782, in Wharton, ed., *Diplomatic Correspondence*, 5: 849; Adams to Jonathan Jackson, in WJA, 9: 515. See also Adams to James Warren, 15 December 1782, in *Warren-Adams Letters*, MHSC, 73: 186; Bemis, *The Diplomacy*, pp. 259-63.

5 Vergennes to Luzerne, 19 December 1782, John Adams to Robert R. Livingston, 6 September 1782, in Wharton, ed., *Diplomatic Correspondence*, 6: 152, 5: 703; James Madison to Thomas Jefferson, 11 February 1783, in PJM, 6: 221.

6 Robert R. Livingston to Congress, 18 March 1783, Livingston to the Governors, 18 March 1783, in Wharton, ed., *Diplomatic Correspondence*, 6: 313-16, 326; JMND, 19 March, James Madison to Edmund Randolph, 18 March 1783, in PJM, 6: 358, 360-61. See also JMND, 22 March, in PJM, 6: 375; Robert R. Livingston to Commissioners, 25 March 1783, in Wharton, ed., *Diplomatic Correspondence*, 6: 338-40.

7 Stephen Higginson to Theophilus Parsons, 7 April 1783, in Parsons, *Memoir*, p. 456.

8 Stephen Higginson to Samuel Adams, 20 May 1783, in Samuel Adams Papers, NYPL. See also Jensen, *New Nation*, pp. 265-77.

9 William Lee to John Adams, 9 March 1783, Bruxelles, in Ford, ed., *Letters of William Lee*, 3: 931-32; London, 28 January, *Maryland Gazette* (Ann.), 1 May 1785. See also East, *Business Enterprise*, pp. 221-28; Nettels, *Emergence of a National Economy*, pp. 21-22.

10 Jedediah Huntington to Andrew Huntington, 25 February 1783, in *Huntington Papers*, CHSC, 20: 468; William Cheever to W. D. Cheever, 17 March 1783, in Davis Papers, vol. 10, MHS. See also Boston, 21 March, *Maryland Gazette* (Ann.), 6 April 1782; In Congress, 22 June, *Providence Gazette*, 13 July 1782; James Sullivan to Benjamin Lincoln, 4 November 1782, in James Sullivan Papers, Box 1, MHS.

11 Létombe to Castries, 18 July 1783, Boston, in Nasatir and Monell, eds., *French Consuls*, p. 21; William Nells to William Irvine, 24 May 1783, in Irvine Papers, HSP; Edmund Randolph to James Madison, 24 May 1783, in PJM, 7: 73. See also Henry Laurens to Edward Brudgen [London], 17 February 1783, Bath, Laurens to Elias Vanderhorst [Bristol], 18 February 1783, Bath, in Laurens Papers, SCHS; James Pemberton to John Pemberton, 15 February, 14 May 1783, in Pemberton Papers, HSP.

12 Henry Laurens to James Bordieu [London], 20 May 1783, Paris, in Laurens Papers, SCHS; John Adams to Robert R. Livingston, 27 June 1783, in Wharton, ed., *Diplomatic Correspondence*, 6: 506; Mathew Ridley to William Paca, 26 July 1783, in Ridley Papers, letterbook, MHS.

13 Henry Laurens to Benjamin Franklin, 17 July 1783, in Laurens Papers, SCHS. See also Laurens to William Michaels, 14 August 1783, ibid.; Jensen, *New Nation*, pp. 154-63; Gordon C. Bjork, "The Weaning of the American Economy: Independence, Market Changes, and Economic Development," *Journal of Economic History* 24, no. 4 (1964): 541-60. Douglass C. North, *Growth and Welfare in the American Past* (Englewood Cliffs, N.J., 1966); Laurens to Franklin, 17 July 1783, Bath, Laurens to William Michaels, 14 August 1783, Bath, in Laurens Papers, SCHS.

14 Edmund Randolph to James Madison, 24 May 1783, in PJM, 7: 73; John Adams to James Warren, 20 March, 21 March 1783, in *Warren-Adams Letters*, MHSC, 73: 191-92, 194. See also John Adams to Abigail Adams, 4 December 1782, in Feinstone Collection, DL; John Adams to Abigail Adams, 27 February 1783, in Adams Mss. Trust, MHS; William Lee to Arthur Lee, 2 April 1783, William Lee to John Adams, 2 April 1783, Bruxelles, in Ford, ed., *Letters of William Lee*, 3: 940, 943; Francis Dana to John Adams, 29 July 1783, St. Petersburg, in Wharton, ed., *Diplomatic Correspondence*, 6: 617.

15 JCC, 23: 720-21, 28: 8-38; PTJ, 6: 211-12.

16 John Adams to Francis Dana, 24 March 1783, in Adams Mss. Trust, MHS; JCC, 24: 225-27, 267; JMND, in PJM 6: 452.

17 John Adams to Robert R. Livingston, 5 February 1783, in Wharton, ed., *Diplomatic Correspondence*, 6: 242; James Madison to Thomas Jefferson, 6 May 1783, in PJM, 7: 18; JCC, 24: 320-21. A report on 19 June was referred to a

committee composed of Williamson, Hamilton, and Madison, but nothing was done. On 5 August Samuel Huntington and Higginson replaced Hamilton and Madison, and the subject was brought up again on 15 September. See JCC, 24: 404-5, and below, note 33.

18 *Secret Journals*, 3: 366-68. See also JCC, 24: 354-55; James Madison to Thomas Jefferson, 10 June 1783, in PJM, 7: 128-29.

19 Stephen Higginson to Theodorick Bland, January 1784, in Campbell, ed., *Bland Papers*, 2: 114-15; Higginson to Arthur Lee, 24 January 1784, in MHSP, 8: 180.

20 John Adams to James Warren, 20 March, 21 March 1783, in *Warren-Adams Letters*, MHSC, 73: 191-92, 196-97.

21 Benjamin Franklin to Robert Morris, 7 March 1783, in Wharton, ed., *Diplomatic Correspondence*, 6: 277; John Adams to James Warren, 9 April 1783, in *Warren-Adams Letters*, MHSC, 73: 205. See also Adams to Warren, 13 April 1783, in *Warren-Adams Letters*, MHSC, 73: 210-11; Adams to Arthur Lee, 6 April 1783 (not sent), in Adams Mss. Trust, MHS.

22 John Adams to Arthur Lee, 12 April 1783, in WJA, 9: 518; Adams to James Warren, 21 March 1783, in *Warren-Adams Letters*, MHSC, 73: 196-97; Adams to Robert R. Livingston, 10 July 1783, in Wharton, ed., *Diplomatic Correspondence*, 6: 532.

23 John Adams to Robert R. Livingston, 14 July 1783, in Arthur Lee Papers, HL; Adams to James Warren, 16 April 1783, in *Warren-Adams Letters*, MHSC, 73: 213-15.

24 John Adams to Robert R. Livingston, 16 July 1783, in Adams Mss. Trust, MHS; Adams to Livingston, 18 July 1783, in Wharton, ed., *Diplomatic Correspondence*, 6: 561; Adams to Elbridge Gerry, 6 September 1783, in Adams Mss. Trust, MHS. See also Adams to Livingston, 23 June 1783, in Arthur Lee Papers, HL.

25 Arthur Lee to John Adams, 12 December 1782, in *Warren-Adams Letters*, MHSC, 73: 184; *Maryland Journal* (Balt.), 29 July 1783; James Warren to Adams, 27 October 1783, in Adams Mss. Trust, MHS.

26 Stephen Higginson to Elbridge Gerry, 5 November 1783, in Misc., NYHS; Higginson to Gerry, Dec./Jan. 1783-84, in Knight Collection, MHS.

27 Robert Morris, State of American Commerce, unidentified hand, May 1782, in Arthur Lee Papers, HL; Henry Laurens to James Bourdieu, 28 January 1783, Bath, in Laurens Papers, SCHS.

28 John Adams to Joseph Reed, 11 February 1784, Hague, in Adams Mss. Trust, MHS; James Warren to Adams, 24 June 1783, in *Warren-Adams Letters*, MHSC, 73: 218.

29 James Barr to John Gray Blount & Co., 7 August 1783, in Alice B. Keith, ed., *The John Gray Blount Papers*, 3 vols. (Raleigh, N.C., 1952), 1: 80. See also David Ramsay to Benjamin Rush, 9 September 1783, in Benjamin Rush Papers, Ramsay Letters, HSP; Joseph Clay to George Mead, 22 April 1783, in *Letters of Joseph Clay Merchant of Savannah 1776-1793, Collections of the Georgia Historical Society* 8 (1913): 188.

30 JMND, 1 April 1783, James Madison to Thomas Jefferson, 13 May 1783, in

PJM, 6: 424-25, 7: 39; "The North American No. 1," *Pennsylvania Journal*
(Phila.), 17 September 1783.

Not all southerners opposed commercial reform and not all northerners
supported it. There were southern merchants and merchant sympathizers
who were very active in the commercial reform movement. A few southern
nationalists hoped that commercial reform would spur further extensions in
congressional authority, and, as we shall see, Virginians active in the movement for internal improvements were also desirous of commercial reform.
On the other hand there were New England farmers and manufacturers who
were as opposed to mercantile reform as southern planters. While distinctions were hardly rigid, political leaders tended to align on commercial
reform according to the dominant interest of their state and section.

31 Richard Henry Lee to James Monroe, 5 January 1784, in Monroe Papers, LC;
   Samuel Osgood to Stephen Higginson, 2 February 1784, in Bowdoin-Temple
   Letters, IV, Winthrop Papers, vol. 24, MHS. See also Osgood to Robert Treat
   Paine, 14 February 1784, in Robert Treat Paine Papers, 1770-1784, MHS.
32 Elbridge Gerry to Stephen Higginson, 4 March 1784, in Samuel Adams
   Papers, NYPL; Higginson to Gerry, 28 April 1784, in Misc., NYHS.
33 *Secret Journals,* 3: 396, 409, 412. See also JCC, 25: 626-32.
34 Elbridge Gerry to John Adams, 14 January 1784, in WJA, 9: 521; Stephen
   Higginson to Gerry, 28 April 1784, in Misc., NYHS; Gerry to Adams, 16 June
   1784, in Adams Mss. Trust, MHS. See also Butterfield, ed., *Diary and
   Autobiography,* 3: 168.
35 Jensen, *The Articles,* p. 266. See also John Adams to Abigail Adams, 7
   September 1783, John Adams to Benjamin Franklin, 14 December 1783,
   John Adams to Joseph Reed, 11 February 1784, John Adams to Jonathan
   Jackson, 1 May 1784, John Adams to Jackson, 16 June 1784, John Adams to
   Samuel Adams, 25 June 1784, John Adams to Elbridge Gerry, 25 June 1784,
   in Adams Mss. Trust, MHS.
36 Thomas Jefferson, "Notes for Consideration of the Commissioners," 10
   April 1784, Samuel Hardy to Benjamin Harrison, 10 April 1784, in PTJ, 7: 93;
   JCC, 26: 169-70.
37 JCC, 26: 176-77, 180-85; Thomas Jefferson to James Madison, 25 April 1784,
   in PTJ, 7: 199; James Monroe to Benjamin Harrison, 26 March 1784, in Dreer
   Collection, Members of Old Congress, HSP; Elbridge Gerry to John Adams,
   24 February 1785, in Adams Mss. Trust, MHS.
38 JCC, 26: 343. See also Elbridge Gerry to Joseph Reed, 5 May 1784, in Reed,
   Reed Correspondence, 2: 408; JCC, 26: 343-47; Thomas Jefferson to James
   Madison, 7 May 1784, in PTJ, 7: 228.
39 JCC, 26: 352-63, 367-74. See also Virginia delegates to Benjamin Harrison, 13
   May 1784, Harrison to Virginia delegates, 28 May 1784, in PTJ, 7: 248-49,
   293-94.
40 East, *Business Enterprise*, pp. 243, 261-62; Jensen, *New Nation*, pp. 187-91.
   See also Edward Shippen to Joseph Shippen, 13 June 1783, in Shippen
   Papers, vol. 8, LC; Bourdieu Challet to Alexander Wallace, 3 September
   1783, in Nicholas Low Papers, London, 1783-1786, LC; Charles Pettit to

Joseph Reed, 22 May 1784, in Reed Papers, NYHS; Jacob Sebor to Silas Deane, 10 November 1784, in *Deane Papers*, CHSC, 23: 203.

41 James Madison to Edmund Randolph, 13 September 1783, in PJM, 7: 314-15. See also Robert Morris to John Jay, 27 November 1783, in Johnston, ed., *Jay Papers*, 3: 97; *Boston Gazette*, 29 December 1783; "To the People of America," by "COMMON SENSE," *Pennsylvania Gazette* (Phila.), 17 December 1783.

42 Richmond, 30 November, *Providence Gazette*, 27 December 1783; Henry Remsen to Charles Thomson, 10 December 1783, in Thomson Papers, LC. See also W. A. Low, "Merchant and Planter Relations in Post-Revolutionary Virginia 1783-1789," *Virginia Magazine of History and Biography* 111 (1953): 117; Ulrich B. Phillips, "The South Carolina Federalists," *The American Historical Review* 14 (1909): 528-30; David Ramsay to Benjamin Rush, 11 July 1783, in Rush Papers, Ramsay Letters, HSP; *Connecticut Courant* (Hart.), 30 December 1783; Saladino, "Economic Revolution," p. 200; *Independent Gazetteer* (Phila.), 28 February 1784; Richard P. McCormick, *Experiment in Independence: New Jersey in the Critical Period, 1783-1789* (New Brunswick, N.J., 1950), pp. 112-115.

43 John Jay to Charles Thomson, 14 November 1783, in Johnston, ed., *Jay Papers*, 3: 96; Stephen Higginson to Elbridge Gerry, 25 February 1784, in Misc., NYHS. See also Joseph Jones to Thomas Jefferson, 21 December 1783, in PTJ, 6: 414-15.

44 [Samuel Osgood] to John Adams, 22 November 1783, in Adams Mss. Trust, MHS. See also Salem, 11 March, *Providence Gazette*, 27 March 1784; New York, 22 April, *New Brunswick Political Intelligencer*, 27 April 1784; Philadelphia, 13 April, *Providence Gazette*, 1 May 1784; New York, 3 July, *Providence Gazette*, 10 July 1784.

45 London, 3 May, *Providence Gazette*, 24 July 1784. See also Thomas Jefferson to James Madison, 1 July 1784, in PTJ, 7: 356-57; Worcester, 30 December, *New York Journal*, 13 January 1785.

46 Circular of Philadelphia merchants, 3 January, *Independent Gazetter* (Phila.), 29 May 1784; Charles Pettit to Joseph Reed, 13 February 1784, in Reed Papers, NYHS; New York, 29 January, *Pennsylvania Journal* (Phila.), 4 February 1784; Richmond, 14 February, *New Brunswick Political Intelligencer*, 9 March 1784; Trenton, 24 May, *Pennsylvania Journal* (Phila.), 2 June 1784; Hugh Williamson to the Blounts, 16 February 1784, in Keith, ed., *Blount Papers*, 1: 150; Richard Dobbs Spaight to Gov. Martin, 12 March 1784, in LMCC, 7: 469; John Langdon to Tench Tilgham, 13 April 1784, in Bancroft, *Formation of the Constitution*, 1: 355. On the lucrative West Indies trade, see above, note 13.

47 JCC, 26: 269-70; James Madison to Thomas Jefferson, 25 April 1784, in PJM, 8: 21. See also Jefferson to Madison, 8 May 1784, in PTJ, 7: 232; Abiel Foster to Josiah Bartlett, 1 May 1784, in LMCC, 7: 510.

48 John Adams to Samuel Adams, 25 June 1784, in PTJ, 6: 468; Jonathan Jackson to Callahan, 29 July 1784, in Lee Family Papers, MHS; Adams to Lt. Gov. Cushing, 27 August 1784, in PTJ, 6: 469; Adams to Francis Dana, 4 November

1784, in Francis Dana Papers, Box 1783-1795, MHS; Samuel Choles to Nicholas Low, 2 February 1785, London, in Low Papers, LC; Mathew Ridley to John Jay, 2 May 1785, in Ridley Papers, letterbook, MHS.

49　New York, 2 November, *Pennsylvania Journal* (Phila.), 6 November 1784. See also Roger Sherman to Shipman, Drake, and Powell, 4 May 1784, in Miscellaneous Bound Manuscripts, MHS; Elbridge Gerry to Joseph Reed, 5 May 1784, in Reed Papers, NYHS; New Hampshire delegates to Meshech Weare, 5 May 1784, in LMCC, 7: 514; Tristram Dalton to John Adams, 6 April 1784, in Adams Mss. Trust, MHS; Dalton to Elbridge Gerry, 13 April 1784, in Gerry Papers, MHS.

50　James Monroe to James Madison, 18 December 1784, in PJM, 8: 189; Monroe to Thomas Jefferson, 14 December 1784, in PTJ, 7: 573. See also Tristram Dalton to John Adams, 21 December 1784, in Adams Mss. Trust, MHS; William S. Johnson to Jonathan Sturges, 26 January 1785, in Burnett Collection, Box 10, LC; Pierse Long to John Langdon, 31 January 1785, in Dreer Collection, Members of Old Congress, HSP.

51　*Freeman's Journal* (Phila.), 19 January 1785; *Pennsylvania Evening Herald*, 1, 4 June 1785. The committee was composed of Morris followers—John M. Nesbit, FitzSimons, John Nixon, Isaac Hazlehurst, John Ross, Clement Biddle, and Tench Coxe.

52　New York, 15 June, *Independent Gazetteer* (Phila.), 25 June 1785. See also "Extract of a letter dated New York," 14 March, in Public Record Office, Foreign Office 4, vol. 3; Joseph Bucklin Bishop, ed., *A Chronicle of One Hundred & Fifty Years The Chamber of Commerce of the State of New York 1768-1918* (New York, 1918), p. 42.

53　John Jay to John Adams, 26 November 1785, in Adams Mss. Trust, MHS. See also Elizabethtown, 18 May, *Pennsylvania Evening Herald* (Phila.), 21 May 1785; Portsmouth, 13 May, *Pennsylvania Journal* (Phila.), 25 May 1785; New Haven, 23 December, *Providence Gazette*, 1 January 1785.

54　*Freeman's Journal* (Phila.), 8, 15 June 1785; LMCC, 8: 89n. The committee had among its members John Hancock, Samuel A. Otis, Caleb Davis, Thomas Russell, Jonathan L. Austin, and Stephen Higginson. See chapter 6.

55　Beverly Randolph to James Monroe, 6 March 1785, in Monroe Papers, LC; Richard Henry Lee to Samuel Adams, 14 March 1785, in Burnett Collection, Box 10, LC. See also JCC, 28: 17, 70, 148.

56　Thomas Jefferson to James Monroe, 17 June 1785, in PTJ, 8: 229-31; George Washington to James McHenry, 22 August 1785, Washington to William Grayson, 22 August 1785, in WGW, 28: 227, 233. See chapter 7.

57　JCC, 28: 201-5; James Monroe to Thomas Jefferson, 12 April 1785, in PTJ, 8: 76. This was at roughly the same time that Grayson was trying to expunge the appropriation for a northern capital.

58　John Jay, report to Congress, 17 May 1785, in JCC, 28: 367; Rufus King to Elbridge Gerry, 1 May, 19 May 1785, Gerry to King, 27 May 1785, in Charles T. King, ed., *The Life and Correspondence of Rufus King*, 4 vols. (New York, 1894-97), 1: 93, 98, 101; Létombe to Castries, 24 May 1785, in Nasatir and Monell, eds., *French Consuls*, p. 33.

59 Richard Henry Lee to Thomas Jefferson, 16 May 1785, in PTJ, 8: 154; Lee to
    John Adams, 28 May 1785, in Ballagh, ed., *Lee Letters*, 2: 362. See also
    Joseph Jones to James Monroe, 21 May 1785, in Monroe Papers, 2d ser., LC.
    Jones's opposition to a commerce amendment gave rise to the idea of a
    commercial convention; see chapter 8, note 8.
60 "Extract of a letter from Boston," 8 June, *Pennsylvania Journal* (Phila.), 28
    September 1785; William Grayson to William Short, 15 June 1785, in LMCC,
    8: 141; James Monroe to Thomas Jefferson, 16 June 1785, in PTJ, 8: 216. See
    also JCC, 29: 533, 539; Intelligence from New York, 4 June 1785, in Public
    Record Office, Foreign Office 4, vol. 3; Elbridge Gerry to John Adams, 14
    July 1785, in Adams Mss. Trust, MHS; Monroe to Jefferson, 15 July 1785, in
    PTJ, 8: 296.
61 Tristram Dalton to John Adams, 21 July 1785, in Adams Mss. Trust, MHS.
    See also letter from Charleston (Mass.), 22 June, *New York Journal*, 28 July
    1785; Jacob Sebor to Silas Deane, 1 July 1785, in *Deane Papers*, CHSC, 23:
    213.
62 David Jackson to George Bryan, 18 July 1785, in George Bryan Papers, Box
    1785-1787, HSP; Rufus King to Dr. Killam, 25 July 1785, in Special Collec-
    tions, BL; James Monroe to James Madison, 26 July 1785, in PJM, 8: 330. King
    did not support the southern position. He was simply upset by attacks upon
    the northern delegates' inability to act.
63 William Grayson to George Washington, 25 July 1785, in Washington
    Papers, LC; Lyon G. Tyler, *The Letters and Times of the Tylers,* 2 vols.
    (Richmond, Va. 1884), 1: 120-21.
64 James McHenry to Joseph Clay, 24 June 1785, in Burnett Collection, Box 10,
    LC; McHenry to George Washington, 1 August 1785, in Washington Papers,
    LC; James Monroe to Thomas Jefferson, 15 August 1785, in PTJ, 8: 382. See
    also Monroe to James Madison, 14 August 1785, in PJM, 8: 342. Washington
    advised McHenry against a limited navigation act; see above note 56.
65 James McHenry to George Washington, 14 August 1785, in LMCC, 8: 182-83;
    James Madison to Richard Henry Lee, 7 July 1785, Lee to Madison, 11
    August 1785, in PJM, 8: 315, 340.
66 See articles dated 30 May, *Virginia Journal* (Alex.), 9 June 1785; Philadel-
    phia, 3 June, *Maryland Journal* (Balt.), 10 June 1785; James Monroe to
    Thomas Jefferson, 25 August 1785, in PTJ, 8: 441-42; John Q. Adams to John
    Adams, 3 August 1785, in Adams Mss. Trust, MHS; David Howell to Gov.
    Greene, 23 August 1785, in LMCC, 8: 199.

CHAPTER 6: COMMERCE AND SECTIONALISM

1 Jacob Sebor to Silas Deane, 1 July 1785, in *Deane Papers*, CHSC, 23: 213;
   Arthur Lee to John Adams, 27 July 1785, in Adams Mss. Trust, MHS.
2 Philadelphia, 4 June, *New Jersey Gazette* (Tren.), 13 June 1785; François
   Barbé-Marbois to Castries, 16 June 1785, in Nasatir and Monell, eds.,
   French Consuls, p. 181.

3 "A New Tax on Imported Goods, or not?—That is the Question."
"PHILO-REPUBLICAE," *Freeman's Jounal* (Phila.), 31 August 1785; "To the
Writer of COMMON SENSE," "CINCINNATUS," from the *New York Journal* in
the *Pennsylvania Gazette* (Phila.), 18 February 1784. See also Worcester, 22
January 1784, *Pennsylvania Journal* (Phila.), 31 August 1784; Trenton, 24
February, *Maryland Gazette* (Ann.), 4 March 1784; *New Brunswick Politi-
cal Intelligencer*, 22 June 1785.

4 "To the MECHANICS of Pennsylvania," *Independent Gazetteer* (Phila.), 8
January 1785; Francis Hopkinson to Thomas Jefferson, 20 April 1785, in PTJ,
8: 99. See also Brunhouse, *Counter-Revolution*, pp. 172-73; *Independent
Gazetteer* (Phila.), 26 February 1785; *Freeman's Journal* (Phila.), 11
January 1785; John P. Kaminski, "Paper Politics: The Northern State
Loan-Officers During the Confederation: 1782-1790" (Ph.D. diss., Univer-
sity of Wisconsin, 1972).

5 See a cordwainer petition, "To the Public," *Independent Gazetteer* (Phila.),
26 March 1785; George Lux to Benjamin Rush, 18 February 1785, in Rush
Papers, Corr., 1753-1812, HSP; *Pennsylvania Evening Herald* (Phila.), 4
June 1785; *Pennsylvania Gazette* (Phila.), 4 June 1785; George Bryan to
Samuel Atlee, 23 June 1785, in Burton Alva Konkle, *George Bryan and the
Constitution of Pennsylvania 1731-1791* (Philadelphia, 1922), p. 272.

6 Philadelphia, 1 October, *Virginia Journal* (Rich.), 20 October 1785. See also
Marbois, cadet, to Castries, 30 September 1785, in Nasatir and Monell, eds.,
French Consuls, p. 184; *Independent Gazetteer* (Phila.), 1 October 1785;
Letterbook of Thomas and John Pemberton, 4 October 1785, in Pemberton
Papers, vol. 21, HSP; Arthur Bryan to George Bryan, 3 November 1785, in
Bryan Papers, Box 17, 1785-1787, HSP. The Constitutionalists remained in
power until new developments presaged a Republican sweep in late 1786.

7 Elbridge Gerry to Samuel Holten, 2 April 1785, in Gerry Papers, 1772-1799,
Knight Collection, MHS; "A Friend to the Community," Boston, 1 April,
Virginia Gazette (Rich.), 21 May 1785; Boston, 1 April, *Independent
Gazetteer* (Phila.), 7 May 1785. See also Thomas Cushing to John Adams, 9
April 1785, Tristram Dalton to Adams, 11 April 1785, in Adams Mss. Trust,
MHS.

8 *Boston Gazette*, 18 April 1785; *Independent Gazetteer* (Phila.), 14 May
1785; *Virginia Journal* (Rich.), 12 May 1785. For the reaction of one of the
members of the seven-man committee, see Joseph Russell to Jeremy Belknap, 2 May 1785, in Belknap Papers, vol. 2, MHS.

9 Henry Knox to Henry Jackson, 18 April 1785, in Knox Papers, MHS; Tristram Dalton to John Adams, 19 April 1785, in Adams Mss. Trust, MHS.

10 Rufus King to Elbridge Gerry, 1 May, 19 May 1785, in King, *King Letters*, 1:
93, 98.

11 James Warren to John Adams, 29 January 1785, Mercy Warren to Adams, 27
April 1785, in *Warren-Adams Letters*, MHSC, 73: 249, 252.

12 Elbridge Gerry to Rufus King, 28 March 1785, in King, *King Letters*, 1:
75-76; William Gordon to John Adams, 8 April 1785, in "Gordon Letters,"
MHSP, 63: 513; Mercy Warren to Adams, 27 April 1785, in *Warren-Adams
Letters*, MHSC, 73: 253.

13 "The Spirit of 1775," Boston, 6 April, *Virginia Gazette* (Rich.), 21 May 1785; "Joyce, jun.," Boston, 13 April, *Virginia Journal* (Rich.), 12 May 1785. See also A. E. Morse, *The Federalist Party in Massachusetts to the Year 1800* (Princeton, N.J., 1909), pp. 29-30.

14 Henry Knox to ———, 21 April 1785, in Knox Papers, MHS; *Freeman's Journal* (Phila.), 25 May 1785. See also Boston, 25 April 1785, *Connecticut Courant* (Hart.), 10 May 1785; *Boston Gazette,* 9 May 1785.

15 Nevins, *American States,* p. 216; Morse, *The Federalist Party*, pp. 29-30; James Warren to John Adams, 4 September 1785, in *Warren-Adams Letters*, MHSC, 73: 262. The commercial elite's victory was short-lived. Their policies disturbed the debtor farmers in the West, and by 1786 their displeasure took the form of armed rebellion which eventually carried Hancock back to power.

16 John Adams to Charles Storer, 28 March 1785, in Adams Mss. Trust, MHS; Adams to Thomas Jefferson, 7 August 1785, in Lester J. Cappon, ed., *The Adams-Jefferson Letters*, 2 vols. (Chapel Hill, N.C., 1959), 1: 51; Adams to Mazzei, 23 August 1785, in PTJ, 8: 59n. See also Adams to John Jay, 5 May, 8 May, 19 July, 20 August 1785, in Adams Mss. Trust, MHS.

17 Thomas Jefferson to James Monroe, 17 June 1785, in PTJ, 8: 230-31; Jefferson to John Adams, 28 July 1785, in Cappon, ed., *Adams-Jefferson*, 1: 46. For the model treaty Jefferson proposed, see PTJ, 8: 317-19. See also Jefferson to Adams, 7 July 1785, in Cappon, ed., *Adams-Jefferson*, 1: 38-39. This idea of using the treaty power to give Congress a power over commerce was to have great importance in 1786 during negotiations with Spain; see chapter 7.

18 John Adams to Thomas Jefferson, 4 September, 24 October 1785, in Cappon ed., *Adams-Jefferson*, 1: 61, 86; Adams to Jabez Bowen, 8 September 1785, Adams to Cotton Tufts, 9 September 1785, in Adams Mss. Trust, MHS; Jefferson to Adams, 19 November 1785, in Cappon, ed., *Adams-Jefferson*, 1: 94.

19 Létombe to Castries, 24 May 1785, in Nasatir and Monell, eds., *French Consuls*, p. 33; James Bowdoin, Circular to the Governors, 28 July 1785, in Bowdoin-Temple Letters, IV, Winthrop Papers, vol. 24, MHS; New York, 22 June, *State Gazette of South Carolina* (Chst.), 18 July 1785; James Madison to Thomas Jefferson, 3 October 1785, in PJM, 8: 375.

20 Massachusetts General Court, *Journals of the House*, May 1785 session, pp. 102, 113-14, 146-47, in ESR; Boston, 4 July, *Virginia Journal* (Rich.), 28 July 1785. See also Committee of Tradesmen to Gov. Bowdoin, 7 May 1785, Merchant Committee to Bowdoin, 7 May 1785, in Bowdoin-Temple Letters, IV, Winthrop Papers, vol. 24, MHS; William Smith to John Adams, 2 May 1785, in Adams Mss. Trust, MHS. For Bowdoin's speech regarding commercial reform see below, note 33.

21 Gov. Bowdoin to Gov. Livingston, 7 December 1785, in Misc. Bnd. Mss., vol. 17, MHS. See also PCC, Item 74, pp. 29-32; Gov. Langdon to Patrick Henry, 16 November 1785, in Henry, *Henry Correspondence*, 3: 336; Massachusetts General Court, *Journals of the House*, May 1785 session, in ESR; Bates, *Rhode Island*, pp. 102-3.

22 Tristram Dalton to John Adams, 21 July 1785, in Adams Mss. Trust, MHS;

Gov. Bowdoin to Gov. of Connecticut, 27 July 1785, in *Bowdoin and Temple Papers*, MHSC, 7th ser., 6 (1907): 62. See also Saladino, "Economic Revolution," p. 125.

23 Tristram Dalton to John Adams, 21 July 1785, in Adams Mss. Trust, MHS; *Boston Gazette*, 25 July, 19 September, 1785. See also *Boston Gazette*, 22 August 1785; "ON AMERICAN MANUFACTURES," "*A Plain, but real Friend to America*," *Maryland Journal* (Balt.), 11 October 1785.

24 John Quincy Adams to John Adams, 3 August 1785, in Adams Mss. Trust, MHS; Samuel Adams to Elbridge Gerry, 10 September 1785, in Bancroft, *Formation of the Constitution*, 1: 457; Charles Storer to John Adams, 23 November 1785, in Adams Mss. Trust, MHS. See also Theodore Sedgwick to Caleb Davis, 14 October 1785, in Davis Papers, vol. 12b, MHS.

25 *Boston Gazette*, 10 October 1785; James Sullivan to John Adams, 23 October 1785, Richard Cranch to Adams, 10 November 1785, in Adams Mss. Trust, MHS.

26 François Barbé-Marbois to Castries, 15 August 1785, in Nasatir and Monell, eds., *French Consuls*, p. 182; Thomas Jefferson to William Carmichael, 4 November 1785, in PTJ, 9: 15; Massachusetts General Court, *Journals of the House*, October 1785 session, in ESR; Gov. Bowdoin to John Adams, 12 January 1786, in *Bowdoin and Temple Papers*, MHSC, 6: 85.

27 Tristram Dalton to John Adams, 23 January 1786, in Adams Mss. Trust, MHS. See also Nathaniel Gorham to Caleb Davis, 16 June 1786, in Davis Papers, vol. 13a, MHS; Forest to Castries, 16 January 1786, in Nasatir and Monell, eds., *French Consuls*, p. 92; Charles Storer to Adams, 7 April 1786, Richard Cranch to Adams, 20 May 1786, in Adams Mss. Trust, MHS; Gov. Bowdoin to John Sullivan, 10 July 1786, in Hammond, ed., *Letters and Papers of Major-General John Sullivan*, 15: 463-64; Dalton to Adams, 11 July 1786, in Adams Mss. Trust, MHS.

28 John F. Mercer to James Madison, 26 November 1784, Richard Henry Lee to Madison, 26 November 1784, in PJM, 8: 152, 151. See also Lee to Madison, 27 December 1784, ibid., p. 202.

29 Mann Page to Richard Henry Lee, 14 December 1784, in Lee Papers, UVa. See also Daniel St. Thomas Jenifer to James McHenry, 17 February 1785, in Bernard C. Steiner, *The Life and Correspondence of James McHenry* (Cleveland, Ohio, 1907), p. 89.

30 Gouverneur Morris to John Jay, 10 January 1784, in Johnston, ed., *Jay Papers*, 3: 104-5. See also Morris to Jay, 24 September 1783, in Sparks, *Morris*, 1: 259-64; Jay to Charles Thomson, 7 April 1784, in Thomson Papers, vol. 2, LC.

31 Charles Thomson to John Dickinson, 19 July 1785, in Dickinson Papers, R. R. Logan Collection, HSP. See also John Jay to Thomas Jefferson, 15 June 1785, in PTJ, 8: 209; Jay to Lafayette, 15 July 1785, in Johnston, ed., *Jay Papers*, 3: 161; Jay to John Adams, 26 November 1785, in Adams Mss. Trust, MHS.

32 Samuel Bryan to George Bryan, May 1785, in Bryan Papers, Box 1785-87, HSP. See also David Howell to Gov. Greene, 29 October 1785, in Staples,

Rhode Island, p. 538; Nathan Dane to James Bowdoin, 10 January 1786, in LMCC, 8: 538.

33 Massachusetts General Court, *Journals of the House*, May 1785 session, pp. 173-84, in ESR; *Virginia Gazette* (Rich.), 6 August 1785. The writer of this piece from Jamaica Plain was likely William Gordon.

34 Massachusetts delegates to Gov. Bowdoin, 3 September 1785, in Burnett Collection, Box 10, LC.

35 Rufus King to Nathan Dane, 17 September 1785, in Dane Mss., LC; Dane to King, 8 October 1785, in King, *King Letters*, 1: 67-69.

36 Samuel Adams to Elbridge Gerry, 19 September 1785, in Bancroft. *Formation of the Constitution*, 1: 457; Gerry to Adams, 30 September 1785, in LMCC, 8: 224. See also Rufus King to Caleb Davis, 17 October 1785, in Davis Papers, vol. 12b, MHS; Massachusetts delegates to Gov. Bowdoin, 2 November 1785, in LMCC, 8: 225; Hall, *Politics Without Parties*, 163-65. H. James Henderson misinterprets the delegates' refusal to support a convention as evidencing their opposition to the movement, led he says by James Monroe and other "Virginia nationalists," to give Congress a commerce power. He maintains that Virginia nationalism was based on commercial regulation and agrarian expansion, but he neglects to point out that this combination, so evident in the Potomac interest, was not widespread in the South. Monroe and the other southerners followed a northern lead, not the other way around, and once the Mississippi issue clarified the sectional balance in Congress they withdrew their support; See Henderson, *Party Politics*, pp. 363-66.

37 Elbridge Gerry to John Adams, 8 November 1785, Joseph Palmer to Adams, 28 November 1785, in Adams Mss. Trust, MHS; George Washington to David Stuart, 30 November 1785, in WGW, 28: 328.

38 François Barbé-Marbois to Vergennes, 28 August 1785, in Corresp. Pol., Etats-Unis, vol. 30, Min. Aff. Etrang. Paris, LC; James Madison to Thomas Jefferson, 20 August 1785, in PJM, 8: 344. Edward Bancroft even assured the Ministry that the United States would eventually clamor for semicolonial status in reaction to Britain's navigation system; see Bancroft to ———, 26 August 1784, in Public Record Office, Foreign Office 4, vol. 3.

39 Thomas Jefferson to Richard Henry Lee, 22 April 1786, in PTJ, 9: 399-400. See also Jefferson to James Monroe, 11 December 1785, ibid., p. 95; London, 10 October, *New Brunswick Political Intelligencer*, 4 January 1786; Joshua Johnson to Thomas Johnson, 6 March 1786, in Joshua Johnson letterbook, LC.

40 David Howell to Gov. Greene, 23 August 1785, in Staples, *Rhode Island*, p. 535. See also Richard Henry Lee to John Adams, 1 August 1785, in Adams Mss. Trust, MHS.

41 John Adams to Richard Henry Lee, 6 September 1785, in Adams Mss. Trust, MHS; Lee to ———, 10 October 1785, in Burnett Collection, Box 10, LC. See also Lee to Adams, 16 December 1785, in WJA, 9: 545.

42 Stephen Higginson to John Adams, 30 December 1785, Adams Mss. Trust, MHS: "Some REMARKS upon the bill at present depending before the General

Assembly of Pennsylvania, for the encouragement of Trade and Navigation," "CAUTION," *Freeman's Journal* (Phila.), 7 December 1785; Nathan
Dane to Samuel Phillips, 20 January 1786, Edward Rutledge to John Jay, 29
June 1776, in LMCC, 8: 288, 1: 517-18; Charles Storer to Adams, 23 November
1785, in Adams Mss. Trust, MHS.

43 John Jay to John Adams, 1 November 1785, in Adams Mss. Trust, MHS;
James Madison to Thomas Jefferson, 20 August 1785, in PJM, 8: 344.

44 Vergennes to François Barbé-Marbois, 14 December 1784, in Bancroft,
Formation of the Constitution, 1: 404; "OBSERVATIONS RESPECTING A
NAVIGABLE CANAL FROM LAKE CHAPLAIN TO THE ST. LAWRENCE," submitted
to Lord Dorchester by Silas Deane, 25 October 1785, in *Deane Papers*,
NYHSC, 23: 465.

45 Rufus King to John Adams, 2 November 1785, in King, *King Letters*, 1: 113;
Adams to King, 23 December 1785, in Adams Mss. Trust, MHS; King to
Caleb Davis, 3 November 1785, in Davis Papers, vol. 12b, MHS.

46 Nathan Dane to Edward Pulling, 8 January 1786, in Burnett Collection, Box
11, LC; Benjamin Lincoln to Rufus King, 11 February 1786, in King Papers,
Box 1, NYHS. See also Main, *The Antifederalists,* app. A, pp. 283-84. Main's
attempt to demonstrate that the Federalists rather than Antifederalists (using
the post-1787 labels) advocated disunion is completely beside the point.
Certainly King, Lincoln, and some of the others who proposed subconfederation were strong supporters of the Constitution. But before late 1787 they
were equally strong defenders of the Articles of Confederation. They feared
strong central government partly because they were worried that an intersectional combination might advance measures which conflicted with their own.
Only a special combination of events rendered sectional interests temporarily less important in 1787. It was this unique situation which enabled a new
central government to be established despite the continuous effects of sectional conflict; see chapter 7 and the epilogue.

47 James Monroe to Thomas Jefferson, 19 January 1786, John Jay to Jefferson,
19 January 1786, in PTJ, 9: 187-88, 185.

48 Nathan Dane to Samuel Phillips, 20 January 1786, in LMCC, 8: 288; Charles-
ton (Mass.), 21 February, *Pennsylvania Journal* (Phila.), 15 March 1786. See
also Nathanael Greene to Charles Thomson, 24 April 1786, in Thomson
Papers, vol. 2. LC; Philadelphia, 9 March, *Maryland Gazette* (Ann.), 13
March 1786; David Ramsay to John Elliot, 18 January 1786, in David L.
Brunhouse, ed., *David Ramsay 1749-1815, Transactions of the American
Philosophical Society,* n.s., 55, pt. 5 (1955): 96: *Newport Mercury,* 6 March
1786; *New Jersey Gazette* (Tren.), 3 April 1786; Thomas Farr to Caleb
Davis, 8 February 1786, Chst., S.C., in Davis Papers, vol. 13a, MHS.

49 "ON AMERICAN MANUFACTURES," "A Plain, but real Friend to America,"
Maryland Journal (Balt.), 11 October 1785. See also Staughton Lynd, "A
Governing Class," in *Class Conflict*, pp. 108, 132; E. Wilder Spaulding,
New York in the Critical Period 1783-1789 (New York, 1932), pp. 7-18.

50 Forest to Castries, 13 March 1786, in Nasatir and Monell, eds., *French
Consuls*, p. 93; James Monroe to Thomas Jefferson, 11 May 1786, in PTJ, 9:
511.

51 Rufus King to Theodore Sedgwick, 21 May 1786, in Sedgwick Papers, vol.2, MHS; King to Elbridge Gerry, 6 July 1786, in Burnett Collection, Box 11, LC. On continued mercantile lobbying, see *Freeman's Journal* (Phila.), 25 January 1786; Cochran, *New York*, p. 171; *Maryland Jounal* (Balt.), 24 February 1786; Charles Storer to John Adams, 7 April 1786, in Adams Mss. Trust, MHS; Guillaume Otto to Vergennes, 9 April 1786, in Bancroft, *Formation of the Constitution*, 1: 495; Arthur Lee to Adams, 30 May 1786, in Adams Mss. Trust, MHS; Boston, 3 June, *Pennsylvania Gazette* (Phila.), 21 June 1786; New York, *Pennsylvania Gazette* (Phila.), 19 July 1786; "Extract of a letter from Jamaica to a correspondent in Charleston," 25 February, *Maryland Gazette* (Ann.), 13 April 1786; Montego Bay, 11 March, *Maryland Gazette* (Ann.), 4 May 1786; Kingston, 18 March, *Maryland Gazette* (Ann.), 11 May 1786; Charleston, 8 May, *Maryland Gazette* (Ann.), 8 June 1786.

CHAPTER 7: THE MISSISSIPPI CONFLICT

1 *Secret Journals*, 3: 441; Silas Deane to James Wilson, 24 July 1783, in *Deane Papers*, NYHSC, 23: 168.
2 *Maryland Journal* (Balt.), 1 July 1783. See also James Wilson to William Bingham, 27 May 1783, in Gratz Collection, Box 26, HSP; Brunhouse, *Counter-Revolution*, p. 135; Kate Mason Rowland, *Life and Correspondence of Charles Carroll of Carrollton*, 2 vols. (New York, 1898), 2: 79; Joseph Harrison, "The Internal Improvements Issue in the Politics of the Union 1783-1825" (Ph.D. diss., University of Virginia, 1954), p. 47.
3 Thomas Jefferson to James Madison, 20 February 1784, in PTJ, 6: 548; Madison to Jefferson, 16 March 1784, in PJM, 8:10. See also Adams, *Maryland's Influence upon Land Cessions*, p. 39.
4 Thomas Jefferson to George Washington, 15 March 1784, Jefferson to James Madison, 8 December 1784, in PTJ, 7: 26-27, 558.
5 George Washington to Thomas Jefferson, 29 March 1784, in PTJ, 7: 50. See also Washington to Christopher Choles, 25 January 1783, in WGW, 26: 64-65; George Mason to Washington, 17 February, 9 March 1775, in Rutland, ed., *Mason Papers*, 2: 221, 224.
6 James Madison to Thomas Jefferson, 25 April 1784, in PJM, 8: 19-22; Jefferson to Madison, 25 April 1784, in PTJ, 7: 118-121.
7 Thomas Jefferson to James Monroe, 10 December 1784, in PTJ, 7: 562-65. On the conflict between Alexandria and Baltimore, see Eugene Parker Chase, ed., *Our Revolutionary Fore-fathers The Letters of François Barbé-Marbois 1779-1785* (New York, 1929), p. 169; J. P. Brissot de Warville, *New Travels in the United States of America*, ed. Durand Echeverria (Cambridge, Mass., 1964), p. 327; East, *Business Enterprise*, pp. 164, 172-73; Freeman H. Hart, *The Valley of Virginia in the American Revolution 1763-1789* (Chapel Hill, N.C., 1942), p. 149.
8 James Monroe to Thomas Jefferson, 20 July 1784, in PTJ, 7: 380. See also James Madison to Jefferson, 3 July 1784, in PJM, 8: 92-95; *Virginia Journal* (Rich.), 3 July 1784; Nevins, *American States*, pp. 337, 341-43.

9 Edmund Pendleton to James Madison, 16 June 1783, in PJM, 7: 151; Thomas Jefferson, "Analysis of Votes," 7 October 1783, in PTJ, 6: 335-36.

10 Joseph Jones to James Monroe, 6 December 1783, in Monroe Papers, LC; Jones to Monroe, n.d. [between April and December 1784], in Monroe Papers, 2d ser., LC. See chapter 4.

11 10 August, *Virginia Journal* (Rich.), 19 August 1784; *Independent Gazetteer* (Phila.), 20 November 1784.

12 George Washington to Richard Henry Lee, 14 December 1784, Washington to Thomas Blackburn, 19 December 1784, Washington to Lafayette, 23 December 1784, in WGW, 28: 11, 14, 17; James Madison to Lee, 25 December 1784, Lee to Madison, 27 December 1784, in PJM, 8: 201, 202; Washington to Henry Knox, 5 January 1785, Washington to George Augustine Washington, 6 January 1785, in WGW, 28: 24, 28.

13 "House of Delegates," 28 December 1784, in Madison Papers, LC; George Washington to Charles Carroll of Carrollton, 10 January 1785, in WGW, 28: 29. See also Patrick Henry to Richard Henry Lee, 9 January 1785, in Henry, *Henry Correspondence*, 3: 266; James Madison to Thomas Jefferson, 9 January 1785, in PJM, 8: 222-26; William Nelson to William Short, 11 January 1785, in William Short Papers, LC.

14 Thomas Stone to George Washington, 28 January 1785, in Gratz Collection, Members of Old Congress, HSP; George Mason and Alexander Henderson to Speaker of the House, 28 March 1785, in Madison Papers, LC; Cora Bacon-Foster, *Early Chapters in the Development of the Patomac Route to the West* (Washington, D.C., 1912), p. 42; Paul Clarkson and R. Samuel Jett, *Luther Martin of Maryland* (Baltimore, Md., 1970), p. 65.

15 Christopher Richmond to George Washington, 8 April, 10 May 1785, in Washington Papers, LC; Washington to Nathanael Greene, 20 May 1785, in WGW, 28: 145; Richard Henry Lee to ———, 13 June 1785, in Dreer Collection, Declaration of Independence, HSP.

16 "*The TRUE INTEREST of the MIDDLE STATES," Freeman's Journal* (Phila.), 2 May 1785; George Washington to James Madison, 30 November 1785, in WGW, 28: 337. See also "Extract of a letter from Alexandria," 19 May, *Providence Gazette*, 11 June 1785.

17 George Washington to Robert Morris, 1 February 1785, in WGW, 28: 52; "Extract of a letter from a gentleman in Alexandria," 23 January, *Providence Gazette*, 12 March 1785. See also Morris to Washington, 17 April 1785, in Washington Papers, LC.

18 John Craig to George Washington, 22 March 1785, in Washington Papers, LC; Washington to Craig, 29 March 1785, in WGW, 28: 118-19; "IN COUNCIL," *Freeman's Journal* (Phila.), 29 June 1785. For a discussion of the tristate convention and the bearing it and the Potomac-Susquehanna competition had on the Annapolis Convention, see chapter 8.

19 JCC, 27: 665; Charles Thomson to Thomas Jefferson, 1 October 1784, in PTJ, 7: 433; *Secret Journals*, 3: 517-18. See also François Barbé-Marbois to Castries, 15 November 1785, in Nasatir and Monell, eds., *French Consuls*, p. 177.

20 Samuel Hardy to Patrick Henry, 5 December 1784, in LMCC, 7: 620; JCC, 27: 687-90, 693-95, 705-6. See also James Monroe to James Madison, 14 December 1784, in PJM, 8: 183-84; Richard Dobbs Spaight to Gov. Martin, 7 December 1784, in Gratz Collection, Box 26, HSP; Hugh Williamson to Thomas Jefferson, 11 December 1784, in PTJ, 7: 569; "Extract of a letter, dated Trenton," 12 December, *Pennsylvania Journal* (Phila.), 22 January 1785.

21 Richard Henry Lee to George Washington, 14 February 1785, in Washington Papers, LC; John Jay to John Adams, 11 February 1785, in Adams Mss. Trust, MHS. For the fear of armed conflict see David Sewall to Samuel Holten, 31 [February] 1785, in *Danvers Historical Collections,* 20: 51; "A Letter from Baltimore to a gentleman in Philadelphia," 15 March, *Freeman's Journal* (Phila.), 23 March 1785.

22 *Secret Journals,* 3: 585-86. See also Samuel Flagg Bemis, *Pinckney's Treaty* (New Haven, Conn., 1960), p. 60; JCC, 29: 561-64, 567-69; Richard Henry Lee to James Madison, 30 May 1785, in PJM, 8: 288-89; Daniel Morgan to Col. Posey, 11 July 1785, in Gratz Collection, Box 13, HSP; New York, 15 July, *New Brunswick Political Intelligencer,* 27 July 1785.

23 Van Beckel to the States General, 27 November 1784, in Bancroft, *Formation of the Constitution,* 1: 398.

24 Caleb Wallace to James Madison, 12 July 1785, in PJM, 8: 321. See also a study "on the Trade & Country of the Illinois," ca. 1785, in Holker Papers, vol. 30, LC; Thomas Willing to James Wilson, 20 February 1785, in Dreer Collection, HSP; David Jackson to George Bryan, 4 June 1785, in Bryan Papers, Box 1785-1787, HSP.

25 "Representation and Remonstrance of New Jersey," 14 June 1783, in McCormick, *New Jersey,* pp. 224-27; Alexander Hamilton to Gov. Clinton, 14 May 1783, in LMCC, 7: 165; Stephen Higginson to Samuel Adams, 20 May 1783, in Samuel Adams Papers, NYPL; Nathaniel Gorham to Caleb Davis, 4 June 1783, in Davis Papers, vol. 12a, MHS; David Howell to Moses Brown, 24 August 1783, in LMCC, 7: 279; Howell to Paul Allen, Esq., 18 September 1783, in Brown Papers, JCBL.

26 Bemis, *Pinckney's Treaty,* pp. 62-66; Oliver Pollock to John Jay, 10 February 1785, in Sparks, ed., *Diplomatic Correspondence,* 3: 141; Diego de Gardoqui to Conde de Galvez, 3 August 1785, in Bemis, *Pinckney's Treaty,* pp. 72-73.

27 Elbridge Gerry to John Adams, 14 July 1785, Richard Henry Lee to Adams, 1 August 1785, in Adams Mss. Trust, MHS.

28 Rufus King to Elbridge Gerry, 24 March 1785, in LMCC, 8: 71. See also Guillaume Otto to Vergennes, 10 January 1786, in Burnett Collection, Box 11, LC. Robert F. Berkhofer, Jr., underplays the role of Jefferson and the influence of sectional conflict and concentrates on the relationship of western expansion to a burgeoning nation in "Jefferson, The Ordinance of 1784, and the Origins of the American Territorial System," *William and Mary Quarterly,* 3d ser., 29 (April 1972): 231-62.

29 Richard Henry Lee to Patrick Henry, 14 February 1785, in Henry, *Henry*

Correspondence, 3: 278; Lee to James Madison, 11 August 1785, in PJM, 8: 339.

30 Samuel Holten to Mr. Wood [paraphrasing Washington], 11 September 1783, in Independence National Historical Park Museum, National Park Service, Philadelphia, Pa.; New York delegates to Gov. Clinton, 19 September 1783, in LMCC, 7: 300-301.

31 JCC, 26: 275-79, 28: 375-81; Jensen, "The Creation," pp. 323-24, and *New Nation,* pp. 352-56.

32 Joseph Gardner to George Bryan, 19 March 1785, in Bryan Papers, Box 1785-1787, HSP. See also Henry Drinker to Richard Stellaford, 5 December 1785, in Drinker Mss., letterbook 1762-1786, HSP.

33 Arthur Lee to John Adams, 6 March 1785, in Adams Mss. Trust, MHS.

34 Létombe to Castries, 22 February 1785, in Nasatir and Monell, eds., *French Consuls,* p. 32; John Jay to William Bingham, 31 May 1785, Jay to John Adams, 14 October 1785, in Johnston, ed., *Jay Papers,* 3: 154, 172.

35 William Grayson to George Washington, 15 April 1785, in Burnett Collection, Box 10, LC. See also "A True American," *Maryland Journal* (Balt.), 29 July 1783, and the discussion of sectional balance and western emigration in chapter 4.

36 Charles Carroll of Carrollton to Charles Carroll of Annapolis, 24 July 1779, in Carroll Papers, MdHS; Thomas Jefferson to George Washington, 10 July 1785, in PTJ, 8: 280. See also "Extract of a letter from a man in the western territory ceded by North Carolina, to a friend in Virginia," 20 December, *Pennsylvania Journal* (Phila.), 5 February 1785.

37 George Washington to George Plater, 25 October 1784, Washington to Jacob Read, 3 November 1784, in WGW, 27:483, 485. See also Washington to Henry Knox, 5 December 1784, Washington to Benjamin Harrison, 22 January 1785, Washington to Edmund Randolph, 13 August 1785, Washington to James Warren, 7 October 1785, ibid., 28: 3, 35, 218, 291.

38 Richard Henry Lee to Patrick Henry, 8 December 1784, in Henry, *Henry Correspondence,* 3: 247; Lee to James Madison, 27 December 1784, in PJM, 8: 202-3.

39 Hugh Williamson to Thomas Jefferson, 11 December 1784, in PTJ, 7: 570; George Washington to David Humphreys, 25 July 1785, in WGW, 28: 204-5. See also Washington to Lafayette, 25 July 1785, Washington to Comte de Rochambeau, 7 September, 1785, in WGW, 28: 207, 256.

40 James Madison to Lafayette, 20 March 1785, in PJM, 8: 250-51. See also Madison to Richard Henry Lee, 7 July 1785, ibid., pp. 314-15.

41 George Mason to George Mason, Jr., 8 January 1783, in Rutland, ed., *Mason Papers,* 2: 761. See also Richmond, 29 November, *New Jersey Gazette* (Tren.), 16 December 1783; George Rogers Clark to Patrick Henry, 1777, in James A. James, ed., *George Rogers Clark Papers 1771-1781, Collections of the Illinois State Historical Library* 8 (1912): 30-32.

42 Ebenezer Hazard to Jeremy Belknap, 9 March 1785, in Hazard Letters,

Belknap Papers, MHS. See also "Lucullus to the Western People No. 1," *Freeman's Journal* (Phila.), 21 July 1784; Joseph Jones to James Monroe, 27 November 1784, in Monroe Papers, WML; "Petition to the Virginia legislature," *Freeman's Journal* (Phila.), 12 January 1785. For the formation of a western "ASSOCIATION," see Charles Cummings to Patrick Henry, 16 May 1785, in Burnett Collection, Box 10, LC.

43 Nassau, 8 January, *Pennsylvania Evening Herald* (Phila.), 26 February 1785. See also Boston, 24 January, *Providence Gazette,* 29 January 1785; *New York Journal,* 3 February 1785; Boston, 10 February, *Virginia Gazette* (Rich.), 12 March 1785; New York, 10 February, *Pennsylvania Evening Herald* (Phila.), 15 February 1785; New York, 12 February, *New Jersey Gazette* (Tren.), 21 February 1785; *New Brunswick Political Intelligencer,* 22 February, 1 March 1785; Philadelphia, 23 April, *Providence Gazette,* 7 May 1785; Philadelphia, 23 April, *Providence Gazette,* 7 May 1785; Philadelphia, 14 May, *Newport Mercury,* 4 June 1785; Philadelphia, 24 May, *Providence Gazette,* 4 June 1785.

44 James Monroe to Thomas Jefferson, 25 August 1785, in PTJ, 8: 441-42. See also Monroe to James Madison, 4 August 1785, in PJM, 8: 342; George Washington to Richard Henry Lee, 22 August 1785, in WGW, 28: 231.

45 James Monroe to James Madison, 12 July, 14 August 1785, in PJM, 8: 319, 341; William Appleman Williams, *The Contours of American History* (Chicago, 1966), pp. 126-38.

46 James Monroe to Thomas Jefferson, 19 January 1786, in PTJ, 9: 186-91.

47 James Monroe to Thomas Jefferson, 16 July 1786, in PTJ, 10: 143; Monroe to Patrick Henry, 12 August 1786, in LMCC, 8: 424-25. See also Monroe to James Madison, 31 May 1786, in PJM, 9: 68-71.

48 Rufus King to Elbridge Gerry, 4 June 1786, in King, *King Letters,* 1: 176; Charles Thomson, "Minutes of Proceedings," 16 August, in LMCC, 8: 429, 440. See also Charleston (Mass.), 19 May, *Pennsylvania Evening Herald* (Phila.), 3 June 1786; Caleb Davis to Nathan Dane, 20 March 1786, in Dane Mss., LC; Dane to King, 11 August 1786, in Burnett Collection, Box 11, LC; King to Dane, 17 August 1786, in Dane Mss., LC; King to Jonathan Jackson, 3 September 1786, in LMCC, 8: 458.

49 Guillaume Otto to Vergennes, 10 September 1786, in Bancroft, *Formation of the Constitution,* 2: 391-92.

50 Bemis, *Pinckney's Treaty,* p. 71; James Monroe to Patrick Henry, 12 August 1786, in LMCC, 7: 423-24; Monroe to James Madison, 31 May 1786, in PJM, 9: 68-69.

51 JCC, 30: 85-86; Gardoqui to John Jay, 25 May 1786, in PCC, Item 81, pp. 189-91; JCC, 30: 323. See also Gardoqui to Floridablanca, 16 April 1786, in Bemis, *Pinckney's Treaty,* p. 82.

52 James Monroe to James Madison, 31 May 1786, in PJM, 9: 68; Monroe to Thomas Jefferson, 16 June 1786, in PTJ, 9: 653; Monroe to Patrick Henry, 12 August 1786, in LMCC, 8: 423-24.

53 James Monroe to James Madison, 31 May 1786, in PJM, 9: 69-70. See also
   Monroe to Thomas Jefferson, 16 July 1786, in PTJ, 10:144; Monroe to Patrick
   Henry, 12 August 1786, in LMCC, 8: 423-24.

54 JCC, 30: 323, 31: 467-84, 509; James Monroe to Thomas Jefferson, 16 June
   1786, in PTJ, 9: 653.

55 James Monroe to James Madison, 10 August 1786, in PJM, 9: 92; Monroe to
   Patrick Henry, 12 August 1786, in LMCC, 8: 423-24; Monroe to Thomas
   Jefferson, 19 August 1786, in PTJ, 10: 276.

56 James Madison to James Monroe, 18 August 1786, in PJM, 9: 108. See also
   Monroe to Madison, 14 August 1786, ibid., p. 104.

57 Guillaume Otto to Vergennes, 23 August 1786, in Burnett Collection, Box 11,
   LC; Otto to Vergennes, 10 September 1786, in Bancroft, *Formation of the
   Constitution*, 2: 390. See also James Monroe to Thomas Jefferson, 19 August
   1786, in PTJ, 10: 275-76; Monroe to George Washington, 20 August 1786, in
   LMCC, 8: 447. Otto was wrong. By early 1787 the South broke the northern
   bloc and reestablished its earlier ties with the middle states.

58 JCC, 31: 483-84, 537-52. See also James Monroe to James Madison, 31 May
   1786, in PJM, 9: 69.

59 JCC, 31: 565-613.

60 Guillaume Otto to Vergennes, 10 September 1786, in Bancroft, *Formation of
   the Constitution*, 2: 391; James Monroe to James Madison, 30 August 1786,
   Monroe to Madison, 29 September 1786, in PJM, 9: 109, 134.

61 John Jay to Gardoqui, 6 October 1786, in JCC, 32: 185. See also Jay to Thomas
   Jefferson, 14 December 1786, in PTJ, 10: 596-97. It is quite possible that Jay,
   like Washington and Madison, was concerned that sectional conflict might
   disrupt plans for a constitutional revision; see note 63 and chapters 8 and 9.

62 Henry Lee to George Washington, 8 September 1786, in Washington Papers,
   LC; Timothy Bloodworth to Gov. Caswell, 29 September 1786, Lee to
   Washington, 11 October 1786, in LMCC, 8: 473-74, 481-82. For the effect of
   the Mississippi conflict on the prospects for constitutional reform, see chapter 8.

63 Thomas Jefferson to James Madison, 16 December 1786, in PTJ, 10: 603. See
   also George Washington to Henry Lee, 31 October 1786, in WGW, 29: 35.

64 Address to the Pennsylvania Assembly, n.d., in Thomson Papers, vol. 2, LC.
   See also Hugh Henry Brackenridge, article dated 9 September 1786, in
   Claude Milton Newlin, *The Life and Writings of Hugh Henry Brackenridge*
   (Princeton, N.J., 1932), p. 74; "Extract of a letter from a gentleman in
   Philadelphia, to his friend in this place [Pittsburgh]," 2 September,
   Poughkeepsie Journal, 1 November 1786.

65 Memorial from the Western counties, in PCC, Item 75, pp. 411-12; Resolution,
   29 October, and instructions may be found ibid., pp. 407, 415. See also James
   Madison to Thomas Jefferson, 4 December 1786, in PJM, 9: 189.

66 James Madison to Thomas Jefferson, 4 December 1786, in PJM, 9: 191. See
   also Henry Lee to ———, 28 October, 11 November 1786, in Henry Lee
   Papers, VSL, and chapter 9 for sectional realignment and continuing conflict
   over the Mississippi navigation.

CHAPTER 8: THE ANNAPOLIS CONVENTION

1 Virginia Legislature, *Journals of the House*, October 1785 session, p. 4, in ESR. See also PTJ, 9: 204; Tyler, *The Tylers*, 1: 125. Madison and John Tyler were both on the instructions committee.

2 James Madison to James Monroe, 7 August 1785, in PJM, 8: 334. See also William Grayson to Madison, 1 May 1785, ibid., p. 176; Grayson to ———, 15 June 1785, in Dreer Collection.

3 James Monroe to James Madison, 14 August 1785, Madison to Thomas Jefferson, 3 October 1785, in PJM, 8: 342, 373. See chapter 7 for the port bill in 1784.

4 *Journals of the House*, October 1785 session, pp. 19, 21, 33, 53, 60, in ESR; Tyler, *The Tylers*, 1: 125-28.

5 James Madison to George Washington, 11 November 1785, in PJM, 8: 404. See also "THOUGHTS ON THE COMMERCIAL INTEREST OF VIRGINIA," by "A," *Virginia Gazette* (Rich.), 19 November 1785.

6 James Madison to George Washington, 9 December 1785, in PJM, 8: 438; *Journals of the House*, October 1785 session, p. 65, in ESR.

7 James Madison to George Washington, 9 December 1785, Madison to Thomas Jefferson, 22 January 1786, in PJM, 8: 438, 476-77; *Journals of the House*, October 1785 session, p. 66, in ESR.

8 Edmund Randolph to George Washington, 3 December 1785, in Bancroft, *Formation of the Constitution*, 1: 470; Joseph Jones to James Madison, 12 June 1785, in PJM, 8: 293.

9 Rutland, ed., *Mason Papers*, 2: 844; Kate Mason Rowland, ed., *The Life and Correspondence of George Mason*, 2 vols. (New York, 1892), 2: 92-3; Bancroft, *Formation of the Constitution*, 1: 252; George Mason and Alexander Henderson to the Speaker of the House, 28 March 1785, in Madison Papers, LC.

10 David Stuart to George Washington, 8 December 1785, in Bancroft, *Formation of the Constitution*, 1: 471.

11 James Madison to George Washington, 9 December 1785, in PJM, 8: 439. See also Madison to James Monroe, 9 December 1785, ibid., p. 436.

12 *Journals of the House*, October 1785 session, pp. 71, 112-15, in ESR.

13 Ibid., pp. 137-38, 151; Rowland, *George Mason*, 2: 93.

14 Gordon DenBoer, "The House of Delegates and the Evolution of Political Parties in Virginia 1783-1792" (Ph.D. diss., University of Wisconsin, 1972), pp. 59-64; Hugh L. Grigsby, *The History of the Federal Convention of 1788*, 2 vols. (Richmond, Va., 1890), 1: 46-47.

15 James Madison to Noah Webster, 10 March 1826, in Noah Webster, *A Collection of Papers on Political, Literary and Moral Subjects* (New York, 1843), p. 172.

16 James Madison to James Monroe, 22 January 1786, in PJM, 8: 483. See also Madison to Thomas Jefferson, 22 January 1786, ibid., pp. 476-77.

17 Edmund Randolph to James Madison, 1 March 1786, in PJM, 8: 495; Joseph Jones to Thomas Jefferson, 21 February 1786, in PTJ, 9: 297.

18 See "ELECTORS OF BALTIMORE" attacking the Potomac Company, *Virginia Journal* (Alex.), 27 September 1785; Maryland Legislature, *Votes and Proceedings of the Senate*, November 1785 session, pp. 53-57, in ESR.

19 Maryland Legislature, *Votes and Proceedings of the Senate*, November 1785 session, pp. 77, 84-88, in ESR.

20 For the Potomac interest in Maryland, see Bacon-Foster, *Patomac Route*, p. 59; George Washington to Thomas Johnson and Thomas Sim Lee, 10 September 1785, Washington to Thomas Stone, 3 December 1785, in WGW, 28: 260-61, 339-41; Philip A. Crowl, *Maryland During and After the Revolution A Political and Economic Study* (Baltimore, Md., 1943), pp. 37-39, 90-91. For Maryland's politically based decision to send second-line politicians to the Philadelphia Convention and to keep important men in the legislature for the paper money fight, see William A. Obrien, "Speculative Interests and Maryland Politics, 1780-1788" (M.A. thesis, University of Wisconsin, 1967), pp. 65-67.

21 *Minutes of the Supreme Executive Council*, in *Colonial Records of Pennsylvania*, vols. 14, 15 (Harrisburg, Pa., 1851-69), 14: 645, 669-72, 15: 5; *Pennsylvania Archives*, vols. 10, 11 (Philadelphia, 1855-56), 10: 755, 11: 522.

22 *Minutes of the Council of Delaware* (Dover, Del., 1886), pp. 968-71; Read, *George Read*, p. 430.

23 "A Mechanic," 19 November, *Federal Gazette* (Phila.), 22 November 1788.

24 PAH, 3: 665-66; E. Wilder Spaulding, *His Excellency George Clinton Critic of the Constitution*, 2d ed. (Port Washington, N.Y., 1964), p. 183; Nevins, *American States*, p. 284; John Jay to Egbert Benson, 12 September 1783, in Johnston, ed., *Jay Papers*, 3: 75.

25 Robert Troup, quoted in Nevins, *American States*, p. 284; Egbert Benson, "Memoir, Read Before the Historical Society of the State of New York, December 31, 1816," NHSC, 2d ser., 2 (1849): 135. Hobart and Benson had both attended the Hartford Convention in 1780.

26 McCormick, *New Jersey*, pp. 176-78, 218, 233, 208-9, 239; Abraham Clark to John C. Symmes and Josiah Hornblower, 9 December 1785, in Miscellaneous Manuscripts, Rutgers University Library, New Brunswick, N.J.; New Jersey Legislature, *Journals of the General Assembly*, February 1786 session, pp. 12-13, in ESR.

27 JCC, 30: 96-97. See also Henry Lee to George Washington, 2 March 1786; Nathaniel Gorham to James Warren, 6 March 1786, Charles Thomson to Pinckney, Gorham, and Grayson, 7 March 1786, in LMCC, 8: 315, 318, 319-20; William Grayson to James Madison, 22 March 1786, in PJM, 8: 508.

28 *Journals of the General Assembly*, February 1786 session, p. 72, in ESR; Charles Pinckney, Speech before the General Assembly, 13 March 1786, in LMCC, 8: 323. See also Guillaume Otto to Vergennes, 17 March 1786, in Bancroft, *Formation of the Constitution*, 1: 486.

29 McCormick, *New Jersey*, pp. 242-43. When New Jersey revoked the 20 February act it made clear the determination to still "counteract, so as they can, every local system of N.Y., until they come fully into the impost duty" ("Extract of a letter from Trenton," 24 March, *Maryland Gazette* [Ann.], 13 April 1786).

30 Nathaniel Gorham to Caleb Davis, 1 March 1786, in Davis Papers, vol. 13a, MHS; "To *the Honourable* the REPRESENTATIVES *of the* PEOPLE *of* VIRGINIA," *Maryland Journal* (Balt.), 28 March 1786; Charleston (Mass.), 14 April, *Pennsylvania Gazette* (Phila.), 3 May 1786. Davis supported the idea of calling a convention; see his letter to Nathan Dane, 20 March 1786, in Dane Mss., LC.

31 William Grayson to James Madison, 22 March 1786, Madison to James Monroe, 22 January 1786, in PJM, 8: 510, 483.

32 James Madison to James Monroe, 19 March 1786, Madison to Monroe, 21 June 1786, in PJM, 8: 505, 9: 83. See also Madison to Monroe, 14 March 1786, ibid., 8: 498.

33 Thomas Rodney, "Diary," 3 May 1786, in LMCC, 8: 350; Pinckney quoted in Andrew J. Bethea, *The Contribution of Charles Pinckney to the Formation of the American Union* (Richmond, Va., 1937), pp. 26-27.

34 John Jay to George Washington, 16 March 1786, in Washington Papers, LC; Benjamin Rush to Richard Price, 25 May 1786, in Butterfield, ed., *Rush Papers*, 1: 388.

35 William Grayson to James Madison, 28 May 1786, in PJM, 9: 63-64; George Washington to John Jay, 18 May 1786, Washington to Lafayette, 10 May 1786, in WGW, 28: 431, 421-22. See chapter 9 for further discussion on the type of convention to have.

36 Henry Lee to George Washington, 7 August 1786, in Washington Papers, LC; Charles Thomson, "Minutes of Proceedings," in Thomson Papers, vol. 2, LC; "Minutes of Proceedings," 16, 18 August, Timothy Bloodworth to Gov. Caswell, 28 August 1786, in LMCC, 8: 427-28, 438, 455. See also JCC, 31: 494-501.

37 Stephen Mix Mitchell to William S. Johnson, 9 August 1786, James Monroe to Patrick Henry, 12 August 1786, in LMCC, 8: 418, 424. See also Guillaume Otto to Vergennes, 17 June 1786, in Corresp. Pol., Etats-Unis, vol. 31, Min. Aff. Etrang. Paris, LC. There is little evidence to support H. James Henderson's contention that Virginians like Monroe, Madison, Richard Henry Lee, and George Washington were more involved in national politics than the 1781-83 nationalists (*Party Politics*, p. 399). The Annapolis Convention, or at least what eventually occurred, was hardly only a Virginian effort. See chapter 9 for a discussion of post-1783 nationalist theories.

38 James Madison to Thomas Jefferson, 12 August 1786, in PJM, 9: 95; John Langdon to Patrick Henry, 27 March 1786, in PCC, Item 77, pp. 125-26. See also *Freeman's Journal* (Phila.), 5 April 1786; James Monroe to John Sullivan, 16 August 1786, in LMCC, 8: 430; Staples, *Rhode Island*, p. 562. Connecticut also had its lucrative navigation system to defend.

39 Massachusetts General Court, *Journals of the House*, February 1786 session, *Journals of the Senate*, February 1786 session, *Journals of the House*, May 1786 session, in ESR; Elbridge Gerry to Rufus King, 23 June 1786, in Gerry Papers, vol. 2, MHS; Stephen Higginson to John Adams, July 1786, in Jameson, ed., *Higginson Letters*, 1: 735.

40 Nathaniel Gorham to Caleb Davis, 23 February 1786, in Davis Papers, vol. 13 MHS; Jabez Bowen to John Sullivan, 18 August 1786, in Emmet Collection,

Annapolis Convention, NYPL. See also James Bowdoin to Gov. Collins, 10 July 1786, in *Proceedings of the Assembly, Colonial Records of Rhode Island,* vol. 10 (Providence, R.I., 1865), p. 214.

41 Rufus King to Jonathan Jackson, 11 June 1786, in LMCC, 8: 389; Stephen Higginson to John Adams, July 1786, in Jameson, ed., *Higginson Letters,* 1: 734. See also King to Adams, 5 May 1786, Adams to King, 14 July 1786, in King Papers, Box 1, NYHS. For another attack on "tory" sympathies, see Pierce Butler to Thomas FitzSimons, 30 May 1786, in Sweet Collection, Box B, SCHS.

42 James Madison to Thomas Jefferson, 12 August 1786, Madison to Jefferson, 12 May 1786, Edmund Randolph to Madison, 12 June 1786, in PJM, 9: 96, 50, 75. See also Daniel Carroll to Madison, 13 March 1786, ibid., 8: 496.

43 James Monroe to Patrick Henry, 12 August 1786, in LMCC, 8: 424-25. See also Monroe to James Madison, 14 August 1786, in PJM, 9: 104; Monroe to Thomas Jefferson, 19 August 1786, in PTJ, 10: 276-77. Theodore Sedgwick was one northerner who was very interested in a northern confederacy; see Segdwick to Caleb Strong, 6 August 1786, in LMCC, 8: 415.

44 James Madison to James Monroe, 15 August 1786, Monroe to Madison, 3 September 1786, Monroe to Madison, 12 September 1786, in PJM, 9: 107, 113-14, 123. See also Monroe to Madison, 10 August 1786, ibid., pp. 91-92.

45 James Read to George Read, 3 September 1786, in Read, *George Read,* p. 420; 8 September, *New York Journal,* 14 September 1786. See also Alexander Hamilton to Richard Varick, 1 September 1786, in PAH, 3: 683; Egbert Benson to John Lansing, Jr., 8 September 1786, in John Lansing Manuscripts, NYPL.

46 13 September, *Freeman's Journal* (Phila.), 20 September 1786; James Madison to Ambrose Madison, 8 September 1786, PJM, 9: 120; Boston, 21 August, *New York Journal,* 31 August 1786; Boston, 25 August, *Freeman's Journal* (Phila.), 6 September 1786; PAH, 3: 685.

47 "Extract of a letter from a gentleman now attending the meeting of a Convention . . . at Annapolis to a friend in Trenton," 9 September, *New Jersey Gazette* (Tren.), 18 September 1786; Philadelphia, 15 September, *Boston Gazette,* 25 September 1786.

48 James Madison to James Monroe, 11 September 1786, in PJM, 9: 121-22; Madison to Noah Webster, 12 October 1804, in Webster, *A Collection of Papers,* pp. 169-71; Benson's Minutes and the Address, in PAH, 2: 686-89. The Annapolis address was widely reprinted.

49 Rufus King to James Bowdoin, 17 September 1786, in LMCC, 468; Tench Coxe to Benjamin Franklin, 19 September 1786, in *Pennsylvania Archives,* 11: 60; St. George Tucker to James Monroe, — 1786, in Monroe Papers, LC.

50 Guillaume Otto to Vergennes, 10 October 1786, in Bancroft, *Formation of the Constitution,* 2: 399-401; "Letters from an American Farmer," in *The Antifederalists,* ed. Cecelia M. Kenyon (Indianapolis, Ind., 1966), p. 203.

51 Henry Knox to George Washington, 14 January 1787, in Sparks, ed., *Letters*

to Washington, 4: 157. See also Nathan Dane to Rufus King, 11 August 1786, in Burnett Collection, Box 11, LC; Washington to Knox, 26 December 1786, in WGW, 29: 123.

52 Rufus King to John Adams, 2 October 1786, King address, October 1786, Dane address, November 1786, in LMCC, 8: 475, 479, 504.

53 James Monroe to James Madison, 7 October 1786, Edward Carrington to Madison, 18 December 1786, in PJM, 9: 143, 218-19.

54 Thomas Jefferson to James Madison, 16 December 1786, in PTJ, 10: 602-6; James Monroe to Madison, 7 October 1786, in PJM, 9: 142-43; Henry Lee to St. George Tucker, 20 October 1786, in LMCC, 8: 489; Otto to Vergennes, 10 November 1786, in Bancroft, *Formation of the Constitution*, 2: 403.

CHAPTER 9: A HOOP TO THE BARREL

1 Pelatiah Webster, *A dissertation on the Political Union and Constitutions of the thirteen United States* (Philadelphia, 1783), p. 3; "Paragraph from an address by John Dickinson while President of Pennsylvania," ca. 1783, in Dickinson Papers, R. R. Logan Collection, HSP. See also Thomas Paine, "American Crisis, No. 13," in Conway, ed., *Writings of Paine*, 1: 374; Alexander Hamilton to George Washington, 24 March 1783, in PAH, 3: 304.

2 Jonathan Trumbull, "Last Advisory Legacy," October 1783, in I. W. Stuart, *Life of Jonathan Trumbull Sen. Governor of Connecticut* (Boston, 1859), p. 606; Oliver Ellsworth to Trumbull, 10 July 1783, in William G. Brown, *The Life of Oliver Ellsworth* (New York, 1905), pp. 103-4.

3 "The North American No. 1," *Pennsylvania Journal* (Phila.), 17 September 1783; Thomas Pownall to James Bowdoin, 9 December 1783, in *Bowdoin and Temple Papers*, MHSC, 6: 26; "A Message from the President and the Supreme Executive Council to the Assembly," 18 August 1783, in *Minutes of the Supreme Executive Council, Colonial Records of Pennsylvania*, vol. 13 (Harrisburg, Pa., 1853), p. 650. See also John Dickinson to Charles Thomson, [12] June 1783, in Thomson Papers, vol. 1, LC. See chapter 3 for federalists' perception of what would occur if the Confederation ceased to operate effectively.

4 Charles Thomson to Benjamin Franklin, 13 August 1784, in Thomson Papers, letterbook, HSP; "The North American No. 1," *Pennsylvania Journal* (Phila.), 17 September 1783; Jeremy Belknap to Ebenezer Hazard, 27 February 1784, in *Belknap Papers*, MHSC, 2: 307; Ebenezer Huntington to Andrew Huntington, 12 August 1783, in G. W. F. Blanchfield, ed., *Letters Written by Ebenezer Huntington During the American Revolution* (New York, 1914), p. 106. See also Thomas Hartley to Thomas FitzSimons, 7 October 1784, in Provincial Delegates, vol. 6, HSP; Jonathan Jackson to John Adams, 10 August 1785, in Adams Mss. Trust, MHS.

5 "A Fellow Citizen," in *The Political Establishments of the United States in*

a Candid Review of Their Deficiencies With a Proposal for Reformation (Philadelphia, 1784), pp. 9, 21; Jeremy Belknap to Ebenezer Hazard, 3 March 1784, in *Belknap Papers*, MHSC, 2: 309. See also John Jay to James Lovell, 10 May 1785, in Johnston, ed., *Jay Papers*, 3: 143; Jay to John Adams, 4 May 1786, in Adams Mss. Trust, MHS.

6 Noah Webster, *Sketches of American Policy* (Hartford, Conn., 1785), pp. 40, 44.

7 James Wilson, JMND, 27 January 1783, in PJM, 6: 134; "Philodemus," *Conciliatory Hints, Attempting by a Fair State of Matters, to Remove Party Prejudices* (Charleston, S.C., 1784), p. 12.

8 "A Plain Politician," in *Honesty Showed to be a True Policy; or, a General Impost Considered* (New York, 1786), p. 6; "Extract from a well written piece under the signature of Solon" [from the *Albany Gazette*], *Boston Gazette*, 9 October 1786; *New Jersey Gazette* (Tren.), 4 September 1786. See also "NESTOR," *New Jersey Gazette* (Tren.), 6 November 1786; "Letter from New York," 23 April, *New York Journal*, 11 May 1786; "Plan for a New Federal Government," *Independent Gazetteer* (Phila.), 25 October 1786.

9 Alexander Hamilton to George Washington, 17 March 1783, in PAH, 3: 292; Washington to Lafayette, 25 July 1785, in WGW, 28: 208. See also Philip Schuyler to Alexander Hamilton, 4 May 1783, in PAH, 3: 349; Nathanael Greene to Charles Pettit, 29 July 1783, in Reed Papers, NYHS.

10 Robert Morris to George Washington, 2 September 1783, in Washington Papers, LC; James Mercer to J. F. Mercer, 23 September 1783, in Mercer Papers, VHS; Gouverneur Morris to Nathanael Greene, 18 May 1783, in Personal Papers, Misc., LC.

11 Stephen Higginson to John Adams, 8 August 1785, in Jameson, ed., *Higginson Letters*, 1: 742. See also Rufus King to Samuel Holten, 21 November 1785, Nathan Dane to James Bowdoin, 10 January 1786, King to Adams, 1 February 1786, David Ramsay to Benjamin Rush, 11 February 1786, Secretary of Congress to George Read, 1 March 1786, Nathaniel Gorham to Bowdoin, 5 April 1786, Dane to Bowdoin, 10 June 1786, in LMCC, 8: 257, 282, 297, 301, 313, 337, 387.

12 George Turner to Winthrop Sargeant, 19 February 1786, in Winthrop Sargeant Papers, MHS. See also James Bowdoin to Nathaniel Gorham, 24 June 1786, in Bowdoin-Temple Letters, IV, Winthrop Papers, vol. 24, MHS; *New York Journal*, 23 February 1786; letter to the editor, 5 June, *Pennsylvania Evening Herald* (Phila.), 7 June 1786; Boston, 15 June, *New Jersey Gazette* (Tren.), 10 July 1786; "ON GOVERNMENT," *Salem Mercury*, 28 October 1786; Boston, 5 December, *Pennsylvania Gazette* (Phila.), 21 December 1786.

13 Jeremy Belknap to Ebenezer Hazard, 9 March 1786, in *Belknap Papers*, MHSC, 2: 432. See also John Jay to Thomas Jefferson, 9 January 1786, in Johnston, ed., *Jay Papers*, 3: 178; Cotton Tufts to John Adams, 12 January 1786, John Thaxter to Adams, 22 January 1786, in Adams Mss. Trust, MHS; John Lathrop to Richard Price, March 1786, in "Price Letters," MHSP, 17:

337; George Washington to Henry Lee, 5 April 1786, in WGW, 28: 402; Rufus King to Jonathan Jackson, 11 June 1786, in LMCC, 8: 389; Jay to Jefferson, 14 July 1786, in PTJ, 9: 135.

14 Charles Pettit to Jeremiah Wadsworth, 27 May 1786, in LMCC, 8: 330; Menasah Cutler to Winthrop Sargeant, 6 October 1786, in Sargeant Papers, MHS; Henry Knox to George Washington, 23 October 1786, in Noah Brooks, *Henry Knox* (New York, 1900), p. 193; James Madison to James Madison, Sr., 1 November 1786, in PJM, 9: 154. See also Hall, *Politics Without Parties*, pp. 166-227; Robert A. East, "The Massachusetts Conservatives in the Critical Period," in Morris, ed., *Era of the American Revolution*, pp. 349-91.

15 John Jay to John Adams, 4 October 1786, in Adams Mss. Trust, MHS; David Humphreys to George Washington, 9 November 1786, in Frank L. Humphreys, *Life and Times of David Humphreys*, 2 vols. (New York, 1917), 1: 377. See also William Plumer to L. Plumer, 22 July 1786, Plumer to John Hale, 13 August 1786, Plumer to Hale, 20 September 1786, in William Plumer Papers, letters 1781-1786, LC; Lynn W. Turner, *William Plumer of New Hampshire 1759-1850* (Chapel Hill, N.C., 1966), pp. 23-24; *Boston Gazette*, 25 September 1786; Rufus King to Adams, 3 October 1786, in King, *King Letters*, 1: 190; *Freeman's Journal* (Phila.), 18 October 1786; Guillaume Otto to Vergennes, 20 September 1786, in Bancroft, *Formation of the Constitution*, 2: 396; Stephen Mix Mitchell to William S. Johnson, 14 September 1786, in Burnett Collection, Box 11, LC; Hartford, 30 October, *Boston Gazette*, 6 November 1786; *New York Journal*, 28 December 1786.

16 Staples, *Rhode Island*, p. 549; John P. Kaminski, "Democracy Run Rampant: Rhode Island in the Confederation," in *Human Dimensions*, ed. Martin, pp. 243-69; Peregrine Foster to Dwight Foster, 23 April, 11 July 1786, in Foster Papers, Box 7, MHS. See also David Humphreys to George Washington, 24 September 1786, in Humphreys, *Life of Humphreys*, 1: 363; James Pemberton to John Pemberton, 25 November 1786, in Pemberton Mss., vol. 47, HSP; Richard Price to James Bowdoin, 22 January 1787, in *Bowdoin and Temple Papers*, MHSC, 6: 130.

17 Silas Deane to Samuel Blackley Webb, 16 July 1785, in Ford, ed., *Webb Correspondence*, 3: 49; Charles Pinckney, Address before the New Jersey General Assembly, 13 March 1786, in LMCC, 8: 328.

18 Peter Thacher, "Oration delivered at Boston," 5 March 1777, in Niles, ed., *Principles and Acts*, p. 47; Samuel Adams to Samuel Cooper, 25 December 1778, in Cushing, ed., *Writings of Samuel Adams,* 4: 108; James Sullivan to John Adams, 23 October 1785, in Adams Mss. Trust, MHS; Richard Henry Lee to Martin Pickett, 5 March 1786, in Ballagh, ed., *Lee Letters*, 2: 411.

19 Simeon Baldwin to Backus, 4 August 1786, in Baldwin Family Papers, Box 5, YL. See also Guillaume Otto to Vergennes, 20 September 1786, in Corresp. Pol., Etats-Unis, vol. 32, Min. Aff. Etrang. Paris, LC; Rufus King to Theodore Sedgwick, 22 October 1786, in Sedgwick Papers, vol. 2, MHS; George Washington to John Jay, 15 August 1786, in Johnston, ed., *Jay Papers*, 3: 208; King to Elbridge Gerry, 5 August 1786, in King, *King Letters*, 1: 188; Charles Storer to Abigail Adams, 12 September 1786, James Warren to John

Adams, 22 October 1786, in Adams Mss. Trust, MHS; Abigail Adams to Mrs. Cranch, 20 January 1787, in C. F. Adams, ed., *Letters of Mrs. Adams* (Boston, 1848), p. 315; King to Gerry, 11 February 1787, in King, *King Letters*, 1: 201.

20 Samuel Osgood to John Adams, 12 November 1786, in Adams Mss. Trust, MHS; Stephen Higginson to Henry Knox, 12 November 1786, in Thomas Wentworth Higginson, *Life and Times of Stephen Higginson* (Boston, 1907), p. 77. See also Higginson to Knox, 25 November 1786, in Jameson, ed., *Higginson Letters*, 1: 743.

21 John Jay to George Washington, 27 June 1786, in Johnston, ed., *Jay Papers*, 3: 205; James Sullivan to John Adams, 16 December 1786, in Adams Mss. Trust, MHS. See also Ezra Stiles to Thomas Jefferson, 14 September 1786, in PTJ, 10: 386; Henry Knox to Washington, October 1786, in Francis S. Drake, *Life and Correspondence of Henry Knox* (Boston, 1873), p. 92; Benjamin Hitchbourn to Adams, 24 October 1786, Jay to Adams, 1 November 1786, in Adams Mss. Trust, MHS; Ebenezer Wales to Caleb Davis, 4 November 1786, in Davis Papers, vol. 13a, MHS.

22 William Plumer to John Hale, 21 September 1786, in Plumer Papers, letters 1781-1786, LC; Ralph Wormley to [Richard Henry Lee], 8 February 1787, in Arthur Lee Papers, HL; James Madison to Edmund Pendleton, 24 February 1787, in PJM, 9: 295. See also David Humphreys to George Washington, 20 January 1787, in Bancroft, *Formation of the Constitution*, 2: 409; Stephen Mix Mitchell to Col. Wadsworth, 3 May 1786, in Gratz Collection, Box 9, HSP; Charles Carroll of Carrollton to John Fitzgerald, 22 January 1787, in Carroll Papers, MdHS; Samuel Newman to Samuel Bradford, 1 February 1787, in Cushing Papers, MHS; Louise Dunbar, *A Study of Monarchical Tendencies in the United States from 1776-1801*, University of Illinois Studies in the Social Sciences, vol. 10 (Urbana, Ill., 1922), pp. 55-75.

23 William Grayson to James Monroe, 22 November 1786, in Bancroft, *Formation of the Constitution*, 2: 405; Stephen Higginson to Henry Knox, 20 January, 8 February 1787, in Jameson, ed., *Higginson Letters*, 1: 744, 747-51; Knox to Higginson, 25 February 1787, in Morse, *Federalist Party*, p. 41n; *Pennsylvania Journal* (Phila.), supplement, 14 March 1787.

24 *Maryland Journal* (Balt.), 11 October, 14 October 1785. See also David Ramsay to Benjamin Rush, 31 January 1785, in Rush Papers, Ramsay Letters, HSP; Benjamin Greene to Stephen Salisbury, 20 February 1785, in Salisbury Papers, Box 5, AAS; Thomas Pinckney to James Madison, 2 September 1785, in Pinckney Family Papers, Box 2, LC; Edward Rutledge to John Jay, 12 November 1786, in Johnston, ed., *Jay Papers*, 3: 217; Charles G. Singer, *South Carolina in the Confederation* (Philadelphia, 1941), p. 95.

25 Henry Lee to James Madison, 25 October 1786, in PJM, 9: 295; George Washington to Henry Knox, 26 December 1786, in WGW, 29: 122.

26 James Madison to James Monroe, 5 October, 30 October 1786, Madison to George Washington, 1 November, 7 December 1786, in PJM, 9: 146, 152, 155, 199-200. See also Patrick Henry to Col. Joseph Martin, 4 October 1786, Henry to Mrs. Annie Christian, 20 October 1786, in Henry, *Henry*

Correspondence, 3: 374, 380; Madison to Thomas Jefferson, 19 March 1787, in PJM, 9: 319.

27 *Minutes of the Supreme Executive Council*, 14: 645; "Extract of a letter from a gentleman in New York, to his friend in this city, dated 28 March," Hartford, 10 April, *Pennsylvania Gazette* (Phila.), 26 April 1786; William Grayson to ———, 15 June 1786, in Dreer Collection, Members of Old Congress, HSP.

28 David Duncan to William Irvine, 25 January 1787, Pitt., in Irvine Papers, vol. 9, HSP; George Muter to Col. James Madison, 21 February 1787, Pitt., in MHSP, 2d ser., 27 (1903): 454. See also Muter to Madison, 20 February 1787, Ky., in PJM, 9: 279; "Extract of a letter from Davidson county, in the western part of North-Carolina," Nashville, 20 October, *Poughkeepsie Journal*, 7 March 1787.

29 William Grayson to James Monroe, 22 November 1786, in Monroe Papers, LC; James Madison to Edmund Pendleton, 9 January 1787, Madison to George Washington, 18 March 1787, Madison to Thomas Jefferson, 19 March 1787, in PJM, 9: 245, 316, 320; Larassagne to William Irvine, 1 April 1787, in Irvine Papers, vol. 9, HSP.

30 James Monroe to James Madison, 7 October 1786, Abraham Clark to Madison, 23 November 1786, Madison to George Washington, 7 December 1786, in PJM, 9: 142-43, 177, 200. See chapter 8 for Monroe's attempt to secure middle state support.

31 James Madison to Edmund Randolph, 2 April 1787, in PJM, 9: 361. See also Edward Carrington to Madison, 18 December 1786, Madison to Thomas Jefferson, 15 February 1787, Madison to George Washington, 21 February 1787, ibid., pp. 218, 268-69, 286; Benjamin Hawkins to Thomas Jefferson, 8 March 1787, in Burnett Collection, Box 12, LC. For the political change in Pennsylvania, see Brunhouse, *Counter-Revolution,* p. 191; *Freeman's Journal* (Phila.), 1 November 1786. See also chapter 7.

32 James Madison to George Washington, 15 April 1787, in PJM, 9: 386; William Blount to John Gray Blount, 14 March, 18 April 1787, in LMCC, 8: 558, 585. See also Madison to Edmund Randolph, 15 April 1787, in PJM, 9: 379.

33 Nathaniel Mitchell to Gov. Collins, 10 February 1787, in Gratz Collection, Box 9, HSP; Mitchell to Gunning Bedford, 10 February 1787, in LMCC, 8: 538.

34 Rufus King to Elbridge Gerry, 18 February 1787, in LMCC, 8: 541; James Varnum to Benjamin Bourn, 21 February 1787, in Burnett Collection, Box 12, LC. See also C. W. Peale to Dr. B. Ramsay, 22 February 1787, in Peale LBFs, APS; William Shippen to Thomas Lee Shippen, 24 February-1 March 1787, in Shippen Papers, HSP; Edmund Randolph to [Edward Carrington], 11 April 1787, in Emmet Collection, NYPL.

35 Willaim Irvine to James Wilson, 6 March 1787, in LMCC, 8: 551; Arthur St. Clair to John Nicholson, 19 March 1787, in Miscellany, Dreer Collection, HSP; William Shippen to Thomas Lee Shippen, 4-29 March 1787, in Shippen Papers, HSP; St. Clair to Thomas FitzSimons, 10 March 1787, in LMCC, 8: 554; Thomas Willing to William Bingham, 19 March 1787, in H. L. Carson Autograph Collection, HSP.

36 William Grayson to Richard Henry Lee, 22 March 1787, in Lee Papers, UVa; Lambert Cadwallader to Samuel Meredith, 27 March 1787, in Misc., Dreer Collection, HSP.

37 Rufus King to Elbridge Gerry, 11 April 1787, in King Papers, Box 1, NYHS; JMND, 11 April, in Madison Papers, 5th ser., LC. See also James Madison to Edmund Randolph, 15 April 1787, Madison to George Washington, 16 April 1787, in PJM, 9: 379, 386; JCC, 32: 167-69.

38 William Grayson to William Short, 16 April 1787, in William Short Papers, LC. See also John Rutherford to General Robertson, 29 April 1787, in Eastburn Collection (TYP), NJHS.

39 James Madison to Edmund Randolph, 11 March 1787, in PJM, 9: 308; JCC, 32: 152. See also Madison to Thomas Jefferson, 19 March 1787, Madison to James Madison, Sr., 1 April 1787, Madison to Randolph, 15 April 1787, in PJM, 9: 319-20, 359, 380; JCC, 32: 177-204.

40 John Jay to John Adams, 12 May 1787, in Adams Mss. Trust, MHS. See also JCC, 32: 279-80; Arthur Lee to George Washington, 13 May 1787, in Burnett Collection, Box 12, LC.

41 Benjamin Hitchbourn to John Adams, 6 January 1787, in Adams Mss. Trust, MHS. See also Temple to Carmarthen, 4 January 1787, in Bancroft Transcripts, America and England, vol. 2, NYPL; Philadelphia, 2 January, *Providence Gazette*, 13 January 1787; John Collins to ———, 17 January 1787, in Gratz Collection, Box 21, HSP.

42 David Humphreys to George Washington, 20 January 1787, in Humphreys, *Life of Humphreys*, 1: 394-96; George Clymer to ———, 11 February 1787, in *The Collector: A Magazine for Autograph and Historical Collectors*, 57 (November 1943-November 1944): 174.

43 James Madison to Edmund Randolph, 18 February 1787, in PJM, 9: 272; William Irvine to James Wilson, 6 March 1787, in LMCC, 8: 551; JCC, 32: 71-74.

44 David Humphreys to George Washington, 20 January 1787, in Humphreys, *Life of Humphreys*, 1: 395; Rufus King to Elbridge Gerry, 2 January, 11 February, 18 February 1787, in LMCC, 8: 527, 539, 541; Edward Rutledge to Arthur Lee, 21 March 1787, in Lee, *A. Lee*, 2: 316.

45 Stephen Higginson to Henry Knox, 3 March 1787, in Higginson, *Higginson*, p. 108; George Washington to John Jay, 10 March 1787, in Johnston, ed., *Jay Papers*, 3: 239.

46 "FATHERS, FRIENDS, AND FELLOW CITIZENS," *Boston Gazette*, 2 April 1787. For the "Revolution of 1787," see Hall, *Politics Without Parties*, pp. 227-56. Hall, like Robert A. East in his "Massachusetts Conservatives," ignores the effect of the spring capital fight on the eastern leaders, which makes the final decision to go to Philadelphia and to reform the Articles of Confederation that much more complex and interesting.

47 Theodore Foster to Dwight Foster, 6 April 1787, in Foster Papers, Box 7, MHS; William Grayson to James Monroe, 30 April 1787, in Bancroft, *Formation of the Constitution*, 2: 418-19.

48 Edward Carrington to Gov. Randolph, 2 April 1787, in LMCC, 8: 569; Boston, 4 April, *New Jersey Journal* (Tren.), 18 April 1787. See also James Madison

to Edmund Randolph, 2 April 1787, in PJM, 9: 361-62; David Humphreys to George Washington, 24 March 1787, in Humphreys, *Life of Humphreys,* 1: 405; Bates, *Rhode Island,* p. 405; Temple to Carmarthen, 7 June 1787, in Bancroft, *Formation of the Constitution,* 2: 425.

49 Gov. Bowdoin to Rufus King, 6 March 1787, in *Bowdoin and Temple Papers,* MHSC, 6: 167. See also Theodore Sedgwick to John Sedgwick, 13 May 1787, Col. John Sedgwick to commanding officers of companies of the 14th regiment, Conn., 13 May 1787, in Charles F. Sedgwick, *General History of the Town of Sharon, Litchfield, Conn.* (Amenia, N.Y., 1898), pp. 81-82.

50 Gov. Bowdoin to Massachusetts delegates, 16 May 1787, in *Bowdoin and Temple Papers,* MHSC, 6: 186; Henry Knox to James Sullivan, 21 May 1787, in Bancroft, *Formation of the Constitution,* 2: 423. See also Bowdoin to George Washington, 14 May 1787, in *Bowdoin and Temple Letters,* MHSC, 6: 184.

51 William Grayson to William Short, 16 April 1787, Grayson to James Monroe, 29 May 1787, in LMCC, 8: 581, 608. See also Grayson to James Madison, 24 May 1787, in PJM, 9: 412.

52 Peregrine Foster to Dwight Foster, 8 June 1787, in Foster Papers, Box 7, MHS; Elbridge Gerry to James Monroe, 11 June 1787, in Bancroft, *Formation of the Constitution,* 2: 428; George Mason to George Mason, Jr., 20 May 1787, in Rutland, ed., *Mason Papers,* 2: 880; Theodore Sedgwick to Henry Van Schaack, 13 March 1787, in Van Schaack, *Memoirs,* pp. 153-54. See also William Coleman to William Plumer, 28 March 1787, Plumer to Coleman, 31 May 1787, in Plumer Papers, letterbook, vol. 1, LC; "AN ORATION: delivered by Joel Barlow at Hartford, Conn., to the Society of the Cincinnati," 4 July 1787, in Niles, ed., *Principles and Acts,* p. 148; Douglass G. Adair, " 'Experience Must be Our Only Guide:' History, Democratic Theory, and the United States Constitution," in *The Reinterpretation of Early American History,* ed. Ray Allen Billington (San Marino, Calif., 1966), pp. 129-48.

53 Philadelphia, 27 December, *Connecticut Courant* (Hart.), 8 January 1787; Salem, 31 March, *Pennsylvania Evening Herald* (Phila.), 14 April 1787. See also a letter of 26 January, *Pennsylvania Evening Herald* (Phila.), 16 May 1787.

54 James Varnum to Benjamin Bourn, 21 February 1787, in LMCC, 8: 545; James Madison to James Monroe, 25 February 1787, in PJM, 9: 298; William Bingham to Lord Landsdowne, 4 March 1787, in Robert C. Alberts, *The Golden Voyage The Life and Times of William Bingham 1752-1804* (Boston, 1969), p. 175; Charles Thomson to John Sullivan, 31 March 1787, in LMCC, 8: 566.

55 Stephen Higginson to Henry Knox, January 1787, in Jameson, ed., *Higginson Letters,* 1: 743; James Madison to Thomas Jefferson, 19 March 1787, in PJM, 9: 318; George Washington to Madison, 31 March 1787, in WGW, 29: 191.

56 James Madison to Edmund Randolph, 8 April 1787, Madison to George Washington, 16 April 1787, in PJM, 9: 369, 383.

57 John Jay to George Washington, 7 January 1787, in Johnston, ed., *Jay*

Papers, 3: 228; Jay to John Adams, 21 February 1787, in Adams Mss. Trust, MHS.

58 Henry Knox to Stephen Higginson, 28 January 1787, in Drake, *Henry Knox,* p. 94. See also Knox to Benjamin Lincoln, 14 February 1787, ibid., p. 95.

59 Stephen Higginson to Henry Knox, 8 February 1787, in Jameson, ed., *Higginson Letters,* 1: 746-49; James Madison to Thomas Jefferson, 19 March 1787, in PJM, 9: 318.

60 George Muter to James Madison, 20 February 1787, in PJM, 9: 280-81; Charles Carroll of Carrollton to Daniel Carroll, 13 March 1787, in Carroll Papers, MdHS; *Poughkeepsie Journal,* 21 March 1787; Richard Henry Lee to Thomas Lee Shippen, 17 April 1787, in Ballagh, ed., *Lee Letters,* 2: 417; James Pemberton to James Phillips, 18 May 1787, in Dreer Collection, HSP; Philadelphia, 19 May, *Providence Gazette,* 2 June 1787.

61 William S. Johnson to Hugh Williamson, 31 March 1787, in Burnett Collection, Box 12, LC; William Grayson to William Short, 16 April 1787, in LMCC, 8: 581. See also William S. Johnson to Samuel W. Johnson, 12 April 1787, in Burnett Collection, Box 12, LC; Mary Smith to Abigail Adams, 12 April 1787, in Adams Mss. Trust, MHS; Henry Knox to Mercy Warren, 30 May 1787, in *Warren-Adams Letters,* MHSC, 73: 295; Richard Platt to Winthrop Sargeant, 7 May 1787, in Sargeant Papers, MHS.

62 Samuel H. Parsons to William S. Johnson, 4 June 1787, in Charles S. Hall, *Life and Letters of Samuel Holden Parsons* (Binghamton, N.Y., 1905), p. 502.

EPILOGUE

1 Philip Schuyler to Henry Van Schaack, 13 March 1787, in Van Schaack, *Memoirs,* p. 153; David Humphreys to George Washington, 24 March 1787, in Humphreys, *Life of Humphreys,* 1: 405. See also James Madison to Edmund Randolph, 24 February 1787, in PJM, 9: 294; *Pennsylvania Journal* (Phila.), supplement, 14 March 1787; PAH, 4: 93, 147. For the continuing story of New York during the ratification fight, see Steven R. Boyd, "The Impact of the Constitution on State Politics: New York as a Test Case," in *Human Dimensions,* ed. Martin, pp. 270-303.

2 Thomas McKean to John Adams, 30 April 1787, in McKean Papers, HSP; Richard Henry Lee to George Mason, 15 May 1787, George Mason to George Mason, Jr., 1 June 1787, in Rutland, ed., *Mason Papers,* 3: 878, 892.

3 George Read to John Dickinson, 6 January 1787, in Dickinson Papers, R. R. Logan Collection, HSP; James Sullivan to Rufus King, 25 February 1787, in King, *King Letters,* 1: 213; Edmund Snow to James Pemberton, 18 March 1787, in Pemberton Mss., vol. 47, HSP.

4 James Madison to Edmund Pendleton, 24 February 1787, in PJM, 9: 295; "THOUGHTS FOR THE DELEGATES to the CONVENTION . . . ," "CAUTION," from a late New York paper, *Connecticut Courant* (Hart.), 16 April 1787.

See also John Rutherford to General Robertson, 29 April 1787, in Eastburn Collection (TYP), NJHS; Temple to Čarmarthen, 15 April 1787, in Bancroft, *Formation of the Constitution,* 2: 417; David Ramsay to Thomas Jefferson, 7 April 1787, in PTJ, 11: 279-80; Forest to Castries, 9 June 1787, in Nasatir and Monell, eds., *French Consuls,* p. 101. The following may also be seen for evidence of the comparatively widespread interest in disunion and subconfederation after September 1786: Benjamin Rush to Richard Price, 27 October 1786, in Butterfield, ed., *Rush Papers,* 1: 408; William Blount to Richard Caswell, 28 January 1787, in Burnett Collection, Box 12, LC; "A serious paragraph from a Boston paper of Feb. 15," *Pennsylvania Packett* (Phila.), 2 March 1787; Madison to Edmund Randolph, 25 February 1787, in PJM, 9: 299; Otto's reports, 5 March 1787, in Corresp. Pol., Etats-Unis, vol. 32, Min. Aff. Etrang. Paris, LC. The alternative of subconfederation was on many men's minds, and not all these proposals or thoughts came from future supporters of the Constitution. As in 1785 and 1786 the notion of disunion reflected the powerful impact of sectional interests on revolutionary politics; see the discussion in chapter 6. For an analysis of the conflicts in the Philadelphia Convention, see Merrill Jensen, *The Making of the American Constitution* (New York, 1964).

5 James Warren to John Adams, 22 October 1786, in *Warren-Adams Letters,* MHSC, 73: 279.

6 Samuel Adams to Richard Henry Lee, 3 December 1787, in Cushing, ed., *Writings of Samuel Adams,* 4: 324; Abraham Yates, "History of the Movement for the United States Constitution," in Lynd, *Class Conflict,* p. 241; George Bryan, "Miscellaneous Tract," in Bryan Papers, Box 1785-1787, HSP. See also Steven R. Boyd, "The Constitution in State Politics: From the Calling of the Constitutional Convention to the First Federal Elections" (Ph.D. diss., University of Wisconsin, 1974).

7 James Madison to James Monroe, 18 August 1786, in PJM, 9:108.

8 *Journal of the Massachusetts Ratifying Convention* (Boston, 1856), pp. 247-48, 154, 25.

9 Samuel Henshaw to Theodore Sedgwick, 14 June 1787, in Sedgwick Papers, MHS.

10 James Madison to Thomas Jefferson, 19 March 1787, in PJM, 9: 318-19. See also Madison to George Washington, 16 April 1787, ibid., p. 383. It can even be argued that by early 1787 many southerners were willing to support major revision of the Articles of Confederation because they could count on middle state support and still had the promise of future states entering the Union and bolstering their strength. Henderson focuses on the latter, which is quite valid; however, he pays scant attention to the spring capital fight or the political revolution in Massachusetts, which, together, demonstrated the intricate balance between sectional interests and other considerations in the late Confederation period; see his "The Structure of Politics," pp. 191-92; *Party Politics,* pp. 404-20.

11 *Debates and Proceedings in the Congress of the United States, 1789-1824,* 42

vols. (Washington, D.C., 1834-56), 1: 857, 861. See Madison's "The Federalist No. 10" for the change in his political ideas, in Jacob E. Cooke, ed., *The Federalist* (New York, 1961), pp. 56-65. For a continuation of the story of sectionalism in American politics, see Kenneth R. Bowling, "Politics in the First Congress, 1789-1791" (Ph.D. diss., University of Wisconsin, 1968), and "Dinner at Jefferson's: A Note on Jacob E. Cooke's 'The Compromise of 1790,' " *William and Mary Quarterly,* 3d ser., 28 (1971): 629-40.

Index

Adams, John, 9, 10, 11, 12, 17, 18, 22, 25, 26, 30, 54, 77-78, 81-82, 88, 106, 141; replaces Deane, 17; elected peace commissioner, 20-21; conflict with Vergennes, 28-29; Congress censures, 29; attacks France and the Morris faction, 83-84; minister to Great Britain, 98; and commercial reform, 87, 99, 101, 106

Adams, Samuel, 9, 11, 52, 77

Albany Plan, 12

Alexandria, Va., 70, 112

Alsop, John, 17

American Revolution: theories on, 5; and sectionalism, 11

Anarchy, 8, 55, 152, 153

Annapolis, Md.: as federal residence, 60, 65, 66, 68, 69, 70, 71, 72, 112-13

Annapolis Convention, 102, 108, 114, 127, 130-35, 143-47, 153; and Mt. Vernon, 113; Virginia resolution, 130; delegates to, 130, 134, 135, 137, 141, 141-42, 143; instructions of New Jersey delegates, 137; nationalists' ideas on, 138-39; and closure of Congress to reform, 140; New England fears of, 140-42; southern fears of, 142; call to a general convention, 144

Aristocracy, 37, 55, 104, 141, 142, 161

Armstrong, John, 47, 134, 143

Army, Continental: sectional conflicts in, 10, 14; mutinies in, 34-35; half-pay demands of, 43; and congressional power, 43-44; commutation of the half-pay, 45, 48, 53; and second impost, 45-47; fear of mutiny of, 1783, 46-47; mutiny in the Pennsylvania Line, 1783, 60

Arnold, Jonathan, 48

Arnold, Peleg, 157

Articles of Confederation, 15, 24, 31, 43-44, 56, 57, 90, 104, 124, 128, 142, 147, 148-50, 154, 161, 162-64, 165, 166, 167; and sectionalism, 5, 15, 57-58; federalist document, 7; debates on, 12; and sectional compromise, 13; and western lands, 13-14, 15; proposed amendments of, 1778, 15; independent convention, 31-32, 50-51, 158, 163; nationalist movement, 32; ratification of, 32; proposed amendments of, 1978, 32-33; proposed impost amendment, 1781, 34-35; and second impost, 45-46, 49; proposed amendment of Article 8, 48-49; federalist ideas on reform, 56; and commercial reform, 86-88, 89-90, 91-93; proposed amendments, 1786, 138-39; opposition to extracongressional reform, 145-46

Baltimore, Md., 81, 93, 110, 112, 113, 114, 132, 142

Bancroft, Edward, 67

Bank of North America, 95

Barbé-Marbois, François, 30, 76, 115

Bartlett, Josiah, 9

Bassett, Richard, 134

Beatty, John, 70

Beaumarchais, Caron de, 17

Bedford, Gunning, 134

Belknap, Jeremy, 151

Benson, Egbert, 135, 143, 144, 146, 166; ideas on Annapolis Convention, 135

Bingham, William, 157

Bland, Theodorick, 27, 45, 46, 50, 62, 68

JACKET DESIGNED BY H. LAWRENCE HOFFMAN
COMPOSED BY FOTOHEADS, INC., GRAND RAPIDS, MICHIGAN
MANUFACTURED BY CUSHING-MALLOY, INC., ANN ARBOR, MICHIGAN
TEXT IS SET IN TIMES ROMAN, DISPLAY LINES IN OPTIMA

Library of Congress Cataloging in Publication Data
Davis, Joseph L   1946—
Sectionalism in American politics, 1774-1787.
Includes bibliographical references and index.
1. United States—Politics and government—1783-1789.
2. United States—Politics and government—Revolution,
1775-1783. 3. Sectionalism (United States) I. Title.
E303.D38   320.9'73'03   76-11310
ISBN 0-299-07020-4